D1560366

ROADS
TO ANTIETAM

ROADS
TO ANTIETAM

BY
JOHN W. SCHILDT

 Burd Street Press

First Printing, 1985
Second Revised Printing, 1997

First Printing by
Antietam Publications,
Chewsville, Maryland 21721

Second Revised Printing by
Burd Street Press, Division of White Mane Publishing Co., Inc.
Shippensburg, Pennsylvania 17257

This Burd Street Press publication
was printed by
Beidel Printing House, Inc.
63 West Burd Street
Shippensburg, PA 17257-0152 USA

In respect for the scholarship contained herein, the acid-free paper used in this book meets the guidelines for permanence and durability of the Committee on Production Guidelines for Book Longevity of the Council on Library Resources.

For a complete list of available publications
please write
Burd Street Press
Division of White Mane Publishing Company, Inc.
P.O. Box 152
Shippensburg, PA 17257-0152 USA

ISBN 1-57249-044-6 (formerly ISBN 0-936-773-00x)

Library of Congress Cataloging-in-Publication Data

Schildt, John W.
      Roads to Antietam / by John W. Schildt.
          p.   cm.
      Originally published: Chewsville, Md. : Antietam Publications,
1985.
      Includes bibliographical references and index.
      ISBN 1-57249-044-6
      1. Antietam, Battle of, Md., 1862. I. Title.
E474.65.S344   1997
973.7'336--dc21   97-26926
                                                            CIP

*With thanks for the friendship, inspiration, and memories
shared with Civil War Round Tables.*

CONTENTS

ILLUSTRATIONS

CHAPTER I

EARLY SEPTEMBER

The creaking of wheels, the smell of sweaty leather harness, the rumble of horse drawn vehicles, and the tramp, tramp, tramp of perspiring men through clouds of dust comprised some of the sights and sounds of September 1862.

The month brought the first invasion of the North by the Confederate Army of Northern Virginia. Robert E. Lee crossed the Potomac and threatened Washington and Baltimore.

To meet this serious threat, Lincoln named a new commander, and the newly reorganized Army of the Potomac moved from the shadow of the nation's capital in pursuit of the invader. The two armies met in battle on South Mountain and at Antietam Creek.

Approximately 125,000 men took part in the campaign. They had their memories. So did the farmers and the folks in the little towns in their paths. They all had their memories and their stories. What was it like for the folks who lived in those exciting days when the artillery, ambulances, supply wagons, cavalry, and infantry of two armies marched by?

Roads to Antietam is an attempt to share the story as told by the soldiers and civilians. Through their stories, the sights and sounds of 1862 come alive.

SEPTEMBER 1

—ARMY OF NORTHERN VIRGINIA—

Robert E. Lee was hurting as the Maryland Campaign began. Due to rain on August 31, the general put on a pair of rubber overalls along with a poncho. While standing talking to some officers someone shouted, "Yankee Cavalry." As Lee reached for the reins

1

to control his frightened horse, he tripped and fell forward. Using his hands to break his fall, he injured both wrists, breaking a small bone in the one and badly spraining the other. Both hands were placed in splints and Lee was forced to ride in an ambulance.

William Owen of the famed Washington Artillery says the whole army "crossed Bull Run at Sudley Ford, moving toward Germantown." He also noted that Lee was in an ambulance due to his bandaged wrists.

William saw the body of General Phil Kearney "lying upon the porch of a cabin near the roadside. He is a very soldierly-looking man, with heavy mustache and goatee; one arm is gone—lost at the gates of Mexico. Lee, Longstreet, and many others knew him well."[1]

There was elation and confidence in the Army of Northern Virginia. William Nelson Pendleton summarizes Second Manassas:

> The battlefield was near that of July 21, 1861, and the position of the two armies on that occasion reversed. Jackson captured Manassas Junction, with its immense depot of army stores of all sorts, on the 26th of August, and held it until nightfall on the 27th. During this time the starving and destitute soldiers were allowed to supply themselves fully from the captured stores, and the great amount of material which could not be removed was burned.[2]

Pendleton was elated. "General Lee's movements have been masterly, Jackson and Longstreet have fought with accustomed skill, energy, and success. We are in a fair way to shake Yankeedom to its centre. God be praised! Oh, that a just peace might come without more bloodshed."[3]

But peace was not to come for a long while and the bloodiest battle of the war was just over the horizon.

Second Manassas and Chantilly provided the background to set things in motion for the Maryland Campaign and started the men in the blue and the gray on the move.

—*ARMY OF THE POTOMAC*—

Rain fell on the Army of the Potomac putting an additional damper on their spirits, already lowered by the defeat at Second Bull Run.

During that September Monday, the men in blue and those in gray moved by divergent roads until they clashed at Chantilly. Generals Phil Kearney and Isaac Stevens fell in the savage fighting.[4]

There was unrest, despair, and pessimism in the ranks of the Union army.

In August the Ninth Corps had been brought back from the successful campaign in North Carolina to join the Army of the Potomac. The men embarked at Newport News. On the third they landed at Aquia Creek and the next day marched to Fredericksburg. Here they were to spend the major portion of the next month watching Fredericksburg and patrolling the Rappahannock River line. Meanwhile Lee was moving around Culpeper Court House.

With all the losses and bickering, General Burnside looked upon August as the gloomiest month of 1862. He was amazed to see the petty jealousy, the vanity, and the competition among the officers. It seemed as though they would rather fight each other than the Confederates. There was little or no team spirit. And they almost seemed to rejoice in one another's failures.[5]

Elements of the Ninth Corps performed rather well at Second Manassas. But Pope's army was suffering from fatigue, lack of supplies, low morale, and poor support from the various commanders.

The Ninth Corps mourned the death of Isaac Stevens. He had distinguished himself as a scholar and gentleman, both at West Point and the days following. President Franklin Pierce placed him in charge of the Pacific Railroad Survey, and then he became governor of Washington Territory. In 1857 he was elected to the House of Representatives and became chairman of the campaign for Breckinridge's presidential attempt in 1860. At Chantilly he had seized the colors of his old regiment, the 79th New York, and was leading his men forward, when he was shot through the head. One of their former division commanders would not be with them on the "Roads to Antietam."[6]

In the series of battles climaxing at Chantilly, the Union army lost over 7,000 men as prisoners, 2,000 wounded and killed, plus 30 pieces of artillery, 20,000 stands of small arms, and great amounts of military supplies.

But perhaps the main blow was that of the damage to morale and prestige. The Union troops were once again demoralized, and still another commander had proven incompetent.

Part of the Ninth Corps had fallen back from Second Manassas to Washington. But General Burnside had been at Fredericksburg and returned to confer with his superiors. A detachment of the Ninth Corps had been on garrison duty at Fredericksburg.

With the Ninth Corps down at Fredericksburg, Charles Johnson wrote that the clouds sponged out enough water to soak the men. Then when morning came they marched through Fredericksburg for the last time. Part of the time it sprinkled and part of the time it poured. The railroad station had been burned and the columns of dark smoke added to the darkness of the skies.

On through the rain the Ninth Corps marched to Aquia Creek. It was a miserable march. When the men reached the spot, they were utterly exhausted. Two days of rainfall had soaked the men and dampened their spirits. They barely got their tents up when another downpour occurred. After some sleep, good strong coffee revived them. The Ninth New York was situated on a bluff overlooking the silvery Potomac.[7]

Before leaving Fredericksburg, three bridges across the Rappahannock, a machine-shop, and all the army warehouses were burned. General Burnside was walking to and fro watching the destruction and sending orders to his regimental commanders. He was weary from the exertion of campaigning and being on guard.[8]

About this time a poor woman with three little children passed him carrying small articles of household furniture. Burnside recognized this Fredericksburg lady as a friend of the Union. He talked to her and dispatched an ambulance to get the rest of her belongings brought to the depot. She and the children were evacuated along with the troops.

Burnside, like the troops, found the night march a terrible ordeal. Several times he dismounted, waded into knee-deep mud and helped push wagons out of the mud.

Meanwhile, George B. McClellan, ever an opportunist and somewhat egotistical, was riding toward Washington. He met with Henry Halleck, commander in chief of the Union armies in his office, and was given verbal orders to take charge of the defenses of Washington, but told not to interfere with Pope's command.

Marsena Patrick's command was on patrol duty that morning. Somewhat later he met John Buford and Joe Hooker. Patrick then attended a council meeting at Fairfax Courthouse. John Pope, Irvin McDowell, William Franklin, and others were present. The result was a lot of marching and counter marching, and mass confusion for Patrick. Finally he was ordered to cover the retreat of the Union army.[9]

John Pope confessed his failures. Writing to headquarters in Washington from Fairfax Courthouse he said, "Unless something is done to restore tone to this army it will melt away before you know it...The enemy is in heavy force and must be stopped in some way."

In response Halleck telegraphed the following message to Pope, "You will bring your forces as best you can within or near the line of fortification. General McClellan has charge of all the defenses..."

Things were so bad that a steam ship was prepared to evacuate the President, the cabinet, and Government officials should the enemy appear. And government clerks and employees were armed and formed into emergency companies. The general feeling was that Bull Run had "brought the country to the verge of the grave." Secretary of War Stanton was all for moving the government elsewhere.

Thus at 7:30 a.m. two men appeared at the home of George B. McClellan. They were none other than Henry Halleck and President Abraham Lincoln. Mr. Lincoln talked about Pope's beaten army and 30,000 stragglers choking the roads leading into Washington. Both Halleck and Lincoln considered Washington lost.

According to George B. McClellan, Lincoln then asked him as a personal favor to "take steps at once to stop and collect the stragglers," to prepare a proper defense, and to take command of all troops coming into the city. It was a verbal request, no orders being given by anyone, and simply placing McClellan in defense of Washington. George readily agreed. After they left, this directive was issued, "Major-General McClellan will have command of the fortifications of Washington and of all the troops for the defense of the capital."

Later in the day, in a heated cabinet session, Lincoln had to defend his choice and his actions. The cabinet could hardly believe their ears. The President must be mad. They talked in tones of disbelief, causing Mr. Lincoln much distress. Only Montgomery Blair did not denounce McClellan. Secretary Chase said that giving the army to McClellan "would prove a national calamity." But Lincoln said McClellan was the best man available at the moment.

Oliver O. Howard, a general in the Second Corps gives us a vivid and accurate description of the emotional temperature of those early September days.

> Could the reader have seen with Mr. Lincoln's eyes— sad, earnest, deep, penetrating as they were—the condition of the Republic on September 2d and 3d, when the Union army with broken ranks and haggard looks came straggling and discouraged to the protection of the encircling forts of Washington, he would have realized the crisis. Divisions in council—envy and accusation among military leaders, unsatisfied ambition struggling for the ascendency—waves of terror gathering forces as they rolled from Washington through Maryland and Pennsylvania northward—a triumphant, hostile army, well organized, well officered, and great in numbers, under a chief of acknowledged character and ability, within twenty miles of the capital—these served to blow the crackling embers, and fan the consuming flame.

> But Abraham Lincoln, who cried to God for strength, was equal to this emergency. He brought Halleck over to his mind.

He checked the secret and open work of his ministers which he deemed too abrupt; he silenced the croakings of the war committees of Congress; he stirred all truly loyal hearts by cogent appeals to send forward men and money; he buried his personal preferences and called back McClellan, his former though fretful lieutenant.[10]

Josiah Favill, a young officer with the 57th New York, echoed the feeling of General Howard saying that the Confederates were not going to just continue the fighting, "but carry the war into Africa," or invade Maryland and Pennsylvania. He adds:

As a choice of evils McClellan has been placed in command again, and is directing the present operations; the excitement North is tremendous. That the rebel army should be advancing into the Northern states is something no one dreamed possible and the people are quick to recognize the fact that war at home is quite a different affair to war at the other fellow's home.

The militia are under arms hurrying to the defenses of Washington, and Baltimore, and everybody is on the tip toe of expectation for: "Grim visaged war is at their very doors."[11]

SEPTEMBER 2

—ARMY OF NORTHERN VIRGINIA—

It was summer, but summer was drawing near an end. Until now things in the east, militarily at least, had gone their way. McClellan had been turned back during the Seven Days Campaign as he advanced on Richmond. Then Pope had met disaster at Second Manassas. The Confederacy had reached its peak. Foreign powers were looking with interest and respect at what was taking place. If the Confederacy could win a battle north of the Potomac, then great political events might occur, including foreign recognition of the Confederacy. Morale was low in the North. One more disaster might lead the people to ask for peace. It seemed as though the Army of Northern Virginia could not be stopped. Yes it was summertime, the summer of the Confederacy.

However, autumn was just around the corner, three weeks away. Just as the days became shorter and the nights cooler in autumn, the leaves changed color, and dropped to the ground, a change was coming slowly but surely to the hopes of the Confederacy. They were about ready to go from their summer to the autumn of their existence. And that change occurred as the men of North and South met on the banks of the Antietam Creek.

Lee realized now was the time to strike. The Union troops that had been routed at Second Manassas had not yet been reorganized. If there was ever a moment to give Maryland an opportunity to throw off the oppressive yoke, now was the time. Thus General Lee wrote to President Jefferson Davis stating his reasons for taking his army north.

1. The Union army would be drawn away from Richmond and Virginia.

2. The farmers would have the opportunity to harvest the crops that had not been stripped by the armies.

3. A Southern victory north of the Potomac would lift the morale of the South and badly lower that of the North.

4. Success in Maryland might foreshadow foreign intervention and perhaps final independence.

5. Success north of the river might lead to a negotiated peace.

So the stakes were high, and like Napoleon, Lee was ready to risk a knock-out blow, hoping to win the war with one major stroke.

Lee also hoped Marylanders might join his army, and maybe the citizens might rebel or leave the Union, thus surrounding Washington.

After the engagement at Chantilly, Jeb Stuart and his troopers headed the Confederate advance toward the Potomac. At the side of the Confederate cavalry chieftain rode young John Pelham, in charge of the Horse Artillery.

Many of the infantrymen who followed wore captured U.S. clothing. In fact, a lot of the wagons had U.S.A. stamped on the canvas. But what they lacked in materials, the Rebels made up for in spirit and enthusiasm.

James Longstreet, commander of Lee's First Corps was not too happy about the decision. He, like the authorities in Richmond and like many private soldiers, thought the policy should be defensive warfare. Yet Lee knew that he could not win the war by staying on the defensive, he had to meet and defeat the enemy in battle. And with less manpower, industry, and railroads, it was unlikely the South could wear down the larger and more resourceful North.

Longstreet lamented that Lee was not as well equipped as an invading army should be. But hopefully the Marylanders would be friendly and supply a lot of help. Lee really had little choice. He could stay in Virginia, strengthen his lines and await another attack, or he could carry the war to the North. This time he chose to be the aggressor.

Longstreet also felt that although the Yankees had been soundly beaten at Second Manassas, they would bounce back quickly. James believed that the Confederate army needed rest after a lot of marching and fighting. But Lee was ready to move north.

Things looked good. Along the Warrenton Turnpike, Hood's Texans and others in the Army of Northern Virginia, saw the guns, canteens, blankets, tin cups, and frying pans, thrown away by Pope's Army after Second Manassas.

Jubal Early, one of Jackson's subordinates, said that the army rested today and watched the movements of the enemy. "Provisions now are very scarce, as the supply in the wagons with which we had started, was exhausted."

Provisions in the haversacks captured at Second Manassas were also about gone. Early's diet was fresh beef without salt or bread and an ear or two of green corn roasted over the fire. Longstreet's men were even worse off as they had not shared in the spoils of Manassas.[12]

The bulk of the Army of Northern Virginia camped at Dranesville. "On to Maryland! is now the cry, and the heads of the columns are directed toward the Potomac."

—ARMY OF THE POTOMAC—

As the dawn broke Tuesday morning, September 2, it brought a clear, very cool day. The troops who had been engaged in combat at Chantilly tried to make fires. They got a lot of smoke but little heat to dry their soaked uniforms or to help their shivering.

For many of the Confederates it was a light day. For the Yankees, they continued falling back to the confines of Washington. Skirmishes took place at Fairfax Court House, Falls Church, Vienna, and Flint Hill.

John Pope and the Union Army of Virginia fell back to the fortifications of Washington. President Lincoln and his cabinet met to consider the command situation. Something had to be done. Mr. Lincoln was having poor success with his commanders. There is some indication the command was offered to Burnside, but he declined and suggested George B. McClellan. Secretaries Stanton and Chase were very much opposed to such a move, but Lincoln prevailed.

One writer says that General McClellan and Staff rode into Washington today, "Though an unnumerable herd of stragglers mingled with an endless stream of wagons and ambulances, urged on by uncontrollable teamsters...Disorder reigned unchecked and confusion was everywhere."

Matthew Graham says, "a gunboat, with steam up, lay in the river of the White House, as if to announce to the army and the inhabitants the impending flight of the administration."[13]

Lincoln must have had mixed feelings about McClellan. In private, according to his secretary, John Nicolay, "Father Abraham" expressed grave doubts about McClellan. John Hay says that it almost seemed like McClellan wanted Pope to be defeated so he could regain command. And for years a controversy raged as to whether or not McClellan withheld support at Second Manassas. Lincoln remarked that McClellan seemed full of envy, jealousy, and spite. "He acts as chief alarmist and marplot for the army." But now "Little Mac" was back in command. If the politicians were not satisfied, the soldiers were. They loved McClellan.

George Kimball of the 12th Massachusetts was at Hall's Hill that evening. The men were weary from defeat and fatigue. Most of the men were discussing recent events in negative terms. Suddenly a staff officer galloped up and shouted, "Little Mac is back here on the road, boys."

It was a transforming moment. "From extreme sadness we passed in a twinkling to a delirium of delight. A Deliverer had come. A real 'rainbow of promise' had appeared."[14]

On this cool and windy Tuesday, David Strother rode from Fairfax Court House toward Alexandria. "After riding several miles through a quiet and secluded region we came in view of our camps on Munson's and Upton's Hills."[15] In the distance could be seen the unfinished dome of the Capitol in Washington.

As the dome of the Capitol was unfinished, so George McClellan had a big job ahead of him, the task of reconstructing the army so it could meet the enemy, give battle, and perhaps get on the road to ending the war.

Henry Halleck wrote to McClellan saying,

> There is every probability that the enemy, baffled in his intended capture of Washington, will cross the Potomac, and make a raid into Maryland or Pennsylvania. A movable army must be immediately organized to meet him again in the field...[16]

Rufus Dawes says this was a dark day for Lincoln's administration.[17]

McClellan was reasonably sure that Lee intended to invade, so he moved the Second, Ninth, and Twelfth Corps to the Maryland side of the Potomac.

Elements of the Ninth Corps mustered and marched down the bluffs at Aquia Creek to board transport boats headed for

Washington. Charles Johnson fell asleep. When he awakened, he saw a dock, a long bridge, and "the dome of the Capitol of our Country." Johnson and his comrades marched through the city to Georgetown where they made camp. Afterwards Charles read a paper that carried a horrible story. Two women had been murdered close to his home town back in Minnesota.[18]

By 5:00 p.m. General Burnside had just about completed his evacuation from Aquia Creek. The teams, stores, beef cattle, etc. were loaded. He did not know what to do with the trains and engines and asked whether he should bring them to Washington or destroy them.

By 12:30 p.m. George McClellan was able to report that elements of Banks' Corps were headed toward Rockville and Poolesville to watch and check the Confederates should they try to cross the Potomac below Point of Rocks. Sumner's Corps was in position near Tennallytown.

Additional cavalry and a battery of artillery were sent to Edwards Ferry. The Rebels were shelling the canal boats, but McClellan thought that it was more of a sport with them than a serious intention to cross.

Marching through Northern Virginia

White's Ford

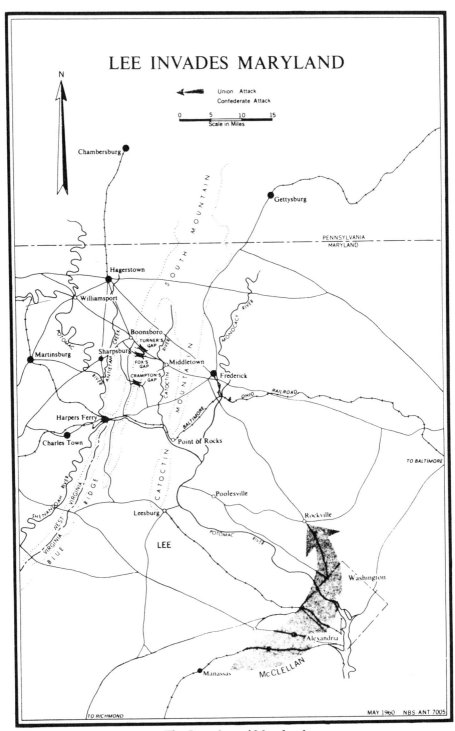

LEE INVADES MARYLAND

Union Attack
Confederate Attack

0   5   10   15
Scale in Miles

N

Chambersburg

Gettysburg

SOUTH MOUNTAIN

PENNSYLVANIA
MARYLAND

Hagerstown

Williamsport

Boonsboro
TURNER'S GAP

Martinsburg

Sharpsburg

FOX'S GAP

Middletown

CRAMPTON'S GAP

Frederick

ANTIETAM CREEK

CATOCTIN RIVER

MONOCACY RIVER

C A T O C T I N   M O U N T A I N

Harpers Ferry

Charles Town

BALTIMORE

Point of Rocks

OHIO   RAILROAD

TO BALTIMORE

POTOMAC RIVER

SHENANDOAH RIVER

WEST VIRGINIA

BLUE RIDGE

VIRGINIA

CATOCTIN

Poolesville

Leesburg

Rockville

LEE

POTOMAC   RIVER

Washington

Alexandria

Manassas

McCLELLAN

TO RICHMOND

MAY 1960   NBS ANT 7005

The Invasion of Maryland

Courtesy—National Park Service

CHAPTER II

CROSSING THE RIVER

—ARMY OF NORTHERN VIRGINIA—

The Union army used the first week in September to regroup and reform. In the meantime, the Confederate Army of Northern Virginia was preparing to cross the Potomac. Now was indeed "the most propitious time" to carry the war northward.

In the early hours of Thursday, September 4, 1862, units of "the flower of Lee's Army" started to cross the Potomac at White's Ford. The river was only two or three feet deep. Although the army was not properly equipped, Lee wanted to invade, and militarily he had to invade. So, farmers living near the river mounted their horses, and like Paul Revere, galloped off to tell others, "The Rebels are coming. The Rebels are coming."

Some of the Confederate soldiers were as disturbed as the farmers. They had signed up to fight a defensive war, not to invade another state. But it was too late now, the invasion was in progress. However, most of the men were in high spirits. Perhaps if they were successful, the war might be brought to an end. They could go back to their jobs and families and live in peace. Maybe one more big battle would do the job. And they knew they could trust Robert E. Lee. A short dip in the waters of the Potomac elevated their spirits too.

By nightfall the Horse Artillery reached Goose Creek near Leesburg. As the cavalry, infantry, and artillery filed into campsites, the nearby countryside was illuminated by campfires. After eating, and drinking their coffee, the soldiers sang, and cheered. They believed in themselves, in their leaders, and they had once again been victorious. Now it was northward, and perhaps one more final victory. It was the summertime of the South. John Pelham took time to write to his parents:

We whipped General Pope last week at Manassas. Now General Lee is leading us into Northern territory. Tomorrow, we'll cross the Potomac and enter Maryland, where they tell us a lot of men are anxious to join our cause. I understand that General Jackson wants to invade Pennsylvania in order to strike the coal mines and railroads so as to cripple the enemy's industry and transportation. If all goes well I hope the war will be over soon and we can all be together again—at least that is my prayer.[1]

Colonel Thomas Munford and the Second Virginia Cavalry, forming the advance of the Army of Northern Virginia, had entered Leesburg on September 2. They found the town in possession of Cole's Maryland Cavalry and the Loudoun Rangers. Munford divided his regiment and sent part of it east of Leesburg to cut off the escape of the Union cavalry. "Between Mile Hill and Big Spring, the converging forces met the Federal cavalry in a sharp skirmish which resulted in several casualties on both sides...After a spirited chase about thirty Union prisoners were captured. Munford then moved on through White's Ford to Poolesville, Maryland."[2]

Daniel Harvey Hill's infantry was the first of the foot soldiers to reach Leesburg. After a brief pause they continued north on old Route 15 to clear and protect the river crossings. Then came Jackson's command, followed by Pete Longstreet.

The disabled Lee and Jackson both made their headquarters for a time at the Harrison home on North King Street. On the fifth the townspeople stood and watched as Lee, Longstreet, Jackson, and Stuart met in the Harrison home for a conference and to plan strategy.

The infantry of the Army of Northern Virginia received a great welcome in Leesburg. The windows were full of lighted candles. The streets were crowded with women and children. Many folks said, "God bless you." Some saw Hood's Texans and shouted, "hurrah for the Texas Brigade." The men from the Lone Star State returned the greeting with vigor.

But there was no time to enjoy the welcome in Leesburg. Jubal Early and others passed through the town and camped for the night at Big Springs several miles from town. (A marker denotes the spot today.) Tomorrow the river, then Maryland, and perhaps Washington, and maybe independence.

Randolph A. Shotwell was the son of a Presbyterian minister, born on December 13, 1844. His father was a native Virginian while his mother came from Massachusetts. Dr. Shotwell accepted a call to Rutherford, North Carolina in 1858, and when the war broke out, young Randolph enlisted, becoming a member of the famous

Eighth Virginia Infantry. After the war he sought political office, but in the days of Reconstruction that was difficult. However, he did very well as a newspaper and magazine editor.

The first week in September 1862 found Randolph and his comrades very happy. Not only were they heading northward after thwarting Union attacks of over one year, but for many men in the Eighth Virginia, Loudoun County was home. Although they were a "hard looking set," many buggies and other horse drawn vehicles brought ladies and residents of Leesburg to the regimental bivouac.[3]

Thursday morning the Eighth Virginia entered Leesburg, "amid a reception committee consisting of the entire community, white and black, old and young, male and female..." It was a touching sight to witness the breathless anxiety of many a parent, watching for the son of whom nothing had been heard in long months, and who might have fallen only a few days before at Manassas, almost within sight of home.

Despite the gaiety, there was quiet with some, and then tears. Their loved ones were not in the ranks. They were among those who had fallen on other fields. Some parents thought their sons just had to be in the ranks.

A group of pretty girls asked, "Is that the Eighth Virginia?" When told that it was, one girl clapped her hands, and exclaimed, "Oh, I'm so glad! God bless you boys, I declare I love every one of you." Naturally, Colonel Hunton's men were glad to respond with cheers to such kind words.

By nightfall, the Eighth Virginia was camped at the "Big Spring" three and a half miles from Leesburg on the Nolan's Ferry road. According to Shotwell, the limestone spring was one of the biggest in the area. He described it as being twenty-five feet across with ice cold, sparkling water, two to six feet deep. Shotwell says the spring furnished water this night for 30,000 men, and was second only to the spring at Darksville in size.

Soon after camp was made, the Virginians were asleep. They were tired and realized a big campaign was ahead of them, and their fate might be "death, sickness, or capture." Little wonder that some of the Loudoun County men slipped home to be with "Polly and the babies."[4]

Heros Von Borcke, Jeb Stuart's chief of staff, describes the excitement.

> Every regiment was preparing for the march, officers were riding to and fro, and the long artillery trains were moving off along the turnpike, their rumbling noise combining with the rattle of the drums and the roll of the bugles to wake the echoes for

miles around...Many a youthful hero looked forward to his triumphant entry into the Federal capital...[5]

The 10th Virginia headed one column approaching the Potomac. The flags were flying and the band blaring the strains of "Maryland, My Maryland." Cheers swept through the ranks. The men were elated. They had reached the Potomac. Another step perhaps toward victory. Many took their shoes off and rolled up their trousers.

Von Borcke, the romanticist, writes:

It was, indeed a magnificent sight...There were few moments...from the beginning to the close of the war, of excitement more intense, of exhilaration more delightful, than when we ascended the opposite bank to the...strangely thrilling music "Maryland, My Maryland."[6]

There were some problems though. With men and wagons descending upon the Potomac, a traffic jam soon resulted. General Jackson ordered his chief quartermaster, Major John A. Harman, to clear the river. Harman had had experience with a stage coach line and in transportation prior to the war. A profane man, he got the job done, even though he "put the fear of God" into the men and animals. All seemed to be afraid of him. After some choice words to the animals and drivers, the traffic jam was unsnarled. Harman reported to Jackson and told him, "There's only one language that will make mules understand on a hot day..."

So the army crossed. And the men had their thoughts and later their memories. A few left them for us to read and from them we gather what it was like on the trek north.

Jed Hotchkiss, Stonewall Jackson's mapmaker, describes the gala crossing:

We started about sunrise and went, by a private road to White's Ford and there crossed the Potomac into Maryland...The 10th Virginia Regt. of infantry, preceded by a band, and bearing a Virginia flag, was in the advance; as the band reached the Maryland shore it struck up the air, "Maryland, My Maryland," amid the shouts of the soldiers. It was a noble spectacle, the broad river, fringed by lofty trees in full foliage; the exuberant wealth of the autumn wild flowers down the margin of the stream, and a bright green island stretched away to the right...We went to a lock in the canal and there intercepted a boat load of melon on the way to the Washington market, which our men bought.[7]

Jackson was presented with one of the best melons. He ordered a field of corn to be purchased and roasting ears given the men. The husks and stalks were to be given to the horses. Fires were to be started so the men could prepare the corn for their haversacks.

Robert Poague, a gunner in the Rockbridge Artillery, got into trouble during the crossing of the Potomac. Jackson had issued an order forbidding the men to ride on the gun carriages or caissons. However, the artillerymen had mounted them during the crossing of Goose Creek. Reaching the Potomac, Poague gave the order for the men to mount again.

Major Frank Paxton of Jackson's staff was present, supervising the crossing. He informed Poague that he would be reported for violating the order. Sure enough, the next day orders came placing a number of the battery commanders under arrest. For several days the batteries operated under this irksome order. Then Jackson found out that Shoemaker, the chief of artillery, had given his permission for mounting during the crossing of water, and the officers were released from arrest.

Late in the day, John Pelham limbered up the guns of the Horse Artillery from the camp site near Goose Creek and started for White's Ford where Jackson's infantry was in the process of fording. Seeing that it would be awhile before he could cross, Pelham ordered his men to unhitch the horses and let them graze on the bank of the river. Pelham and Breathed rode to a knoll to watch the infantry cross to Maryland. Some of the soldiers took off their shoes. Others rolled up their trousers. The Potomac was two and a half feet deep at the time. The rays of the setting sun danced on the river and from the muskets and the standards of the flags. It was a picturesque scene.

Suddenly they were joined by an officer on a cream-colored mare. He splashed into the Potomac and turned and faced the troops in mid-stream doffing his familiar kepi to the soldiers who cheered and cheered. It was none other than "Old Jack" himself. The cheers were followed by the Rebel yell, and then on the Maryland shore, a regimental band struck up the tune "Maryland, My Maryland."

It was almost midnight before Pelham was able to cross. "Keep the muzzles pointed up." This was the order to keep water out of the gun barrels. He too gave orders that none were to ride on the caissons. The added weight would make the wheels sink deeper in the river bottom.

At one point the guns stalled in the water, so the walking artillerymen put a shoulder to the wheel and pushed. Reaching the Maryland shore, Pelham's men bivouacked in a grove of trees. It had been an exciting day and the invasion had begun with great promise.

A lot of black cooks and servants followed the Army of Northern Virginia into Maryland. They were allowed to roam at will, the same as back home. "They foraged for their masters wherever they went," and were quite good at supplementing rations. Somehow they always found chickens, flour, and butter. Although having the freedom to escape in Maryland, none seemed to want to. Many of the blacks accompanying the Rebel army expressed fear of the Yankee army.[8]

The columns of Confederate infantry approaching the Potomac were dirty, tattered, and unshaven. The brims and tops of their hats were full of holes or nonexistent. Many shirts were without buttons. The weapons were the only items that were clean and neat. Most were shoeless. What an army! Some of the veterans had never seen the army so filthy, ragged, and so low on provisions.

Some of A.P. Hill's men were lying by the roadside waiting their turn to cross. While they waited, along came General Lee and General Hill. Powell Hill gave the order, "Move out of the road, men." But Lee would not have them disturbed. "Never mind, General, we will ride around them. Lie still, men." So Hill's Light Division remained in place and the two generals detoured around them.

Henry Kyd Douglas says that the troops crossed the Potomac in fours, "well closed up, shouting, laughing, singing, with a brass band in front playing, 'Maryland, My Maryland,' it was an inspiring scene."[9]

Jubal Early was in the column crossing at White's Ford, about seven miles above Leesburg. "This ford was an obscure one on the road through the farm of Captain Elijah White, and the banks of the river had to be dug down so that the wagons and artillery could cross."

The Chesapeake and Ohio Canal posed another problem and a bridge had to be hastily constructed across it for the wagons and the artillery. Early camped at Three Springs.[10]

Jackson instructed Jubal Early to let the men help themselves from the Maryland cornfields, getting enough for two days. The men had already helped themselves. Beef without bread, and pork and green corn constituted a poor diet, but were better than nothing. However, it was a weakening diet for men on a long march, and produced a lot of diarrhea.[11]

For Randolph Shotwell and the men in the Eighth Virginia, crossing the Potomac was almost like a carnival. Many of them just about stripped. And it seems that the crossing was more relaxed for Longstreet and his corps than Jackson's command. Shotwell says that many were in the state of Adam and Eve before the temptation.

The soldiers waded and splashed like a group of school boys at the old swimming hole. Some slipped and fell on the slippery rocks on the river bottom. Some wrestled in the water and played.

The Eighth Virginia was a very fun loving unit, so perhaps that accounts for the carnival-like atmosphere. Meanwhile, on the banks of the river, the bands played "Maryland, My Maryland," and wagons and army wagons pulled up ready to cross.

Many eyewitness accounts tell of Lee's army being ragged when they entered Maryland. But at least they were clean. "The whole army was well washed for once." They had gotten rid of hundreds of vermin infesting their clothing. For many it was the first bath they had had in a long time. Even Shotwell had to admit that there was "a wide interval between 'sympathizing with,' and 'serving with, the half-clad, half-shod, half-fed, half-armed, unshaven, unshorn,...sunbrowned, battle-scarred,' Rebel rag-tag."[12]

Regardless of one's feelings concerning the war, we have to admit the Confederate soldier was a special breed, deeply motivated, otherwise he certainly would not have been in the army.

There was a lot of commotion in Frederick on September 5. The report reached town that Stonewall Jackson had crossed with 12,000 troops at Noland's Ferry. John Bender was arrested for circulating the sensational report. But the report became a reality. Jackson's command had indeed reached Frederick County, and according to Jacob Engelbrecht was camped on the farm of Benjamin M. Moffatts, three miles below Buckeystown.

Thomas Gorsuch, the provost marshal, was given orders to destroy the Federal stores. Thus about 10:00 a.m., the supplies stored in Kemp Hall were brought out into Church Street and the torch applied to beds and cots. Other items were burned at the Depot and Hessian Barracks.[13]

South of Frederick, "Stonewall" Jackson was in pain. A Southern sympathizer had given him a horse. The horse reared into the air and threw Jackson heavily to the ground, stunning him and injuring his back. For a time, Jackson had to relinquish his command to D.H. Hill, and like General Lee, rode in an ambulance.

After crossing the Potomac, Fitz Lee's column trotted to Poolesville. Some of the folks along the route were very warm and friendly, others were remarkably cool. The Confederates expected this because they realized that Montgomery County was not really devoted to the Southern cause. However, there was a very warm welcome in Poolesville. Von Borcke says the enthusiasm of the citizens "rose to fever heat." Some of the young men mounted their horses and insisted on joining the Confederate cause.

Among those wishing to enlist were two young merchants. They offered to sell everything in their places of business for Confederate money. The Rebel troopers soon cleaned them out "to the last pin." The soldiers were like children, buying everything in sight, whether they needed it or not. After all, over a year of war had kept them from buying nice things in Virginia. If the invasion did not go well, it might be a long time before they had another such opportunity.

Von Borcke made a number of odd purchases, a box of cigars, some white sugar, some lemons, and a pocket knife. He felt as happy as a king with his new treasures. Perhaps he gave some of the lemons to Jackson who sucked them regularly for his health.

Jeb Stuart says that "the reception of our troops in Maryland was attended with the greatest demonstrations of joy, and the hope of the inhabitants to throw off the tyrant's yoke stirred every Southern heart with renewed vigor and enthusiasm."

This may have been true in Poolesville and for the cavalry, but certainly not for all the infantry. Again, some of the response may have been in fear.

Wade Hampton and his men halted for the night in Poolesville.[14]

Jackson says that his command crossed during the day and encamped near Three Springs. Only the Black Horse Cavalry was nearby, so he directed Captain Randolph to guard his flanks against any surprises.[15]

—*ARMY OF THE POTOMAC*—

Meanwhile, the Yankee cavalry was moving from Falls Church to Tenallytown, thence to Seneca Mills and Muddy Run.[16]

At 11:30 a.m. Alfred Pleasonton reported that he had explored the river road and found it picketed by Confederate infantry. The First Massachusetts was picketing all the fords. Pleasonton had word that Longstreet had crossed into Maryland during the night. He also spoke of the shelling of the canal boats at Edwards Ferry. At 5:00 p.m. he reported 3,000 Confederate infantry on the Maryland side of the Potomac.[17]

As midnight drew near, Captain Crowninshield for the First Massachusetts Cavalry reported no Rebels at Edwards Ferry, but dust at Whites Ferry, seven miles up the river. The dust indicated the Rebels were moving toward Frederick in large numbers. "A rebel deserter told Captain Crowninshield that Jackson, Longstreet, Smith, and Hill were crossing, and that they had sixty pieces of artillery, and a force of between 30,000 and 45,000 men." This report was sent from Muddy Branch.[18]

That morning Captain Chamberlain of the First Massachusetts Cavalry took 100 men to patrol the fords of the Potomac. In Poolesville he encountered Fitz Lee's Rebel cavalry.

As the men from Massachusetts advanced to meet the enemy, some Southern sympathizers in Poolesville placed stones and other barricades in the street behind them. When driven back by the men in gray, chaos resulted as many horses were thrown by the obstacles. As a result, Captain Chamberlain and thirty of his men were captured.[19]

The men in the Sixth Wisconsin were hungry today. Their food and supplies had been burned at Manassas. They told Captain Noyes that they wanted more than Army rations. Previously they had given him $300 worth of excess money. Now he used this money to get them milk, canned turkey, peas and beans. It was the first time that many of them had eaten canned food.[20]

The Sixth Wisconsin stopped in front of the White House. It was a very hot and sultry night. The break was between 9:00 p.m. and midnight.

One member of the unit says that they could see the tall form of "old Abe" in shirt sleeves, water pail and dipper in hand, stepping over and among the boys lying all over the ground, giving them water to drink.[21]

When the Army of the Potomac started north, the Eighth Ohio was reluctant to leave the Washington area. They had been amply supplied with food from the gardens in the big city and from Georgetown. Watermelons, cakes, pies, and fresh vegetables comprised the daily menu. If they had stayed long, the soldiers from Ohio would have gained a lot of weight.

The only negative note was that they had not been paid since duty at Luray. The army was only six months behind in their pay.

When the Eighth arrived in Rockville on the fifth, it seemed the whole army was massed in the area.[22]

The movement filled the highways, such as they were. Cavalry went in front, on the flanks, and covered the rear. Then came the infantry and artillery, followed by the long wagon trains containing food, ammunition, and other supplies.

Each unit was supposed to have its course charted for the day. A time was designated for departure. If two roads met, the unit reaching the junction first had the right of way. The other column filed into a field and prepared coffee. Normally the men in blue marched four abreast permitting room for orderlies and couriers to travel back and forth.

SATURDAY, SEPTEMBER 6, 1862

—*ARMY OF NORTHERN VIRGINIA*—

Frederick was captured by the Rebels. Jacob Engelbrecht writes, "This morning about 10 o'clock the Rebels took possession of our good city of Frederick without opposition—no soldiers of the U.S. being here. About five or six thousand Cavalry and Infantry and also three Batteries of Artillery...No commotion, or excitement, but all peaceably and quiet the soldiers are around the town purchasing clothing—shoes, caps and eatables...Many of our citizens left town last night."[23]

It was an exciting day. The men in gray had reached Fredericktown, and the threat of battle loomed on the horizon. Colonel Bradley T. Johnson, a native of Frederick, was immediately appointed provost marshal. Jackson was quick to tell the folks why the Confederate army was there. "Remember the cells of Fort McHenry...the insults to your wives and daughters! The arrests! The midnight searches of your house!...rise at once and strike for Liberty and right." The people who had not taken cover listened with respect, but made little effort to respond.

General Lee wrote to President Jefferson Davis that "two divisions of the army have crossed the Potomac, and I hope all will cross today. Navigation of the Chesapeake and Ohio has been interrupted and efforts will be made to break up the use of the Baltimore and Ohio Railroad."[24]

Jackson was still hurting, and kept D.H. Hill in command of his columns, but then he got back on his horse and rode to a point above the bridge over the Monocacy. En route, he heard one of the soldiers say, "I wonder if the general has roasting ears in his haversack, too?" When the troops stopped for lunch, Jackson reached into his haversack, pulled out a roasting ear and joined the men in the ranks in gnawing on the ear. Jed Hotchkiss says that Headquarters were established four miles from Frederick, close to the Monocacy Junction of the B & O Railroad. Lee's tents were nearby.

During this Saturday, Winder's Brigade crossed the Potomac "in excellent order and high spirits, following the Monocacy road, crossing the river of the same name, and encamped within seven miles of Frederick City."[25]

David R. Jones and his division crossed the Potomac today, marched through Buckeystown and encamped on the banks of the Monocacy River.[26]

The artillery reserve of the Army of Northern Virginia was placed in the rear and therefore did not move until September 7. Writing from Leesburg this first Saturday in September, William Pendleton says:

> We are to cross into Maryland. Most of the army crossed last night and this morning; we go tomorrow morning...There

will be a great deal of warm work in the operations now entered upon. May God guide, strengthen, and direct us in them.[27]

Robert Poague and the captains in the Rockbridge Artillery fared rather well camping near Frederick. They went to a Dutch farmhouse and got "first rate meals." Although not Southerners, they took the Confederate money. Poague "never enjoyed good things to eat as much in my whole army experience." The word spread and soon some infantry officers joined them. The farm family fed all they could accommodate.[28]

Rebels broke into the office of *The Frederick Examiner.* After forcing the door, the men started to break up the furniture. They turned their attention to papers and books and would have destroyed the press and type had not Mr. William Ross pleaded with the provost marshal of the Rebel army. Guards were then placed at the office.[29]

It's too bad there was not a photographer in Frederick to capture the sights of the Army of Northern Virginia. One writer says that even Jackson "wore a seedy and dirty hat which any Northern beggar would consider an insult to have offered to him...The soldiers had a decayed appearance."[30]

Apparently some wore pants made of U.S. Army tent canvas, the material having been captured at Manassas. Yet the folks at Fredericktown were grateful that the Rebs purchased the stocks of clothing in their stores. They realized, and the Rebels knew, that the Union soldiers would have stolen or taken the goods they wanted.

To see a regiment formed may have looked like a circus. In many cases, no two men were dressed alike. There were blue jackets trimmed in green, grey trimmed in red, trousers were likewise like Joseph's "coat of many colors." And to top it off, many were shoeless, and many were in rags, while most had no undershirts. Still others had no blankets to protect themselves from the chill of the September nights.

Nights and days of marching and sleeping on the ground made the so-called uniforms dusty and greasy. Bugs, lice, and other vermin infested the clothing, requiring, whenever the opportunity, hours of boiling to get rid of the varmints for a short period of time.

Most of the men in the Army of Northern Virginia felt that fighting was not the hardest part of being a soldier, but marching with heavy loads, hungry, lousy, and poorly clothed was almost more than some could take.

They agreed with Lee's policy in Maryland of "touch not, taste not, handle not," so different from Union acts in the South. But the fresh fruit was a great temptation. Lt. Bob Coe of the Eighth

Virginia was actually arrested for breaking ranks and stuffing his pockets with apples.

Some Confederate soldiers, although respecting Lee, were bitter. They knew of paths eighteen and thirty miles wide desolated by the Yankees in Virginia, and wanted to get even. European observers were amazed by the conduct of Lee's army. They believed, "to the victors belong the spoils." A writer from the *London Times* thought it was a great mistake on the part of Davis and Lee to wage dignified and gentlemanly warfare.

Randolph Shotwell felt the war might have been won if Southern armies had invaded Northern soil and lived off the land. "Let the hardships and losses of war once begin to fall upon Yankee pockets, and the Peace would soon have dawned. But a different policy led to a different end."[31]

—*ARMY OF THE POTOMAC*—

Things were happening on the Union side, too.

Elements of the First and Ninth Corps were coming together at Leesboro, Maryland, forming the right wing, under the leadership of Ambrose Burnside.

New units were arriving in Washington and were ordered to report to the various corps. Orders specified the Ninth Corps at Leesboro six miles out the Seventh Street Road; Franklin's Corps on the grounds of the Virginia Theological Seminary; and Sumner's Corps at Rockville.

Marsena Patrick went to headquarters in Arlington. Patrick learned that both Pope and McDowell were to be relieved. McClellan was to be placed in command of all forces around Washington. Patrick felt sick, perhaps it was because he heard the talk that the Southern Confederacy deserved to be recognized.[32]

From Monday through Friday the Sixth Corps remained in camp near Alexandria, collecting horses and transportation. But today the men under William F. Franklin crossed the Long Bridge, tramped through Georgetown on to Tenallytown, completing the first steps on the road north.

At 4:05 p.m. General McClellan ordered the First Corps to move at once from the Virginia side of the Potomac near Upton's Hill, and proceed via the Long and Aqueduct Bridges, using the Seventeenth Street Road to Leesborough.[33]

Alfred Pleasonton sent back reports today saying 30,000 Confederates had crossed the river, and that their objective was Washington. Three different dispatches quoted the 30,000 figure.[34]

The Confederates had been in Barnesville and were now within three miles of Clarksburg. Loyal Union citizens had been compelled to take down their flags. They were threatened by those loyal to the South who boasted that by nightfall the Rebels would occupy Clarksburg.

The Yankee cavalry reached Clarksburg, and by nightfall scouts were looking over the countryside as far as Hyattstown. The First U.S. Cavalry rode to Brookville to "scout in the direction of the Baltimore and Ohio Railroad." The Eighth Illinois and the Third Indiana advanced towards Darnestown and picketed the roads toward Poolesville and the Potomac.

At 6:15 p.m. Mr. Diffey, a supervisor with the Baltimore and Ohio Railroad, sent word to government sources saying that 5,000 Confederates had already passed a spot near Frederick Junction and they were still coming as far as the eye could see. Telegraph lines had been cut at the east end of the bridge, but the Confederates "were quiet and orderly."[35]

"The Clustered Spires of Fredericktown"
Courtesy—The Frederick News-Post

CHAPTER III

"THE CLUSTERED SPIRES OF FREDERICKTOWN"

During this first week in September, the war that the folks of Frederick had read about came home to their doorsteps. Union troops had come and gone for over a year, and the city had been used for a supply depot. Now Frederick was an occupied city and the Confederate army ringed the city.

It was a day full of events, excitement, and alarm, depending on who you were and what your hopes were. The men in gray felt sure they were on the verge of great success, while the citizens of Frederick were full of anxiety. It was a warm day and Jed Hotchkiss was busy making another map for Jackson.

Robert Moore, a cannoneer in the famed Rockbridge artillery from the Shenandoah Valley, hoped, along with his comrades, to reach Baltimore. All his dreams were about what he was going to do when they reached that Maryland city.

Although orders were given to stay in camp, Moore and Steve Dandridge slipped out, evaded the provost guard, crept through a field of corn and made their way to Frederick.

Dandridge had a few U.S. dollars. So the two of them went to a small store and had some wine, bread and butter. They had their canteens filled with whiskey for future use.

Moore and Dandridge did some more shopping and sat down to a nice big watermelon purchased from a fruit stand. Then bells rang in Steve's head. He remembered a girl he knew who was staying in Frederick. She was supposed to be at the home of a Mr. Webster. To his delight he found her in and was invited to stay for dinner. Moore excused himself and went back to camp.

That night officers had to break up a fight between the Rockbridge Artillery and Raines' Battery from Lynchburg.

27

While encamped near the "clustered spires," the Confederate artillerymen feasted daily on apple dumplings.[1]

William Owen looked for something to eat as soon as he got across the Potomac. Food had been short, consisting mainly of corn plucked from the fields along the route of march. "We call this...the 'Green corn campaign'." Most of the folks said they were Rebels, primarily because it was expedient to say so. The young ladies were wild to see General Lee. After lunch, Owen and several others lined up a column of girls in family carriages and started off to find "Uncle Robert." He was surrounded by the girls, hugged and kissed, and became very red in the face. The younger soldiers were wishing all the time the girls would turn their attention toward them.[2]

D.R. Jones marched from the Monocacy near Buckeystown today to Monocacy Junction and went into camp near the "Clustered Spires of Fredericktown."

Major H.J. Williams of the Fifth Virginia Infantry entered Frederick today and encamped about two miles from town on the Emmitsburg Road. This was at Worman's Mill. "Our short sojourn in the land of promise brought a salutary change in the general appearance and condition of the troops. The ragged were clad, the shoeless shod, and the inner man rejoiced by a number and variety of delicacies to which it had been a stranger for long, long weary months before."[3]

Watermelons must have been plentiful in September of '62. The 21st Virginia Infantry came upon a string of B & O Railroad cars, apparently near Monocacy Junction. One of the cars was loaded with watermelons. The men broke ranks and made their selections. They then entered Frederick with the watermelons under their arms. Perhaps the folks wondered if they had a new weapon. The Virginians went to the Frederick agricultural grounds and made camp. They raided a large Union hospital. John Worsham, an enterprising member of the 21st, skipped camp to see the town. He was invited into several homes, and treated very nicely. At several places he was offered something to eat. In the course of the evening, he "ate enough for six."[4]

Late afternoon, the Texas Brigade passed through Buckeystown, and made camp south of Frederick, near the Monocacy and the B & O bridge. They were to remain here for two days. The time was spent resting and bathing in the river. The men bathed with their clothes on. That way they saved a duplication of effort.

In September of '62, George Neese was a gunner in Chew's Battery, and was attached to Munford's cavalry. At midnight the guns and the artillerymen plunged into the Potomac. The water was two and a half feet deep. What a way to begin the Sabbath.

Neese left the "Southern Confederacy...and landed in the United States, in Montgomery County..." He marched most of the night, through the morning, and about 2:00 p.m. reached a point near Frederick. He notes that the Potomac was about four hundred yards wide where the artillery crossed, with a "gentle current and smooth bottom."[5]

From a distance, George admired the "Clustered Spires of Fredericktown." The countryside was beautiful, "rich and fertile land, well cultivated." Chew's Battery was ordered to Urbana. En route, they saw Jackson's men destroying the stone and iron railroad bridge over the Monocacy River. It was sunset when the gray cannoneers reached the village of Urbana.

People flocked to the headquarter's tents located south of Frederick. Lee, Longstreet, Jackson, and Stuart were in great demand. The people wanted to see them, but Jackson and Lee were not feeling well, and each of the leaders had a lot to do, so they stayed close to their tents.

On Saturday, Henry Kyd Douglas had a visitor. His mother drove from Ferry Hill on the banks of the Potomac to see her son. She also had the opportunity to meet the famous Generals of the Confederacy. Lee, Jackson, and Longstreet cordially received her.

In late afternoon, Jackson was called to Lee's tent. On the way, he met a carriage with two young girls from Baltimore. Both jumped out and ran to the general. One took his hand, while the other put her arm around old "Stonewall." He was embarrassed and miserable in the situation.[6]

Jackson did not go to Sunday morning services, but in the evening, he wrote out a pass and climbed into an ambulance. Accompanied by Douglas and Morrison, he rode from Frederick Junction into Frederick and the German Reformed Church on West Church Street. The church was chosen as there were no services at the Presbyterian Church.

While Jackson was thinking about church, William Owen and the artillerymen found a grocer who accepted a few hundred dollars and supplied the men in gray good food and drink. "Champagne flowed like water." The end result was a good old headache, cured the next morning by a cold dip in the Monocacy River.

On one side of the Washington Artillery were the tents of James Longstreet and on the other the tent of Jackson. "Old Jack" kidded Longstreet for being the only general with a "bodyguard of artillery."

At the church service Jackson was tired, and soon he fell asleep. "His head sank upon his breast, his cap dropped from his hands to the floor." The prayer of the congregation, and the preaching of the pastor did not disturb him. It took the music of the choir to rouse him.

Henry Kyd Douglas, who was with his commander, learned that Rev. Daniel Zacharias, the pastor of the German Reformed Church, was praised because he had the nerve to pray for President Lincoln in the presence of General Jackson. "Well, the general didn't hear the prayer; but if he had, he would doubtless have felt like replying as General Ewell did, when asked at Carlisle,...if he would permit the usual prayer for President Lincoln, ...'certainly, I'm sure he needs it.' "[7]

On Monday, Jackson was to write home to his wife of the experience. He felt sorrow at falling asleep. He continued by saying, "The minister is a gifted one, and the building beautiful....The town appears to be a charming place...."[8] Jackson also expressed surprise that so many went to church, seemingly unafraid or unconcerned about the presence of the Rebel army.

"Stonewall" also expressed the wish that he might be back home in Lexington surrounded by peace instead of war.

This was a busy day for William Nelson Pendleton. Today he and the Confederate Reserve Artillery left Leesburg and forded the Potomac. The Episcopal cleric was upset, he did not have time to go to church. Throughout the September Sabbath he rode through the Maryland countryside. Finally, as the clock struck the end of the day, he and his command reached their bivouac at Arcadia along Ballenger Creek, south of Fredericktown.[9]

Jacob Engelbrecht wasn't the only resident of Frederick to keep a journal. Catherine Susan Thomas Markell, a Southern sympathizer, also recorded daily events. She notes that on the seventh, General Jackson sat in William Dantz' pew, just two seats from the Markells.

On the eighth Mrs. Markell was honored to have General William Barksdale of Mississippi and his staff as dinner guests. She also sent fruit to General Jubal Early. The general's brother carried the pears, plums, and grapes in a big red bandana. Later in the day, Generals Lafayette McLaws and Joseph Kershaw took tea at the Markell residence. "Some twenty officers and girls were at the Markell home until almost midnight."

—ARMY OF THE POTOMAC—

While the Confederates were relaxing in Frederick, the Eighth Illinois and the Third Indiana cavalry regiments dashed into Poolesville and captured some Confederates. Major Chapman led the charge.

The weather was fair and pleasant, and in Washington, David Strother went to the Willard Hotel. There he heard that Pope was no longer in command of the Army of the Potomac. McClellan was in command again.

David also heard from John W. Garrett, the President of the Baltimore and Ohio Railroad that 5,000 Confederate troops had moved toward Frederick. Strother, a Virginian who cast his lot with the North, felt it was absurd for the Confederacy to think it could conquer the North. In the evening sixty pieces of artillery and 20,000 infantry marched up G. Street, heading eventually to Frederick.[10]

George McClellan was putting his reorganized army in motion. McClellan wrote to his wife,

> Again I have been called upon to save the country. The case is desperate, but with God's help I will try...to do my best....My men are true and will stand by me to the last. I still hope for success, and will leave nothing undone to gain it....My hands are full, so is my heart.[11]

At noon today, Alfred Pleasonton sent a dispatch to General Marcy saying cavalry pickets had questioned a man who said that Longstreet's Corps had crossed the Potomac yesterday, and had headed north on the Chesapeake and Ohio Canal towpath. Jackson's men were on ahead of Longstreet. The Confederates were "badly cared for, many of them without shoes."[12]

By 6:40 p.m. Colonel Farnsworth reported Poolesville in Federal hands. He had driven the Fifth Virginia Cavalry and its sixty-man detachment from the town. Most of the Rebel cavalry had gone to Barnesville on Saturday. A black man told the Union officer that he had taken some ladies to Barnesville to see the Rebels. "They told the ladies they were going to Frederick, and from thence to Baltimore." The Rebel train finished crossing at Conrad's Ferry that morning, and passed in the direction of Frederick.[13]

Governor Curtin of Pennsylvania seemed to have direct sources. He reported 35,000 Confederates in Frederick, "shoeless, unclad, taking possession of all stores having shoes, army goods, or other supplies, paying for the same in Confederate scrip. Announced their destination as Baltimore."

A source told Governor Curtin that Jackson had made the statement that he was going to Philadelphia via Adams and York Counties and Lancaster. The Pennsylvania Governor was sure that invasion was coming through the Cumberland Valley. Many folks from Hagerstown and Western Maryland arrived in Harrisburg late Saturday night and in the early hours of the Sabbath.[14]

In September of '62, James Oliver was a young doctor from Athol, Massachusetts, serving with the 21st regiment from that state as a physician. He lived a long life, and after the war he was a country doctor and member of the Massachusetts Legislature, and Chairman of the Education Committee.

Dr. Oliver did not reach the regiment until after Chantilly. He found the battle "a staggering blow to the 'unit.' " The whole country and the army were terribly depressed after the defeat of Second Bull Run. The army was demoralized. Although he did not care for General Pope, Oliver felt Pope had not been properly supported.

Oliver broke camp in Alexandria on September 4 and marched to a spot north of Washington, D.C. On the seventh the tramp toward Frederick began. At this point, Oliver began to realize the difficulties of a regimental surgeon. The troops were tired from the Virginia campaigns, "and disgusted with the Army of the Potomac." When the order came to break camp, many went on "sick call." Young Dr. Oliver had a severe task as he sought to separate those who were really sick from those who were just pretending. One hundred fifty men came to see the doctor. He was swamped. But just in the nick of time, Dr. Cutter, who had been with the regiment from the time of muster, arrived. He knew every man and soon had everything straightened out.

Oliver was a wise young man. He saw that troops would try to take advantage of him. After all, a doctor's word in regards to the health of troops was higher than that of a general. He also noted that "The marching in Maryland was not rapid or exhausting." McClellan was proceeding with his usual caution. The country was beautiful and soon the soldiers became more cheerful, and confident."[15]

Charles Johnson placed his journal in his knapsack and placed it in one of the regimental supply wagons. He wondered if he would ever see it again. To aid his memory, he prepared a little notebook to carry with him so he could jot down his thoughts. He was comforted by the fact that " 'Little Mac' is ahead of us, and you know he is our 'best'!"

At sunrise the men of the 35th Massachusetts washed their faces and hands in a horse trough and went to look for breakfast in the houses along 7th Street. They would eat army rations only as a last resort. Every house was full, and the task was difficult. The day became hot and the men marched but four miles.[16]

Matthew Graham says that McClellan started on the "Roads to Antietam" with 87,000 men, leaving 73,000 men, 120 field pieces, and 500 heavy guns to protect Washington.

For the first few days the weather was ideal, although a little warm. The absence of mud made things nicer, and of course being in friendly country was a tremendous change and boost to morale.

This is stated in almost every account. Matthew Graham says the men moved at a leisurely pace, and enjoyed seeing men at work in the fields and ladies hanging the wash. Some women stood in the doorways of their houses, while children came to the edge of the road, or peered from windows. The only disturbing element was the dust. The roads had been ground to powder by the continuous procession of men and wagons. All the men kept an eye for good springs of water. The Ninth New York and other units were part of a great river of blue converging on Frederick.[17]

Some units plodded along and kept very loose organization. Lieutenant Colonel Kimball of the Ninth New York was not about to let this happen to his regiment. He formed a strong rear detachment, and along with his officers kept a constant watch on conditions. In general, the march of the entire army got better with each passing day.

The 35th Massachusetts was assigned to the Ninth Corps and that Saturday evening "fell in, crossed the Long Bridge and marched through the streets of Washington." The regimental historian says:

> ...the people were at leisure, and doors and windows were crowded with spectators. Expectation of battle was vivid, and cheers followed the troops as they hurried through the darkening streets, accompanied by the rumble of heavy wagons and tramp of many feet. A part of the regiment turned off to the arsenal to exchange muskets; the rest marched up Seventh Street, due north, into the dust and pale moonlight of the country roads, the night air hot, but excitement cooling as the city was left behind. On we pushed until past midnight, tramp, tramp, by quiet farms and sleeping countrymen. Men began to express fatigue in emphatic words, then straggling began, and rebukes were of no avail. The rear had almost mingled with the head of the column when, at half past one o'clock, the order came to halt for the night; and, footsore and weary, the men sought shelter in an oak grove beside the road, and, gathering a few dried leaves, rolled themselves in such coverings as they had and slept.[18]

Panicky citizens in the District expected Lee to move directly on the defenses of Washington. Instead, he crossed the Potomac at the Upper fords and invaded Maryland, where he hoped that the people would rise in support of the Confederacy. In that respect, his hopes were dashed. Western Maryland was not the Eastern Shore. The partisans of secession had long since gone south, and Whittier's *Barbara Fritchie*, if only a legend, nevertheless reflected the loyal spirit of the population.[19]

The Irish Brigade shared the enthusiasm with which the rest of the Union army greeted the return of George B. McClellan. The men almost idolized him. It is hard to find a military commander whose presence made such a difference in the morale of the men.

One soldier wrote that marching around Virginia for a week, carrying fifty pounds of equipment, living on one meal a day, and sleeping on the wet ground, could not keep the men from cheering at the news of McClellan's return.

Naturally McClellan had to follow the military strategy of the day, protect Washington, Baltimore, and Philadelphia. So he had to advance between Lee and these cities. Three roads were taken. They were what is now Route 97, leading to the road between Baltimore and Frederick; the main pike from Washington to Frederick through Rockville, Clarksburg, Hyattstown, and Urbana; and the so-called River Road or current Maryland 28, running through Beallsville and Dickerson.

The contrast in Maryland from the devastation in Virginia was most welcome and noticeable. The land and farms in Virginia had been stripped bare. But in Maryland all was fresh and green. Now instead of cold, sullen glares, and icy comments, the men were met with smiling faces, butter, pork, chicken, ripe fruit, good bread, and homemade pies. They never had it so good.

Josiah Favill and his comrades were at Rockville. Everybody was friendly for a change, and the men felt proud to belong "to a gallant army...hurrying to place itself across the path of the invader." Camp was pitched on a lovely hillside. As soon as they were free from command responsibilities, several officers rode into Rockville to visit with the people. The folks were very much impressed with the "sunburnt soldiers on whom so much depends."

Women and children greeted the soldiers with fruit, flowers, and water. The men of the 57th New York and the other soldiers in blue were the heroes of the hour. Many of the soldiers gave buttons to the prettiest girls they could find. It seems as though people everywhere wanted military buttons from the soldiers.

The citizens of Rockville were to have plenty of opportunity to gather buttons. By the next day, hourly reports started coming in of the crossing of the Potomac by the Rebels. Young Favill was very much impressed with the troop build-up. He thought McClellan had an immense army, well equipped and eager for battle, "Brains and genius are only wanting to accomplish the greatest results."

The men seemed to realize that everything depended on them. They knew that if they were defeated, Philadelphia, Baltimore, and Washington would "be the prizes to fall into the hands of the Rebels."[20]

Three soldiers from Massachusetts tramped northward on the "Roads to Antietam." They all took notes, and all three died of wounds received in action.

H.R. Dunham was with Company B, 19th Massachusetts. His journal for the Maryland Campaign was found in the Hoffman barn at Antietam. For the seventh, he says:

> Today is Sunday 7 am but how different from our quiet New England Sunday. Nothing around to remind one that it is God's day of rest. Much would I give if I could be. God help me so to live that if I never spend an earthly Sabbath at home with friends I love, that I meet them all where I can spend an eternal Sabbath with them in heaven. O God, help me to live aright here that I may reign with Christ in Heaven.[21]

> Today my Regt. is on picket duty about four miles from Darnestown.

Wilder Dwight was a Lieutenant Colonel in the Second Massachusetts:
He states:

> The events of the last three weeks are incredible. Disaster, pitiable, humiliating, contemptible!

> It is a hot, sunny, breezy afternoon. We are line of battle with Sumner's corps....We want SOLDIERS, and a General in command....O, it is heavy to see life and hope and peace and honor withering away daily....Nor do I see any evidence of tone or wisdom in power anywhere....

> It has come back to McClellan! I met him in Washington the other day. His manner was gay, confident, elate. His staff were jubilant. Again, he takes the reins, and what do you expect? I must hope, though I know not why.[22]

MONDAY, SEPTEMBER 8, 1862

—ARMY OF NORTHERN VIRGINIA—

Early in the morning, William Pendleton reported to Robert E. Lee at Army Headquarters at Monocacy Junction. With no military duties, Pendleton rode into Frederick to visit some of his former parishioners. He and the family had served all Saints Episcopal Church during the years 1846–1854, prior to leaving for Lexington. He found the church and parsonage both closed. But the church members were glad to see him. He says, "Greater kindness no one ever received."[23]

While Pendleton was visiting and enjoying the day in Frederick, Robert E. Lee was busy. He had planned to wait in Frederick until McClellan made some move, and until he saw how the people of Maryland would respond to the invasion. He wished to be as tactful and diplomatic as possible.

On September 4, Lee had conferred with Bradley Johnson who told his commander not to expect too much from the folks in the Frederick area. Their sympathies were Northern. Lee hoped that ex-Governor Lowe, a Southern sympathizer would come and make an appeal in behalf of the South. But Lowe did not come. Time was passing and he had to do something, so Lee issued his appeal to the people of Maryland and the folks of the North. The document told why the Confederates were in Maryland, and described their aims. Lee said he was not coming as a conqueror but in hopes of a peace between the two sections of the country. He invited the folks of Maryland to join the Confederate cause, and he urged the young men to enlist in the ranks. From the older people Lee asked their prayers and sympathies.

The residents of Frederick County listened to the plea but paid little attention. They remained "passive spectators and disinterested witnesses." They showed "little sympathy" with the Southern cause.

For the most part, the Confederate soldiers obeyed Lee's orders in respect to the protection of private property. Soldier Dickert in Kershaw's Brigade said the campaign was "conducted with kid gloves on."[24]

Primarily the citizens looked with curiosity and wondered when the Rebels would go. They had heard of the greatness of Lee and Jackson. But when they looked at the dirty, ragged soldiers, the awe faded away. And perhaps many wondered just how long the Confederacy could continue. Some wanted to see Jackson sucking his lemon, but he had little time for visitors, press conferences, or entertaining. This was war and he had work to do.

Some storekeepers jumped their prices so that coffee was a dollar. The men in gray, however, listened to Lee and discipline was strict.

> Their behavior towards everyone was very carefully managed—no bad treatment of anyone was permitted (wrote a local citizen). No straggling was allowed, and although no discipline measures were observed, implicit obedience was maintained; for if a man declined or moved tardily a blow of a sabre or butt of a pistol enforced the order. It was stated by the men that four of the army had been shot for straggling since leaving Leesburgh.[25]

But soldiers are pretty keen. George Shreve and the Horse Artillery had roast pig. When questioned about it, they said the pig wondered into camp and they had to kill it in self-defense. No more questions were asked and the troopers enjoyed their meal.

All indications point to a quiet, restrained reception in Frederick. However, the picturesque and romantic Von Borcke saw it differently:

> Entering the good old city of Frederick, I found it in a tremendous state of excitement. The Unionists living there had their houses closely shut up and barred; but the far greater number of citizens, being favourably disposed to the Confederate cause, had thrown wide open their doors and windows, and welcomed our troops with the liveliest enthusiasm. Flags were floating from the houses, and garlands of flowers were hung across the streets. Everywhere a dense multitude was moving up and down, singing and shouting in a paroxysm of joy and patriotic emotion, in many cases partly superinduced by an abundant flow of strong liquors.[26]

Lack of shoes, uniforms, and food all contributed to the misery and appearance of the Rebels in Frederick. Many of them had trouble with a proverbial army problem, lice.

> Every evening, hundreds could be seen, sitting on the roads or fields, half denuded with clothes in laps, busily cracking, between two thumbnails, these creeping nuisances (graybacks or body lice)...the men would boil their clothes for hours—next day these confounded things would be at work as lively as ever...many used to place their under-raiment, during the night, in the bottom of some stream and put a large stone to keep them down; in the morning they would hastily dry them and get a temporary relief...[27]

A lady wrote a classic description of the appearance of the Army of Northern Virginia in Frederick.

> I wish, my dear Minnie, you could have witnessed the transit of the Rebel army through our streets...Their coming was unheralded by any pomp and pageant whatever. No burst of martial music greeted your ear, no thundering sound of cannon, no brilliant staff, no glittering cortege dashed through the streets; instead came three long, dirty columns that kept on in an unceasing flow. I could scarcely believe my eyes; was this body of men moving so smoothly along, with no order, their guns carried in every fashion, no two dressed alike, their officers hardly distinguishable from the privates, were these, I asked myself in amazement, were these dirty, lank ugly specimens of humanity, with shocks of hair sticking through holes in their hats, and dust thick on their dirty faces, the men that had coped and encountered

successfully, and driven back again and again, our splendid legions with their fine discipline, their martial show and color, their solid battalions keeping such perfect time to the inspiring bands of music? I must confess, Minnie, that I felt humiliated at the thought that this horde of ragamuffins could set our grand army of the Union at defiance.

Why it seemed as if a single regiment of our gallant boys in blue could drive that dirty crew into the river without any trouble. And then, too, I wish you could see how they behaved—a crowd of boys on a holiday don't seem happier. They are on the broad grin all the time. O, they are so dirty! I don't think the Potomac River could wash them clean; and ragged! There is not a scarecrow in our cornfields that would not scorn to exchange clothes with them; and so tattered! There isn't a decently dressed soldier in the whole army.

I saw some strikingly handsome faces though, or rather they would have been so if they could have had a good scrubbing. They were very polite, I must confess, and always asked for a drink of water, or anything else, and never think of coming inside of a door without an invitation. Many of them were barefooted. Indeed, I felt sorry for the poor, misguided wretches, for some of them limped along so painfully, trying to keep up with their comrades.[28]

"Yet those grimy, sweaty, lean, ragged men" were the flower of Lee's army. But they were soldiers and well disciplined. Even a Union sympathizer writes in admiration:

In manners, in the conduct of soldiers and the discipline, these bundles of rags, these cough-racked, diseased and starved men excel our well-fed, well-clothed, our best soldiers. No one can point to a single act of vandalism perpetrated by the Rebel soldiery during their occupation of Frederick, while even now a countless host of (Federal) stragglers are crawling after our own army, devouring, destroying or wasting all that falls in their devious line of march. God knows I have no need to praise Confederate forebearance, but the fact that we are confronted by an army perfectly under the control and discipline of tried and experienced officers is incontrovertible. It accounts for the excellence of their fighting, and the almost powerlessness of our own army.[29]

Jed Hotchkiss continued working on his maps in the morning, and in the afternoon rode into Frederick.

The Valley Register, the weekly newspaper covering events in the Middletown area, was published as usual on September 5. At that time all was quiet and peaceful in the Valley. There was no apparent threat to Frederick County, and the few who talked of the threat of a Confederate invasion were considered "all wet." Besides, Middletown was small and there was nothing an invading army would want.

However, things changed drastically in a few days. The editor, George Carlton Rhoderick, being pro-Northern, fled, as did many others when the reality of the Confederate invasion became known. And *The Valley Register* was not published on September 12. Instead columns of blue-clad troops would follow those in gray who had already tramped through the town on the main road. And a few days later, the little German farming village would become a hospital with patients in some of the buildings until January of 1863.

Mr. Rhoderick fled to Pennsylvania but when he returned, being a good reporter, he obtained first-hand information from those who witnessed the stirring days. Those who saw the Confederate troops in Frederick and Middletown agreed that the Army of Northern Virginia "was in the most forlorn and starving condition, ragged, shoeless, hatless, and filled with vermin." Their conduct was good with the exception of tearing down the United States flag and tramping it in the dust.

That September Monday, Captain Edwards Motter, a native of the Valley, returned home with the Confederates, and boasted of what they were going to do. They hauled down the Union flag at George Crouse's, and tore it to shreds.

That morning Chew's Battery and Munford's cavalry started south from Urbana toward Poolesville. It was an eighteen-mile journey. One mile from their destination, the Confederates saw the Yankee cavalry. These were, according to George Neese, "the first Yanks we saw since our arrival in the United States."[30]

One mile from town, Neese and his comrades went into position on a hill, near the edge of a woods. George felt that only the fire of the battery kept the Rebel cavalry from being wiped out.

Neese was really surprised at the warm response. The blue artillery forced the Confederate battery to move, and after they got the range, dropped shells right in their midst. George says, "I believe that the confounded Yankees can shoot better in the United States than they can when they come to Dixieland. They did better shooting with their artillery today than any I have seen since I have been in service."

The action was fierce. And not until the end were the Confederates assured of safety. Neese thought,

> If today's proceedings is an average specimen of the treatment the dear Yanks intend to give us in the dear United States, I think the best thing we can do is go back to Dixie right away.[31]

After a ten-mile withdrawal, the Rebel artillery and cavalry camped for the night at the southern base of Sugar Loaf Mountain. Neese slept in a straw stack.

Neese was very much impressed with the little town of Barnesville, and the beauty of Sugar Loaf Mountain. He and his comrades were aware of a Yankee signal station near the top, commanding a view of everything.

John Chamberlayne took time to write to his sister Lucy from a spot along the B & O Railroad at Monocacy Junction. He relates: "A dirtier, more ragged, exhausting set would be hard to find, the world over. To one who sees and knows the conditions and privations of this army, their endurance and great deeds especially within the last month makes food for the extremest wonder."

Chamberlayne went on to extol the virtues of the Army of Northern Virginia, but added cautiously, "Our work is not half done, but the army has by experience gained such confidence in itself and its leaders that it may be said to be irresistible. Whatever Lee's plans are, they will be good, and his army can carry them out."

Then the young artillery officer talked about Frederick County, saying, "People are kind enough generally, but they fear us with a mortal terror; many of them seem to think us Goths and Vandals and Huns, they tremble sometimes when spoke to, and are astonished to see us without torch and tomahawk...."

"The Valley of the Monocacy is beautiful; like parts of Loudoun and Orange,...only softer, more highly cultivated and settled more thickly than either....This county, Frederick is as Yankee as Hartford or Cape Cod."

Ham told about having dinner in town on the seventh and talking with a pretty young girl by the name of Miss Schley. She told the Confederate officer that she had friends in both armies.

Chamberlayne concluded by saying he was lonesome, and missed his books and old familiar faces. "I do so long to be home again, where people have time to think of something besides powder and lead, and where there will be talk of other than dead and wounded....The most comfortable thing I know is that all things must cease and therefore if we don't the war will."[32]

For Jacob Engelbrecht, the situation was almost unbelievable.

Is it possible?—the Good old city of Frederick is in possession of the Confederate Army under Genl. R.E. Lee, but the City I believe under Genl. Thos. J. Jackson...—the different divisions are encampt 2 or 3 miles around the city and number about 80,000, Col. Bradley Johnson...Rev. Brig. Genl. Wm. N. Pendleton....The men had leave of absence to visit the town and make purchases....There were at least ten thousand in town, a complete Jam, all the Stores & Shops were Sold out....The Rail Road Iron Bridge at the Monocacy Junction was destroyed yesterday also the Georgetown bridge nearby. Pickets are Stationed all around town 3 or 4 miles & all the farmers wishing to go home & come in must have passes—Genl. James Coopers house (Fredk A. Schelys) has been taken as Headquarters.—the Basement of the Court House has been taken as the Guard House.[33]

Stuart ordered Munford to drive the Yankees from Poolesville. Three regiments were sent to perform the task, along with four cannon. The shot and shell flew back and forth. The Yankees charged and were driven back. The crossroads commanding the approach to Sugar Loaf Mountain was held and remained in Confederate hands for another three days.[34]

All of the Confederate cavalrymen agreed that life in the Urbana area was like an oasis in the desert. There was nothing to do but to await the Union advance, make patrols, and mingle with the good people of the area. Of course, a major interest was girls. The staff officers accepted the kind hospitality of Mr. Cockey, a Southern sympathizer who invited them to make cavalry headquarters in his yard. Stuart and Major Von Borcke enjoyed the lovely Ann Cockey, the cousin of Martha and Virginia. Ann was from New York and visiting and definitely Yankee. Nevertheless, she enjoyed the soldiers and the attention they paid to her. Pelham and Breathed double dated the sisters. They strolled through the orchards and talked of many things, of life in Alabama, the course of the war, and the future. Every moment that could be spent away from duty was in company with the Cockey girls.

Stuart knew how to take advantage of a good thing. So it was decided to decorate a large vacant building which had been used as an academy, and hold a ball. Colonel Blackford of Stuart's staff describes the gala evening in Urbana.

> On the edge of the village stood a large, vacant building which had been in peace times used as a female academy, and the staff was soon busied in having a large room prepared there. The walls were decorated with regimental Confederate flags collected from the regiments around, an army band furnished the music, and lovely moonlight lit the beauty and fashion of the country on their way as they assembled in response to our invitation. The officers came prepared for any emergency, fully armed and equipped, picketing their horses in the yard and hanging their sabres against the walls of the dance hall. As the delightful strains of music floated through the vacant old house,

and the dancing began, the strange accompaniments of war added zest to the occasion, and our lovely partners declared that it was perfectly charming. But they were destined to have more of the war accompaniment than was intended by the managers, for just as everything had become well started and the enjoyment of the evening was at its height, there came shivering through the still night air the boom of artillery, followed by the angry rattle of musketry. The lily chased the rose from the cheek of beauty, and every pretty foot was rooted to the floor where music had left it. Then came hasty and tender partings from tearful partners, buckling on of sabres, mounting of impatient steeds, and clattering of hoofs as the gay cavaliers dashed off to the front.

McClellan's advance guard had struck our outposts, but after a sharp skirmish they withdrew for the night and we hastened back "covered with glory," at least in the ladies' eyes. Dancing was resumed and was at its height again when, alas, it was doomed to a final interruption. Heavy tramping of feet in the passage attracted the attention of the lady who was my partner, standing at the time next the door of the ballroom. Looking out, she clasped her hands and uttered a piercing scream. The scream brought all the dancers trooping out to see what was the matter now, and there on stretchers the wounded were being carried by to the vacant rooms upstairs.

It was no use talking to them of any more dancing that night. There, like a flock of angels in their white dresses assembled around the stretchers, they bent over the wounded men, dressing their wounds and ministering to their wants, with their pretty fingers all stained with blood. One handsome young fellow, as he looked up in their faces with a grateful smile, declared that he would get hit any day to have such surgeons to dress his wounds. All that was left for us now was to escort the "lovely angels" home by the light of the moon and to bid a last, tender farewell to them and to the happy days we had spent among them, for we knew that the morrow would bring again war's stirring scenes around us.[35]

There were numerous blacks with the Army of Northern Virginia, serving on general staffs, or as servants. Ned Haines arrived at Monocacy Junction today with letters, money, and other items from home for John Dooley. Ned had served with John's father and brother in earlier actions, and now declared his loyalty to John.

During the interlude, Dooley went into Frederick to visit friends on the staff of the Catholic School in town. Father Paresce insisted on giving John clean clothing, underwear included. John returned to camp feeling like a new man, clean all over.[36]

Henry Berkeley Robinson never made it to Antietam. On the way to the river his artillery unit stopped in Warrenton for a meal at a hotel. There was plenty of coffee, but little food. On September 4 he was near Aldie and had nothing for breakfast except two roasting ears. Reaching Leesburg the next day, he heard news of the crossing into Maryland, but his unit went into camp on the Winchester pike.

On the sixth and seventh, Henry spent time in Leesburg, looking for some pretty girls. The best horses from his unit were taken and given to the batteries going into Maryland. He and his comrades had to put up with a lot of broken down horses to pull guns, wagons, and other plunder from Bull Run to Winchester.

On the eighth, Berkeley's unit started for Winchester. The move was not made until sunset. They covered ten miles on a lovely, moonlight night, and then made camp on the farm of a Mr. Adams, just south of Winchester pike. The next two days were spent on the farm, and Henry and others bought chickens for sixteen cents; butter at twelve and $1/2$ cents; and milk at 25c a gallon.[37]

—ARMY OF THE POTOMAC—

South of Frederick at Rockville, General McClellan was writing another letter saying no one was aware of the great task that had been imposed upon him. "I have been obliged to do the best I could with the broken and discouraged fragments of two armies defeated by no fault of mine." He then had some uncomplimentary remarks to make about McDowell and Pope, blaming them for the deaths of some of the finest men he had commanded.

Little Mac concluded by saying, "I will probably move four or five miles further to the front tomorrow, as I have ordered the whole army forward, I expect to fight a great battle and do my best at it."

President Lincoln wanted to know "How do things look?"

A lively skirmish occurred near Poolesville. Colonel Elon Farnsworth was taking a detachment to occupy Poolesville and picket the fords of the Potomac. En route Farnsworth encountered Confederates on the Barnesville Road. Over forty men were killed or wounded on the two sides in the affair.[38]

Charles Johnson felt that if the Rebels did not skedaddle, "someone will get hurt, for McClellan is the head of us now and he is not a man to make a move for the fun of things." There are many rumors about the purpose and objective of the march. Most agreed though, that the advance in three columns was to confront the enemy. There were also rumors about Burnside taking command of the entire army.[39]

About noon, McClellan reported General Franklin at Muddy Branch, with Sykes, Sumner, and Banks near Rockville. Pleasonton was preparing to advance the cavalry to Barnesville, Hyattstown, Damascus, and Unity. McClellan was sure Lee was beyond the Monocacy.

By nightfall, McClellan had the Army of the Potomac massed between Rockville and Brookville. Although scouting reports were vague and conflicting, George was sure he could thwart an attack on Washington, Baltimore, or Pennsylvania. General Burnside was reporting that both the First and Ninth Corps were improving and in better condition than they were when they left Washington.[40]

Charles Davis and the 13th Massachusetts realized little progress had been made in terms of crushing the so-called rebellion. But at least it was a pleasure "to be again marching among loyal people who are interested in our welfare." As camp was made between Washington and Darnestown, Davis thought about things as they were a year ago. At that time, the 13th Massachusetts had numbered almost 1,000 men. Now there was half that number present for duty.[41]

During the march, some new recruits arrived. Among them was a young, patriotic high school graduate. He was shocked at the appearance of the troops. The uniforms didn't fit, and the blouses and caps were torn and faded.

Soon after his arrival, the new recruit asked where he could get some milk for his coffee. The veterans, always anxious to pull a prank, sent him to the captain. The officer was surprised, but understood the prank, and promptly informed the lad that milk was not provided by the government, it was not G.I.

Instead the captain told him that milk was provided by getting a cow, grabbing the proper instrument, and attempting to aim the stream of milk into a tin cup.

Major Hincks writes, "Woods near Rockville....We are in a magnificent oak grove and a better spot for a camp could hardly be imagined. In these same woods two or three other regiments which comprise our brigade are bivouacked. Within bugle call there may be perhaps 50 or 100,000 men."[42]

Durrell's Battery was in Montgomery County today. The men had the chance to go looking for food. They found a good supply of fruit, potatoes, and corn.[43]

This was a happy day for Edwin Marvin and members of the 5th Connecticut. The wagons containing their knapsacks caught up with them, and the soldiers were able to change clothes after four weeks of wearing the same outfit. Marvin writes, "We shall wash and change now every day until the inhabitants emigrate. We can, perhaps, make it too lively for them to form local attachments."[44]

TUESDAY, SEPTEMBER 9, 1862

—*ARMY OF NORTHERN VIRGINIA*—

Robert Edward Lee was faced with making some decisions. The folks in the Frederick area had not rallied to the Confederate cause. McClellan was advancing slowly toward him, and the Union garrisons at Harpers Ferry and Martinsburg had not been evacuated as he had thought.

Therefore to continue without a threat to his rear, or to his supplies and communications, Lee was forced to deal with these forces. Writing General Orders No. 191 from his tent south of Frederick, Lee ordered Jackson to proceed to Martinsburg, clear the town of Union forces, then continue down the south side of the Potomac and invest Harpers Ferry from Bolivar Heights.

Lafayette McLaws with his own and R.H. Anderson's division, was ordered to seize Maryland Heights on the north side of the Potomac, and James Walker was to endeavor to destroy the Monocacy Aqueduct and proceed to Loudoun Heights, on the east side of the Shenandoah. When the various commands had captured Harpers Ferry, they were to join the rest of the army at Boonsboro or Hagerstown.[45]

This was a bold and dashing move, dividing his army four ways in enemy territory. Longstreet's command would serve as the rear guard, covering the South Mountain passes, with Jeb Stuart and the cavalry patrolling and scouting.

John G. Walker got an early start on Order No. 191. His command left from their Monocacy Junction campsite to destroy the Chesapeake and Ohio Aqueduct over the Monocacy where it empties into the Potomac River. After a trip that took most of the day, they arrived at the aqueduct at 11:00 p.m. and found it occupied by enemy pickets. After an exchange of gunfire, they fled. The Confederates went to work on their task. However, due to lack of tools and the sturdiness of the masonry, they realized it would take days to complete.[46]

The Rebel cavalry was screening and shielding the advance of the main army, south and southwest of Frederick.

George Neese and his comrades watched for the Yankees to come from Poolesville today. But they didn't come. Perhaps it was just as well, for we "were ready to give our United States welcomers an explosive welcome."

Jed Hotchkiss notes that things were astir in the Confederate camp because "marching orders are out." People flocked to Confederate headquarters south of Frederick to see the famous General Jackson. They had heard so much about his Valley Campaign, and how he evaded several Union generals. They wanted to see him in person. Now was the time, because, although the folks in Frederick County did not know it, Jackson would "not pass this way again."

In the midst of military preparations, Mrs. Markell and some friends "visited Generals Lee, Jackson, and Longstreet at their headquarters about 2 miles south of Frederick. We took several bouquets—gave mine to General Longstreet."[47]

—ARMY OF THE POTOMAC—

McClellan left Washington on Sunday. He knew that a portion of the Confederate army had crossed the Potomac into Maryland. But he was not sure what they intended on doing. He didn't know whether the objective was Washington or Pennsylvania. However, he knew he had to stay between the Rebels and Washington.

Thus the First and the Ninth Corps moved to Brookville; the Twelfth and the Second to Middlebrook; while the Sixth Corps stayed between Rockville and the Potomac.

While on patrol, Colonel Farnsworth of the Eighth Illinois observed a Confederate squadron near Monocacy Church. The men in blue were able to divide the Confederate unit and succeed in capturing the flag of the Twelfth Virginia Cavalry. This was quite a trophy for the blue-clad troopers.[48]

That day H.R. Dunham and the 19th Massachusetts marched about 8 miles. "It was very warm. Most of us removed our knapsacks yesterday and are pretty well used up. I did not fall out. Corp...did because of sunstroke & we had to leave him by the side of the road, to come along with the ambulance train. We halted about 5 P.M. and commenced to get our suppers. Today for the first time in one month we had an exchange of clothing and we feel like new men."

Dunham had some bad luck. When he got his knapsack from the wagon, he found its contents had been stolen.[49]

Durell's Battery was under way also, moving to Mechanicsville and Brookville. The folks in the last village welcomed the cannoneers with waving flags and handkerchiefs. Here they learned that they were headed north to fight the Confederates who were also in Maryland.

It was a relief to be in Maryland. The Virginia countryside had been devastated by war. But, everything was fresh and green. Fences were up, the barns in good repair, and there was an abundance of fruit.[50]

On that warm and cloudy day, David Strother left Washington with orders to report to General McClellan in Rockville, David left at the hour of 3:00 a.m. "The road to Rockville was filled with wagons and stragglers. It was hot and dusty and I arrived at the town about sunset."

McClellan's headquarters were located on a hill, half a mile toward Great Falls. After a cordial welcome and an exchange of past memories, McClellan asked Strother to become a member of his staff. Then the two looked at maps. McClellan remarked that Lee had 100,000 troops. David shared important information about the terrain between Frederick and Harpers Ferry.[51]

Members of the 19th Massachusetts and other units were not in good spirits as the Maryland Campaign began. However, a few days in Maryland and the return of George McClellan seemed to rejuvenate them.

Fences suffered terribly as the Army of the Potomac advanced. They were gathered and used primarily for cooking, the weather being warm enough as to do away with campfires throughout the night.[52]

By noon all the Union forces ordered forward were in motion. McClellan's intelligence reported the Confederates massed around Frederick. Captured cavalrymen talked of going to Gettysburg or York. And by 8:15 Sugar Loaf Mountain with its strategic summit and lookout was in Union hands.[53]

Reports coming to McClellan had Jackson's headquarters at New Market, east of Frederick. This indicated to "Little Mac" that Jackson intended to move toward Baltimore. General Burnside was therefore ordered to take and hold Ridgeville and push toward Westminster.

Burnside had his problems. Yesterday he reported his men in good condition. But apparently he did not know the whole story. General Crawford's brigade, of what was to become the Twelfth Corps, was in bad shape. It had been almost wiped out at Cedar Mountain in early August. To make matters worse there had been no time to rest or reorganize the companies. The four regiments had but 629 men present for duty. The figure was being reduced daily due to fatigue and illness. Lack of proper food, and depression over constant battle defeats made the men ripe for camp diseases.

Crawford says, "Most of our marches have been made during the heat of the day, and we arrived in camp almost invariably at night, when the men worn out, throw themselves upon the ground to seek rest, regardless of the dews and indifference to hunger."[54]

Many simply could not keep up in the column of march. But on the other hand, the army was having a problem with straggling, and Seth Williams, one of the adjutant generals, wrote that McClellan was aware of the lack of discipline.

The safety of the country depends on what this army shall not achieve; it cannot be successful if its soldiers are one half skulking to the rear; while the brunt of battle is borne by the other half.

To meet this problem a strong order came down from Army Headquarters, giving officers authority to court-martial men on the spot. Shootings were threatened if the problem persisted, and each column was to give a strong rear guard, and men at the forks of every road. Flankers with bayonets would keep men in line of march unless there was a necessity to leave the ranks. The men were also asked to prevent damage to the fences and crops of the people of Maryland.[55]

Charles Johnson and his comrades in the Ninth New York received their "dog tents" today. "They are in piece about as large as a blanket and one of these is given to each man to carry....They are no trouble to carry and will keep off dews at least and rain if it is not too heavy....Now we can say...we carry our houses on our backs, even if they look more for canines than men."[56]

In the fall of 1861, the Second Massachusetts camped at Pleasant Hill and then near Seneca, close to Darnestown, Maryland. Nearby was the farm of a Mr. Desellum. He was quite a character and in 1861 and again on the "Roads to Antietam" invited Col. Wilder Dwight and other soldiers to eat with him.

Mr. Desellum had spent his entire life on the farm. His travels were never beyond the borders of the two adjoining counties. His father and his grandfather had all farmed the place, and he was rooted to the family soil.

Desellum and his maiden sister hated Jeff Davis. They were Union all the way. Desellum was well read and intelligent. Twenty-five slaves lived on the place, and apparently had it pretty good. When asked if he owned slaves, Desellum replied, "No, the slaves own me."[57]

Things were pleasant in 1861. But in '62 "immense armies were in motion." Yet Colonel Dwight took time to chat with his old friend, and relate to him what was happening. He also visited with some of the little black children who were glad to see their soldier friend. Tired from strenuous service, the Desellums persuaded Dwight to rest for a while on the couch. Then Dwight mounted his horse, bowed, and waved his hat three times to those who had come to bid him farewell, in this case, a final farewell. He had a rendezvous with death in the West Woods north of Sharpsburg.

George Noyes started with a supply train late this evening to join his division. He traveled five miles and then gave the animals a breather. "The whole country was full of soldiers." George knocked on a door, and his knock was answered by a man in a night cap. He was told that every bed was filled, and there were soldiers sleeping in the parlor and on the kitchen floor. George could see their prostrate forms as the moon shone on the floor. However, he had better luck at a nearby farmhouse and slept in a four-poster bed.[58]

The first Massachusetts Cavalry, along with other horsemen, spent the days of September 5–9 patrolling the towpath of the C & O Canal, checking on the fords of the Potomac, and scouting in advance of the Union infantry as they moved from Rockville toward Frederick.

John Dooley

Courtesy—Georgetown University

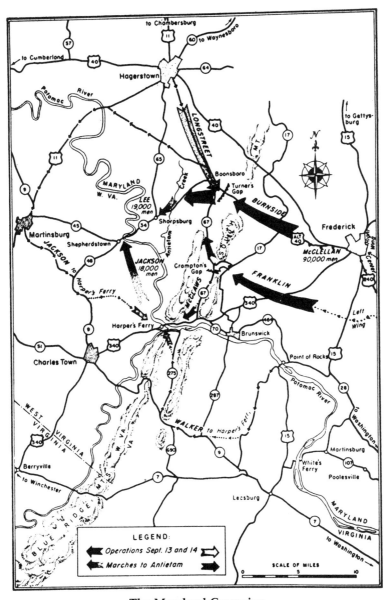

The Maryland Campaign

Courtesy—National Park Service

CHAPTER IV

"ADVANCE AND MANEUVER"

—ARMY OF NORTHERN VIRGINIA—

Long before daylight on Wednesday, September 10, the Army of Northern Virginia struck their campsites at Monocacy Junction and Worman's Mill. Each command was moving out to carry out their assignment in Order No. 191.

Thomas J. Jackson rode into town and turned left onto West Second Street. He hoped to pay a quick visit to Reverend Ross, pastor of the Presbyterian Church. However, at 5:30 a.m. the clergyman was still asleep, so Jackson rode on and rejoined his command where Bentz Street intersects with West Patrick.[1]

Jed Hotchkiss reports leaving camp at 3:00 a.m. Along the route of march he found strong Union sentiment, but all the folks were amazed and thankful for the discipline of the Confederate troops.

Jacob Engelbrecht had a lot to write about that day:

> Going—perhaps Gone—This morning say 3 or 4 o'cl Southern Army. commenced moving westward and have continued ever since (now 10 hours) and still passing through town from the George town road....I suppose 50 or 60 thousand men and several hundred cannon.

At three a.m. on the morning of the eleventh, Jacob wrote again:

> Still Marching—the passing of the Rebel troops Continued all day yesterday, until night & this morning about three hours more....It took them about 17 hours altogether—we estimate the whole number at about seventy thousand....at least 1000 wagons & ambulances—very few Cavalry—only those that came the first day. I saw Nearly the whole of them pass—thinking I would never see the like again—they were generally young and

hearty....Many were barefooted and some had one Shoe & one barefoot—they really looked "Ragged and tough." The first 8 or 10 thousand got a tolerable good supply of Clothing & Shoes & boots but the Stores & Shops were soon sold out & the whole town was with Closed doors and windows (This was from Saturday to Thursday). I suppose the length of the whole Cavalcade waggons—Cannon & men would make a string of about 14 or 16 miles—I was very anxious to see the whole proceedings of an enemy taking a town....I must say that at no time was I the least alarmed....We took it cooly & deliberately....We put ourselves into the hands of the Lord who had watched over us so many years & we were fully assured he would not forsake us in the time of Need....I must say the Rebels behaved themselves well....Our town is as still & quiet as a Sabbath day.[2]

William Owen says they marched through Frederick with "bands playing and colors flying. Many citizens came to the streets or looked out of the windows at the passing columns. The artillerymen marched in front of their guns, singing as they went."[3]

During the passing of the Confederate army through Frederick, the Barbara Fritchie incident occurred.

The next two paragraphs are taken from Miss Eleanor D. Abbott's book on Barbara Fritchie. Miss Abbott was a great-grandniece of "Dame Barbara."

Further confirmation of the flag waving incident is found on page seven of the April 8, 1910 issue of the Atlantic Constitution, a Southern publication, on file in the Congressional Library, Washington, D.C. It comes from the Confederate Captain Frank Meyers, who was at that time a sergeant in the 6th Virginia. He tells that Barbara Fritchie came out on her porch and waved her little flag at them as they were passing her house, and one of the soldiers called to him: "Sergeant, let met shoot it down." Captain Meyers said, "I told him 'no', as we had been given positive orders not to disturb a thing in the town"; so not one of them bothered her.

Mrs. Fritchie's own account of the incident, as told to a niece, goes something like this:

It was early morning, September 10, 1862. The large bunting flag had not yet been placed in the dormer window, as it was not quiet seven o'clock. One of Mrs. Hanshew's children came in, calling excitedly, "Look out for your flag, the troops are coming!" (Mrs. Hanshew had heard the Confederates were en route through the town, and had sent the child to warn her aunt not to display the flag, but she misunderstood.) Thinking the Union troops were coming, Mrs. Fritchie took her small silk flag from between the leaves of the family Bible and stepped out on the front porch. Immediately one of the men came to her and told her she had better go in, or she might be harmed. Realizing her mistake, and that she was in the midst of Confederate soldiers, she nevertheless refused to go in. Then a second soldier came and tried to take the flag from her, saying he wanted to put it on his horse's head. A third soldier threatened to shoot it out of her hand if she didn't go in. An officer rode forward, turned angrily upon the man and said, "If you harm a hair on that old lady's head I'll shoot you down like a dog." Then turning to the trembling old lady, he said, "Go on, Granny, wave your flag as much as you please." A little after seven o'clock, when her companion, Miss Yoner, went to call her to breakfast she found Mrs. Fritchie in the parlor quite excited, "They tried to take my flag, but a man would not let them; and he was a gentleman."

Barbara Fritchie herself told the above account to Miss Caroline Ebert, her husband's niece, who came to see her, shortly after the flag-waving incident. In 1913, as plans were being made to erect a monument in Mrs. Fritchie's honor, she related the story to Mrs. J.H. Abbott and Miss Eleanor D. Abbott, and made an affidavit before a notary public.[4]

Mrs. Markell and her friends fed over three hundred Confederates as they marched westward. Mr. Markell was a storekeeper, and the family lived in a nice house on West Patrick Street. Some of the soldiers apparently mistook the home for a hotel. According to Mrs. Markell, the mother of Henry Kyd Douglas was with her. In fact, Mrs. Douglas was displaying a pretty rebel flag. A young lady took the flag and gave it to Henry Douglas when he rode past the Markell home. Mrs. Markell also pinned a small Confederate flag to the hat of a South Carolina soldier as he marched by.

John Dooley noticed a lot of noise as the Confederates passed through Frederick. Some was made by the soldiers. Frederick had seemed very lukewarm. Even those leaning toward the South were careful in showing their feelings because of spies and the fear of retaliation.

One of the great evils of the war was the division of families and neighbors over loyalty to the North or the South. John sensed this evil in Frederick.[5]

Dooley took time to stop a few moments at the Novitiate. He wanted to say goodbye to his friends. But his presence gave Father

Ward an anxious and embarrassing moment. Some paroled Yankee officers arrived seeking the Father's help in procuring assistance for the wounded and sick Union soldiers in Frederick. But Father Ward was most diplomatic and handled the situation well.[6]

Dooley mused as he walked, and lamented that rich farm and countryside had been tramped down by soldiers of war. "Hamlets and whole towns were plundered, their peoples outraged, and the houses left masses of charred and smoking ruins."

But some were bold enough to cheer in Frederick and this made John happy. After all, the Army of Northern Virginia was the last agent of free government, and without States Rights the situation would be worse than when the colonies were ruled by England.

One elderly lady looked at the Texas Brigade and said, "The Lord bless your dirty, ragged souls." A little boy wanted to know if they were really "Texicans." Others were amazed at the "Bonny Blue Flag." At one point a strong breeze just about tore the flag from the bearer and wrapped it around the neck of a pretty girl.

William Owen and his comrades were all struck with the beauty and freshness of the Middletown Valley. "How peaceful it looked; and yet armies were to tramp over it."

After leaving Frederick, the men of the Confederacy climbed the Catoctin Mountain at Braddock Heights, and beheld the beauty of the Middletown Valley. Perhaps they felt like Daniel Webster who remarked that in all his travels he had never seen anything to equal the Middletown Valley.

Down the mountain and through the streets of Middletown surged the warriors. Stonewall Jackson for the first and last time beheld the village, and received a cool reception "as two very pretty girls with ribbons of red, white, and blue in their hair and small Union flags in their hands ran to the curbstone, and laughingly waved their colors defiantly in the face of the general. He bowed and lifted his cap with a quiet smile and said to his staff, 'We evidently have no friends in this town.' The girls abashed, turned away, and lowered their tiny battle flags." For hours the waves of gray pressed westward. The people who watched them march by seemed cold and sullen. There were no cheers, no welcome of any kind. Mingled with the tread of the infantry was the clatter of sabers and the grinding of artillery wheels. War had come at last to Middletown Valley and it would become even more real in a week, as the homes and churches of the community became part of a vast hospital.

Across from the Methodist Church in Middletown, there lived a 17-year-old girl by the name of Nancy Crouse.

As the men in gray marched by, young Nancy clutched a Union flag about her and lost it only when Southern troopers tore it away from her.

Jackson's command crossed South Mountain at Turner's Gap. "Stonewall" dismounted about a mile from town at the home of Mr. John Murdock and ordered headquarters tents to be pitched across the road.

Disregarding Jackson's advice, Henry Douglas rode into Boonsboro to see what he could learn about the Potomac fords and to see some friends. Lieutenant Payne and some of the Black Horse Cavalry were also in town. The Confederate soldiers went into the United States Hotel. Suddenly there was the clatter of hoofs. The men in gray ran out, beat a hasty retreat, pursued by a company of U.S. cavalry. In the process, Henry received a bullet hole through his nice new hat.

Reaching the bivouac area, they found Jackson walking his horse, unmindful of any danger. He sensed the problem, mounted, and rode to the rear, while his men tried a ruse. They stopped, wheeled, and called to imaginary reinforcements. At that the blue column turned back to Boonsboro. Douglas was also able to recover the gloves Jackson had dropped in his hasty retreat.[7]

One of the artillerymen disobeyed orders today, and nearly got killed. Against officers' orders, Private Ashbrook seated himself upon a caisson and lighted up his pipe. Soon an explosion ripped the air, and Ashbrook was airborne, a full twenty feet, all his clothing torn off, and burned from head to feet. As he was rescued, the rest of the shells in the chest began to explode. Men rushed to empty their canteens on the smoking chest, and hurled the smoking shells into a nearby ditch of water.

While the bulk of the Army of Northern Virginia headed westward, Lafayette McLaws and his division tramped to Burkittsville and beyond, headed for Maryland Heights.[8]

Realizing the impossibility of destroying the Monocacy aqueduct, John Walker decided to rejoin the main Confederate army via a march to Jefferson and Middletown. Walker knew that with the main army moving from Frederick, he would be in a most perilous position. Before he could leave, however, orders came from General Lee to proceed to Harpers Ferry and assist Jackson and McLaws in the capture of that place. His orders specified that he was to cross at Cheek's Ford, really Chick's ford named after a native family and road.

However, Yankee troops thwarted Walker in his attempts to cross at Chick's Ford. Under cover of night, he crossed the Potomac at Point of Rocks in the waning hours of the tenth and the first hours of the eleventh.[9]

This was a frustrating day for George Neese and Chew's Battery. They were recalled from Sugar Loaf Mountain to Urbana, started to rest, and then sent back to the same spot for picket and patrol.

—ARMY OF THE POTOMAC—

Meanwhile, although still moving slowly, the Army of the Potomac was heading for Frederick. There seemed to be more alarm in Washington than with McClellan.

Things were becoming tense in Washington. Headquarters for the Defense of the city issued strict orders:

1. No soldier was to be permitted to cross the Potomac or visit the cities of Washington, Georgetown or Alexandria without a pass.

2. No wine, beer, or ardent spirits, unless they were for the hospitals were to be allowed to pass the guards.

3. All fast riding or driving is forbidden in the Cities of Washington and Alexandria. Teamsters must drive their teams at a walk.

4. Wagons were not to halt at crossings, and there was to be a wagon length break after every sixth wagon.[10]

Governor Andrew Curtin again seemed to know more what was going on than McClellan. At 3:00 p.m. he sent a message to Washington saying a paroled Union man saw General Jackson on the National Road between Middletown and Boonsboro. The sheriff of Hagerstown had met a rebel scout who was a personal friend, and the scout urged him to leave Hagerstown immediately.[11]

Part of the First Maine Cavalry was left at Poolesville on detached guard duty. Some of the men had a profound religious awakening.

Another service was performed by the boys of the First Maine while there, which, though not strictly coming under the head of military duty, shows to some extent the morale of the men. A revival meeting was in progress in the Methodist church, soon after the regiment went into quarters there, in which many of the boys took an active part, leading in prayer, in singing, and in the general exercises of the meeting, and introducing many revival hymns, till then unknown to the people of that city, which gave new life to the spirit of the meetings, and received the thanks of the good people of the church

for their services. Many of the boys will remember those meetings, held nightly in the church near headquarters, and what
times of religious excitement they were, exceeding anything
ever seen in their own state. Scores, whites and negroes, would
be affected with a strange power, and there would be singing,
and praying, and shouting, almost to the verge of hysteries,
and wild excitement everywhere. Strong men would be stricken
down in an instant, and prostrated on the floor. Now and then
there would be half a dozen or more prostrate in the aisle or on
the platform at a time.[12]

Some of the men went to the services just for something to do.
Others went out of curiosity, and some went for laughs. But their
down east training made them respect the services.

David Strother was busy making maps for Burnside, Sumner,
and Franklin. He also saw Rush's lancers pass in the distance with
"their red pennants and long lances; they had quite a 'middle ages'
appearance." The new staff officer also signed a paper enlisting the
help of officers in preventing the troops from pillaging Maryland
farms.[13]

As Lee was moving westward, McClellan had his army moving
toward the Frederick-Baltimore Road, via Lisbon and Damascus;
Sumner coming up from Washington toward Urbana and Frederick,
and the left wing stepping toward Buckeystown, with an eye toward the Potomac.

Charles Johnson lauds McClellan, saying he did not think
the Confederates would stay long in Frederick. "McClellan seems
to have put new life into everything."[14]

Marsena Patrick's command received orders to march with
other units to Cooksville. "After repeated halts & rests & delays we
reached a placed called Unity, or near there, where it was decided
we should encamp for the night." Patrick was invited to stay at the
mansion home of the Honorable Bowie Davis. The estate had been
in the family for years. Davis expressed the feeling that the war
was being carried on for "party & personal purposes."[15]

About 2:00 p.m. George Noyes reached his division in camp
near Unity. It looked like a tented city, ten thousand residents at
the edge of a woods. He went to the general's tent and soon had
some roast beef from the hands of a surgeon who was serving as a
cook.

There's something about the fellowship of a military mess that
brings great comradeship. As the officers were eating, there was
the clatter of hoofs, and a courier galloped up with sealed orders.
The message gave instructions to move. But George was tired and

knew the wagon train could not get started immediately, so he curled up in a hay stack for an hour of shuteye. Sharing in the frustration of the hour was a sutler, who had just gotten set up for business.[16]

Equally frustrating was the fact that they only marched three miles, and it took four hours to do it. A cold rain was falling too, making life miserable. The damp night, and the light of the camp fires cast an unusual reddish glow over the area.

From Rockville northward on the "Roads to Antietam," the 14th Connecticut marched with the Irish Brigade. The Irishmen jeered the 14th, called them blue legged devils, and said, "We won't be able to see you for your dust when Bobbie Lee catches up with you."[17]

Like the other soldiers in the Army of the Potomac, the Irish Brigade liked the relaxed pace traveling from Washington to Frederick. They left Georgetown on the third and tramped six short miles to Tennallytown. This brought a two-day halt. Then it was on to Rockville, Clarksburg, and Hyattstown, averaging less than ten miles per day. These were the most "leisurely marches they ever knew."

One of the oddities of the war happened sometime on the twelfth. The Irish Brigade made camp in a field dotted with haystacks. These provided for many the softest beds they had known since leaving home. Even General Richardson took to a stack and soon fell fast asleep in the hay.

When morning came, a soldier who had spent the night sleeping near the top of the stack, slid down and landed on the general. "You scoundrel!" General Richardson shouted. "You've broken my ribs. Who the devil are you?"

The stranger from above gave the division commander a good, swift kick in the seat of the pants, along with a stream of profound oaths.

Suddenly Captain Jack Gosson found himself face to face with Israel B. Richardson. "Oh bless my soul....I'm sorry, sir. I'm sorry. Say, I've got some good stuff here in my pocket, would you care for a drink?"[18] Together the captain and the general drank from a flask and the incident was forgotten.

The Eighth Ohio reached Clarksburg. Toward evening there was a skirmish with the Rebels. Frank Sawyer and his comrades were sent to the front with loaded pieces and fixed bayonets. The skirmish line moved through the Walter's plantation and halted. General Israel Richardson arrived and took dinner with the loyal farmer. He learned that Confederate cavalry had occupied the farm the previous night.[19]

The Sixth U.S. Cavalry made an attempt to dislodge the Confederates at the base of Sugar Loaf Mountain. However, their position was too strong. Late in the day Hancock's Brigade of infantry from Franklin's Corps arrived, and the Rebels retreated.[20]

McClellan was still having problems with Jackson being at New Market, and as late as noon still thought the Confederates to be in Frederick. As late as 10:00 p.m. that night, McClellan was holding that news to be true.[21]

Meanwhile the Ninth Corps was being ordered to move at once to Ridgeville on the Baltimore and Ohio Railroad, by way of Damascus. Hooker was to go to Poplar Springs, four miles east. Sumner and the Second Corps was to move up to Damascus. General Rodman was to stay in Damascus and hold the road to New Market. But Sumner had already moved to Clarksburg, south of Frederick. Banks' old unit was within a mile of Damascus, and Sumner was three miles east of Clarksburg.[22]

THURSDAY, SEPTEMBER 11, 1862

—*ARMY OF NORTHERN VIRGINIA*—

The Army of Northern Virginia continued on its mission to force the surrender of Harpers Ferry and Martinsburg.

From a location near Boonsboro, Lee heard the report that a Union force was approaching Hagerstown from Chambersburg and the north. To meet this threat, he had to divide his army once again. Longstreet was sent to Hagerstown while Daniel Harvey Hill was left as the rear guard. This rumor later proved untrue, but it caused a twenty-five mile round trip march. And with sore feet and meager rations, this was the last thing the men in gray needed.

John Dooley and his comrades had a feast as they marched from Frederick to Hagerstown. They were impressed with the fertility of the farms along the way, so different from war-torn Virginia. Acres of corn with crimson tassels greeted them, with good clover and timothy for the animals. But the prizes were the orchards and the apples, peaches, and pears, hanging heavily upon the trees. Whenever possible, the men slipped from ranks and filled their haversacks and pockets with fresh fruit.[23]

That morning Jackson and his men broke camp and proceeded to a point just west of Boonsboro, and took the road to Williamsport, following what is now Route 68 to the Potomac. The command passed the battleground of Falling Waters, where just over a year before, many of them had received their baptism of fire.

On the southern side of the Potomac, the men marched to Hammond's Mill, $1^1/2$ miles from the North Mountain Depot of the Baltimore and Ohio Railroad. A few prisoners were taken there. It was a warm day with showers. Headquarters was established at Hammond's.[24]

It was hoped that being northwest of Martinsburg, the Union command there would be prevented from escaping to the west. But General White evacuated the town and headed for Harpers Ferry instead.

John Walker's men were exhausted from their Monocacy expedition, so they remained in camp. The next day they would head for the Virginia Heights overlooking Harpers Ferry. Their objective, Hillsboro.

Lafayette McLaws crossed into Pleasant Valley today. He reported on the Baltimore and Ohio Railroad bridge running just under Maryland Heights, with a pontoon bridge just about fifty yards upstream. The railroad bridge was defended by cannon. McLaws realized that once he gained possession of Maryland Heights, the position would be untenable by the Yanks.

McLaws mentions the road through Crampton's Gap and Brownsville Gap as avenues of approach. He also learned of a road from Solomons Gap to the top of the Heights and directed General Kershaw to carry out an attack.[25]

Jeb Stuart remained at headquarters in Urbana covering the advance and maneuver of the Army of Northern Virginia. Lee's brigade held the left at New Market on the Baltimore and Ohio Railroad; Hampton's brigade was in the center at Hyattstown, while Munford's men were spread out toward Poolesville.

With the advance of the Union Sixth Corps, Munford had to fall back from near Sugar Loaf Mountain to Buckeystown.[26]

Chew's Battery went into position near a school house, three miles from Urbana. The Yanks advanced during the day, and the battery fell back to Urbana. This time their location was on the pike where the bridge across the Monocacy crosses the B & O. It was first class range for canister. They were ready to give the Yanks a warm welcome. Camp was made on the banks of the Monocacy.[27]

—ARMY OF THE POTOMAC—

McClellan seemed to love the pomp and circumstance of war. He had a large staff of about fifty men, including two generals and at least six colonels. With the move of army headquarters, tents were pitched in a Seneca meadow.

David Strother engaged in a conversation with an officer about Berkeley Springs. The officer was none other than Randolph B. Marcy, McClellan's father-in-law, and now his son-in-law's chief of staff. Marcy related that information had been received showing the Confederates heading for Hagerstown and the Potomac.[28]

Patrick's command traveled the turnpike and journeyed to Lisbon with Patrick riding in an ambulance, due to his recent illness.[29]

George Noyes was wakened early and told to get ready to move. He shaved by the light of a mirror four inches in diameter, washed in a beaten up tin basin, and carried his camp stool to the officers' mess. What a life.

It was a frustrating march. The mileage was short, and there were frequent halts and much congestion. The route was through pleasant farming country, and the sun was hot. About 6:00 p.m., the column reached Lisbon. After the troops stopped, miles of wagons rolled by, and George thought his supply wagons would never arrive.[30]

That evening the Ninth New Hampshire reached a pasture field near Damascus. They had tramped through the rain and mud, but that was better than the sun and the dust. Tents offered some shelter from the rain, but no help for the rain-soaked uniforms.[31]

A member of the 35th Massachusetts tells us what the march was like.

> The small supply of pork and hard bread, which fastidious appetites had placed in our haversacks at Arlington, was now exhausted. Coffee without milk or sugar, so bitter at first, had become pleasant; raw salt pork was a luxury, with a fine nutty flavor; and hard bread took the place it never afterwards gave up, as the first essential of a soldiers life. The trees along the road were loaded with green apples, and many of the men experimented with a diet of sour apple sauce. Stray fowls were thrown into the pot and devoured almost before they could utter their last expiring clack. We began to understand the saying, that an army moves upon its stomach....
>
> Hot days, dusty roads and bruised feet make the bivouac on the ground at night a welcome rest. The discomfort of marching in close ranks, with perhaps a train of wagons or artillery in the middle of the road, and another column of troops on the other side, all hurrying forward, sometimes at double-quick, must be tried for a few days to be duly appreciated. Experience was gained daily. Lazy fellows found that a pound weight or so of water in a canteen was a heavy lug, and learned to beg their

drink of neighbors and go light themselves. The never ended discussion was begun whether, if in light marching order, a choice must lie between an overcoat or a blanket, which should be carried along. Also the boys discovered that, in view of unexpected orders to move, it was advisable to heat their pots of water first, then put in the precious coffee, and woe to him who mixed his coffee in the cold water, hoping for time to boil it; if he did not get an order to march, or detail for picket, some stumbler would be sure to kick the burning rails and upset the magnificent array of blackening tin diapers...[32]

FRIDAY, SEPTEMBER 12, 1862

—*ARMY OF NORTHERN VIRGINIA*—

Jackson, McLaws, and Walker were moving to seal the doom of Harpers Ferry. Moving cautiously by way of Hedgesville, "Old Jack" approached Martinsburg. Finding the enemy had fled, his men advanced into the streets and "were greeted with a hearty welcome." Jed Hotchkiss says, "the ladies thronged the General and went so far as to cut a number of buttons off his coat, and also attacked the tail of his horse. A.P. Hill marched...6 miles toward Harpers Ferry....I bought some things in Martinsburg; new hats for the General and myself."

The new hat has an interesting story. The purchase was in response to a request by Jackson. However, Jed wondered "what size?" "What fits you will fit me." So Jed bought the new hat. He then took Jackson's old gray hat and put it into his saddlebag for safekeeping. Later he received the general's permission to keep it as a souvenir.

On Thursday, George Neese had gone without food. As the sun went down, an officer said that they could have corn and potatoes if they could find them. Somewhere the items were found, and corn and potatoes were the menu for breakfast. Then Chew's Battery started for Jefferson. Although the countryside was very impressive, George writes that the folks in Jefferson were very "sourish," evidently strongly Union. One lady, however, waved a handkerchief at the men in gray. Camp was made near Jefferson about sunset.[33]

McLaws and his men made ready to attack Maryland Heights. General Semmes was left to protect the rear at Brownsville Gap, and a brigade was sent to protect the rear at Solomon's Gap. Kershaw was to move on the positions on the Heights which the local folks said were heavily fortified. General Cobb was to support the operation. General Anderson took possession of Weverton and guarded against any attack from Frederick. So the Confederates were pretty well in control of the lower end of Pleasant Valley. Toward dark, Kershaw drove in the Union skirmishers on Maryland Heights and was set for an attack on Saturday.

Munford's cavalry fell back to Jefferson. For twenty-four hours they remained in almost constant probing action with the Union cavalry.

While the Union army was approaching Frederick, Generals Jeb Stuart, Fitz Lee, and Wade Hampton, along with their staffs dined at the Markell home. Sweeney, Stuart's musician played the "Southern Yankee Doodle," and "Old Gray Hoss," along with many other favorites. Mrs. Markell was thrilled by the presentation of a portion of the general's plume, and his autograph.

About four o'clock a courier informed the generals that Yankee drums could be heard, and columns of Union infantry could be seen in the distance. Hampton and Lee left, but Stuart was in no hurry. A line of battle was formed in front of the Markell home, and later in the day, a portion of their porch railing was blasted away, and the family retired to the basement for safety.

Benjamin Prather crossed the Potomac with Stuart's cavalry on the first Friday in September. After camping on Enoch Lowe's farm near the Monocacy, he was on patrol duty and this Friday found him in the Burkittsville area.

Prather had a very interesting experience with General Lee. The Commander of the Army of Northern Virginia, according to Prather, was in camp at Mountain Mill where Dr. Thomas Hillery was caring for Lee's injured hands.

During the course of the day, Munford and his cavalry escorted Lee from the Burkittsville area to a rendezvous with Jeb Stuart in Pleasant Valley. But they had some difficulties.

While going through a small stream at John Ahalt's Grist Mill, the left front wheel of the horse-drawn vehicle broke. Prather and another man took the wheel to the blacksmith shop near St. Paul's Church. There the "village smithy" made an emergency repair.

The escort made it to Werner's Tannery where four new wheels were placed on General Lee's ambulance. The cavalrymen took Lee to Stuart who escorted him to a meeting with General Longstreet at Boonsboro.[34]

—ARMY OF THE POTOMAC—

On that cloudy and warm Friday, the headquarters of the Army of the Potomac moved out early, and the tents were struck at eight o'clock. Davis Strother rode with his new friend, General Marcy.

The column halted a mile south of Urbana where in "a lovely grove surrounded by grass fields like shaven lawns" camp was made for the night.[35]

The 19th Massachusetts was drawn up in formation today and strict orders read about foraging. In the midst of the proclamation, a black boy by the name of Henry Johnson appeared. He was an unofficial mess attendant for the officers. Under each arm he had a big crock of homemade butter. The officers tried to get Henry to conveniently disappear. If the officer reading the order saw Henry, he pretended not to notice.

While on the march, it was the custom to spend one day on the road, and two days tramping through the fields. This gave each regiment every third day the advantage of a good road. The men usually marched in "Route Step," meaning walk as you please. When the bugle sounded "Attention," the musket was brought to "carry."[36]

George Noyes rode in the company of the division staff to New Market, eating a fine dinner at a wayside inn, hosted by a charming lady.

Along the way, Noyes heard the story of a cattle driver, who was asked, "To what division do your charges belong?" Without batting an eye, the driver replied, "Hooker's division, sir."

The folks in New Market were glad to see the men in blue. The area seemed like "a land flowing with milk and honey." The town was picturesque. By 7:00 p.m., most were in camp just beyond New Market.[37]

George Noyes fed his horse in an excellent field of oats. As he fed his half-starved mare, he gazed out over the countryside and saw a scene he would never forget, "long columns of troops, their bayonets glistening in the sun, and the mighty coil of armed men stretching down the mountain sides....It was the best view of an army on its march that I have ever enjoyed."

This must have been near Frederick as the troops were approaching the town. In the upper part of a barn were twenty Rebels. Some were sick, and others had been wounded in Friday's cavalry skirmish. They looked pale and thin from their toils and lack of food. The farmer remarked how dirty and ragged the Confederates looked. But Noyes knew that despite their appearance they were excellent fighters. He respected them because of their spirit, and how they stood up under difficulties.

By 2:00 p.m. Noyes and his comrades went into camp along the Monocacy, "a lovely spot now crowded with troops." All around were tents and artillery, and off in the distance, "the clustered spires of Fredericktown." Sounds of martial music filled the air. Headquarters were established in a farmhouse.

John Gibbon and his men reached New Market today. On the way, he encountered John Reynolds, former superintendent of West Point, and now a division commander in the First Corps. Reynolds was a victim of politics, at the urging of Governor Curtin, he as a Pennsylvanian was being recalled to Harrisburg to assume command of the militia as Pennsylvania was being threatened by Lee. Curtin had put great pressure on Lincoln in the matter.[38]

Marsena Patrick was upset over the many delays caused by frequent halts without apparent reason. Then came the rain and an early darkness. It was 9:00 p.m. when the column reached New Market. The supply trains were far behind, so the men went to bed without supper.

The Ninth New Hampshire waited quite a while for an ammunition train to pass near New Market, and at night camped near the Monocacy. The valley seemed to be full of troops. They saw a house damaged by the skirmish on Thursday. Then they headed for the river to wash and bathe. General Reno's headquarters were nearby.[39]

The Ninth New York heard firing as it approached Frederick. Usually the cavalry made the initial contact. Then artillery was brought up in support, and finally infantry. If the situation looked good, new infantry units were sent. This was done for two reasons, the veterans rested, and the troops would have a taste of fire. Normally the enemy disappeared with the advance of the infantry, so this inspired and gave confidence to the new troops.[40]

Rufus Dawes of the Sixth Wisconsin wrote home that day. "My health is good. And I am ready to take my chances." He adds, "Our task is not easy."[41]

As the Ninth and First Corps advanced from the east, in the ranks was the Ninth New Hampshire Infantry and its band.

The regimental band covered fifteen miles that day after snacking on a few ears of green corn in the morning. They had a lot to complain about, "blistered feet, and they felt mean and ugly." There was an amusing incident along the way. Somewhere near New Market, a herd of cattle was being driven past, part of the government supply. A stubborn bull was giving the driver a rough time. He told the members of the Ninth New Hampshire they could have him if they could catch the critter. The men from the granite state charged. And in thirty minutes, the carcass of the bull was being dressed. He would cause no more trouble.[42]

Charles Johnson saw Damascus the previous day, and the beautiful Sugar Loaf Mountain off in the distance. The country was becoming "entrancingly beautiful." Across the lovely landscape there were the seemingly endless files of troops.

That morning Charles wakened from his sleep in a clover field and had a breakfast consisting of milk and crackers.[43]

The Third Wisconsin was among the troops reaching the little village of Ijamsville. In town they heard the Rebels had evacuated Frederick. But other sources said they were making a stand at the Monocacy near Jug Bridge.

Ambrose Burnside, commanding the right wing of the Army of the Potomac, reports that he reached the Monocacy by way of Leesborough, Brookville, and Damascus. Slight resistance was met at the bridge.[44]

The veterans always had a big time when new troops were getting ready to go into action for the first time. They delighted in painting bleak pictures, in making the enemy look like savages, and in terrorizing the men who were already filled with anxiety. The more they succeeded in scaring the new troops out of their wits, the bigger the laugh they got when the recruits moved out. Officers finally had to put a halt to this practice as it was too demoralizing.

Rodman's division of the Ninth Corps came to the support of the cavalry. After crossing the Monocacy, the men marched to half a mile from the edge of Frederick and then filed to the left until the "command reached the open fields across the railroad, and moved in line by brigades, over fences and through tall corn, where the alignment could only be maintained by observing the tops of the numerous colors."[45]

Rodman's division went through the cornfields, potato patches, gardens, and backyards, tearing down wash lines in their advance.

While the Confederate cavalry withdrew from the Monocacy, Jacob Engelbrecht went to the roof of Val Brunner's warehouse at the depot. There with opera glasses he watched the advance of the Ninth Army Corps. The Confederate cavalry gave way before the advance of the infantry. They retreated via Patrick Street as far as Bentz Street. There they turned to the right about, drew sabers, and went galloping toward the Square. Into the streets of Frederick was heard the snorting of horses, the clash of swords, and the cries of men. Most of the action was noise, with none killed, although quite a few were wounded. And Colonel Moore of the 28th Ohio was captured by the men in gray.[46]

General Pleasonton, McClellan's cavalry commander, says, "I entered Frederick about 5 o'clock in the evening....The enemy pickets were driven out of Frederick as we advanced on the Urbana Road, while Burnside's corps pushed them on the New Market Road, from which direction he entered about half an hour before my advance."[47]

The roads were muddy from the previous day's rain. And to make matters worse, due to road congestion, the Eighth Illinois cavalry had to take a route of thirty-three miles to cover the sixteen from the Clarksville area. It was after dark when the column reached Frederick. Abner Hard says, "We received a most hearty welcome and greeting....Passing through the city we encamped about a mile beyond, without blankets, as our baggage had not arrived....On the hills...to the west, and in plain sight, the enemy's campfires were burning....We expected an encounter the next morning."[48]

Jacob Cox says that as Hampton's cavalry went out the west end of Frederick, and the men in blue came in the east side, windows were opened, and National flags displayed. This even though the smell of powder was still in the air.[49]

Once Frederick was cleared, "troops poured into the city from all roads east and south." The Ninth New York made camp on a rocky bluff overlooking the railroad depot. "It was a night of the wildest excitement in Frederick, the streets were crowded with citizens who were glad to see the men in blue. It was a night to be remembered by the tired and footsore troops." A carnival-like atmosphere prevailed. Frederick had rarely ever seen a night like it.

Every house was illuminated. Folks acted like the battle and the war had already been won. Refreshments were offered from every doorstep. Trays and baskets of food were given to the men. Water, lemonade, and stronger drinks were also offered.[50]

For most of the men in the Ninth Corps this was the first night of socialization they had had since leaving home in 1861. Some of the men slept in private homes.

General Burnside's path was blocked numerous times. He received many words and tokens of thanks. He was looked upon as a deliverer.

David Thompson says the experience in Frederick was "a bright one" and provided the topic of discussion at campfires for months afterward.

Charles Johnson notes the reception was extremely enthusiastic. Soldiers were dragged into houses and "given everything that would fill empty stomachs." The cheering exceeded anything Charles had ever heard. Frederick was indeed a lovely and loyal city. Charles wondered why the Rebs did not blow up Jug Bridge over the Monocacy. But he thought they may not have had the time.[51]

One member of the Ninth New York must have had more stamina than others. A friend of David Thompson's "ran the guard," or left camp near midnight, and returned with a crock of butter, apple butter, lard, a live hen, and a three-legged skillet. So in the wee hours of the morning some of the men had a feast.

And it seems that Lieutenants Barnett and Horner, on the way back to camp from a pleasant visit in a Frederick home, were the first to spot the fire at the Frederick jail. Barnett hurried to camp and sought help from Colonel Kimball, while Lieutenant Horner rushed to the jail to help get folks out, and at the same time prevent the escape of the prisoners. Soon three companies of the Ninth New York arrived on the scene to aid the fire fighters.

Some of the soldiers mounted the walls of the jail yard to keep a close eye on the prisoners. The first thought was that some Southern sympathizers set the fire to create a disturbance.[52]

An investigation revealed that the inmates probably set the jail on fire hoping to escape during the excitement that was sweeping the city. Sheriff Michael Zimmerman was able to save most of the furniture. However, the building itself was pretty well gone when the flames were first seen. The fire hydrant had also been turned off, undoubtedly to prevent use by the military. It may have been turned off earlier during the Confederate occupation and never turned back on. But crime does not pay, at least it didn't in 1862, and the prisoners did not escape.

Meanwhile, Ezra D. Simons was having some thoughts at Harpers Ferry. In 1859 he had looked at the coffin of John Brown en route for burial at North Elba, New York. Now he was with the 125th New York Volunteers. It was 7:00 p.m. The men had covered twenty-two gruelling miles, marching under the assumption that they had to carry everything issued to them. The men were just in time to join the forces about to fall to "Stonewall" Jackson.[53]

CHAPTER V

SATURDAY, SEPTEMBER 13, 1862

—ARMY OF NORTHERN VIRGINIA—

Lee's widely scattered army had a variety of tasks. The main body of Longstreet's First Corps had a relaxing day in Hagerstown, while D.H. Hill stood guard at South Mountain. Kershaw's brigade had a difficult day of advance and maneuver on Maryland Heights, while Jackson's command moved to tighten the noose on Harpers Ferry. Jeb Stuart and his cavalry skirmished throughout the day with the Yankees at Jefferson, Braddock, and Catoctin Creek.

As the Yankee cavalry came sweeping over Braddock Mountain, Wade Hampton became concerned about his supply wagons. He made the decision to send them to Burkittsville, rather than to Turner's Gap. The First North Carolina held the Yankees at bay while being subjected to a severe cannon and musketry fire.

Hampton hoped to join up with Munford in Burkittsville. Turning toward that town, he found the Yankees on a parallel road. Hampton ordered Lieutenant Colonel Young to charge those who were threatening his avenue of escape. The charge worked, and Young captured thirty men belonging to the Third Indiana and Eighth Illinois. Thus Hampton made it safely to Burkittsville and joined the small Confederate force holding Crampton's Pass.

Division seems to have been the name of the game for the Confederates in the Maryland Campaign. Not only did Lee have four main elements operating in different locales, but so did Longstreet and McLaws. On September 13 as McLaws prepared for his final assault on Maryland Heights, he had Semmes at Brownsville Gap, Anderson at Weverton, and a unit at Solomon's Gap, and his main attack group.

Kershaw had his work cut out for him. Maryland Heights was rocky with many boulders, and fallen trees. Kershaw had a limited field to advance and maneuver.

The fighting on the thirteenth is very ably described by that great Southern historian, Douglas S. Freeman:

An early start by Kershaw on the morning of Saturday, September 13, carried the seventh South Carolina past the abatis to another and heavier obstacle of logs and stone, 400 yards further south. Barksdale and his Mississippians had already been deployed on the precipitous eastern face of the Heights and there, by sheer tenacity, had been able to keep a line. He now received orders from Kershaw to turn the second abatis and get in its rear.

The Mississippians speedily contrived to creep along the rim of the heights and to get on the flank of the Federals. Kershaw was encouraged by this and was hopeful of bagging all the defenders.[1] However, when a company of the Seventh Mississippi fired into some Union sharpshooters, a panic swept them, and the entire Union line broke into a perfect rout, escaping down the mountainsides to the rear.[2] By 10:30 a.m., Kershaw cleared the barrier completely; by 4:30 p.m., the Confederates had possession of the entire Heights. McLaws closed in from Pleasant Valley and occupied the little settlement of Sandy Hook, which nestles under the east edge of Maryland Heights.[3]

Thus, McLaws' mission was accomplished. Now he had to aid in the capture of Harpers Ferry, and then get back to Lee and the main army. So far, so good. But the picture was in the process of changing. On Sunday Franklin would attack Crampton's Gap, and McLaws would be in deep trouble.

Jackson's men were on the move this Saturday in mid-September. From positions near Martinsburg, they advanced to Halltown on the road from Harpers Ferry to Charles Town. Jed Hotchkiss was detailed to establish a line of communications with General Walker on Loudoun Heights. Crossing the Shenandoah River by way of Keyes Ford, Jed and his mates got some fine peaches, and then went to the top of the mountain. Walker was just getting into position. During the afternoon, artillery was placed, and word was received from McLaws on Maryland Heights. It was a warm day. But Jackson's command could rest in the assurance, "We have the enemy surrounded and hope to take them tomorrow."[4]

Mrs. Angela Kirkham Davis lived in Funkstown in September of 1862. Her husband was a storekeeper. She was a Yankee from Batavia, New York, and her husband was an ardent Unionist. Some of the local folks threatened to burn his place down. When news of the Confederate invasion reached her ears, friendly neighbors suggested she return home. She would not go, but her husband, fearing for his safety, fled to Chambersburg.

She estimated that 40,000 Confederates passed her home in mid-September. Her number is high, unless she counted them going and coming. And still, she would be high. In her eyes, they "were a poor, forlorn looking set of men....They were tired, dirty, ragged, and no uniforms whatever....Many were barefooted, some with toes sticking out of their shoes and others in their stocking feet."

Although in compassion, she offered them water, Mrs. Davis told them in no uncertain terms that she was a Yankee. Therefore, some of the soldiers made her drink the water first, thinking she had poisoned it. They were well behaved, and she heard little or no swearing.

Mrs. Davis saw Robert E. Lee, "an elegant-looking gentleman," riding in an ambulance, guarded by soldiers. His arm was still in a sling because of the August 31 accident.

General Lee promised to warn the women and children of Funkstown in the event a major battle loomed near. But it took place around Sharpsburg instead.[5]

Mrs. Davis was thirty-four in 1862. For the rest of her life she remembered the Confederates marching to and from Hagerstown, and treating a wounded New York officer after Antietam.

It took a while for William Pendleton and the Artillery Reserve to reach Hagerstown. They left Frederick on Wednesday afternoon, and reached the Hub City at noon Saturday. He attributed the slow pace as being necessitated by developments at Harpers Ferry. He found the folks to be cousins to the Yankees and sympathetic to them, "but we treat them kindly."

Pendleton says, "This is beautiful country." The folks seemed to be scared of the Confederate legions. "The weather is delightful; dust, however, a great nuisance. Such clouds of it you never saw." Nelson knew he could not preach in Hagerstown, but hoped he could hold services in one of the army camps.

From Frederick to Boonsboro, the Confederates received a cool welcome; however, things were better in Hagerstown. Folks were much friendlier. The men went shopping in Hagerstown at a dry goods store. Waterproof clothing, and dress patterns for the ladies back home were main items purchased. One merchant had a lot of old hats on a top shelf in his store. They looked to be a hundred years old. They called them the "Brother Jonathan headgear." The Confederates took the entire stock and wore them on the remainder of the "Roads to Antietam" and into the battle itself.

Ned Haines showed his loyalty to John Dooley in Hagerstown. Ned went shopping and found some fine grapes. He met some nice folks who tried to talk him into staying and deserting John. But Ned would have none of it. He said, "I knows too much about them abolishunists."[6] Ned thought they would be nice to him for a while, and then let him shift for himself. He preferred to stay with Dooley.

The Confederates in Jefferson heard the firing from Frederick, as the Rebel cavalry was being pushed back. Chew's Battery took a very rough and narrow road to Burkittsville, and went into position commanding the road leading to Crampton's Gap and overlooking the Middletown Valley.

They were ready to fire as a column approached. At the last minute a courier came galloping forward saying that the advancing men were those of Hampton's C.S.A. cavalry. "Don't fire." So the tragedy was averted. When night came, Chew's battery crossed the mountain and made camp at the western base of the mountain.

D.H. Hill stood alone near Turner's Gap, watching one Union campfire after another shoot forth flame. The enemy was filling up the Middletown Valley. Hill felt like he was the loneliest man in the world.

—*Army of the Potomac*—

As the dawn broke, heralding a bright, sunny, pleasant day in Maryland, units of the Army of the Potomac were ready to march. Units of the Ninth Corps were already in town. A detachment was sent to support the cavalry at Jefferson, and in the afternoon, most of the Ninth Corps marched through Frederick, triggering a great ovation and response. Although there are many glowing descriptions of this day, it is hard to pinpoint units other than those of the Ninth Corps and McClellan himself, as being among those who experienced the great celebration.

From the existing accounts it seems as though the First, Twelfth, and Second Corps were very near Frederick by the end of the day, but did not march through until Sunday on their way to South Mountain.

General Pleasonton was ordered to move the cavalry toward Jefferson and Middletown, with the objective being to scout the South Mountain passes. General Franklin called for infantry support. Thus a portion of Rodman's division was sent to serve with Pleasonton, the main body of the cavalry headed for Middletown, and the rest to cooperate with Rush's Lancers headed for Jefferson.[7]

Later in the day after the Catoctin passes had been cleared, Burnside ordered Reno's Ninth Corps to move at once for Middletown. Hooker was to follow at daybreak on Sunday. To be closer to the front, Burnside went with Reno to Middletown. The First Division moved at 2:00 p.m. and camped for the night one and a half miles from Middletown.[8]

About noon, Jacob Cox was ordered to take his division of the Ninth Corps and proceed to Middletown. General McClellan met Cox in person as the column moved west.

To complete the patrol work, Pleasonton headed toward Middletown, and met Rebel cavalry and artillery at Braddock on top of the Catoctin Mountain. The Union troopers dismounted, and the men who seemingly bore the brunt of the campaign, the 8th Illinois and the 3rd Indiana, went forward as skirmishers. After a severe cannonading and several warm volleys with carbines, the enemy retreated hastily, having previously barricaded the road in several places.

A hasty pursuit followed. The Confederates blew up the bridge on Catoctin Creek west of Middletown, set fire to the barn, and did other damage. However, the creek was shallow, and the Yankee cavalry kept on going until they found the Confederates in a strong position on South Mountain. Pleasonton at this point sent a request to Burnside for infantry support, and the columns started forward from Frederick.

General Pleasonton had found a Confederate rear guard at Turner's Gap, but it was assumed that the cavalry with a little support could sweep it away. McClellan expected the Confederates to be in Hagerstown and Harpers Ferry. He also expected a battle at Boonsboro, but not on the mountain. This was the message he obtained from the Lost Order.

As the Yankees fell back to Middletown and the danger passed for the moment, the ladies of the village came out with big slices of buttered bread. Abner Hard and the men from the Eighth Illinois enjoyed the food and their kindness.[9]

The Union wounded who fell on the Burkittsville and Boonsboro roads were brought back to a church, presumably the Lutheran Church, for treatment.

For the first time, the First Massachusetts cavalry came under fire. While in reserve, a Rebel shell took the legs off two infantrymen. The troopers mounted up and gave chase. Many of the men were thrown from their mounts on the rough and rocky mountain ground. The burning bridge west of Middletown caused them to halt. But they had survived their baptism of fire.[10]

William Pickerall of the Third Indiana Cavalry has some additional comments on this action. He states,

> Encircled with forest crowned mountain ranges, I have seen no lovlier landscapes than the Middletown Valley, as it appeared to me, on the afternoon of September 13, 1862. By the way of the National Road we had entered that Valley over the crest of the Catoctin Mountains, on this glorious September day....

> The presence of two hostile armies on this peaceful scene must have seemed a strange transition to the dwellers of this beautiful Valley.

Pickerall's company from the Third Indiana, and another unit from that regiment, plus four companies from the Eighth Illinois were sent after the Confederate wagon train which residents of Middletown said had gone in a southwesterly direction. Six brass guns and a large cavalry unit were at the rear of the Confederate column. Pickerall felt largely outnumbered.

The Yankees halted and while resting in a meadow, Pickerall was enthralled with the beauty of the valley and cattle resting peacefully in the pastures. "In the distance were the mountain crests, wreathed in the blue haze of a perfect Autumn day's loveliest sunshine."

Two hundred yards away on a little ridge overlooking a rough country road, which was sort of a short cut to Middletown was an old-fashioned schoolhouse (the Quebec School).

For some reason school was in session, although it was Saturday. The teacher and the children seemed to be caught up in the rude awakening of war. The teacher had a rough time keeping the attention of the children. They kept looking out the windows.

For a brief moment, the lads from Indiana relaxed, caught up in the memories of happier days. Half of Pickerall's company, including himself, had been teachers in little country schools. For a moment it seemed as though they were back home in Indiana, home where they wanted to be, and where they ought to be, teaching little children. All too briefly, it was like an oasis in the desert.

Then the major shouted a command and the men had to leave the Quebec School. The Confederates were too strong to be pursued. The men from the midwest had to fall back to Middletown. As the column entered the rough, rocky road, a shot came whizzing over their heads, hitting a hickory tree.

Then from behind a ridge came a large body of Confederate cavalry, sabres drawn, filling the air with oaths, and demanding the surrender of the men in blue. Fence rails were torn down and a lively skirmish followed. Corporal Harvey Williamson of Company

F had his head split open, and was taken to the Lutheran Church in Middletown to a makeshift hospital. There during the night he died. He would never gaze upon another country school, and the folks back home would lament his passing.

The offices of *The Valley Register*, although edited by a pro-Union citizen, escaped harm as the Confederate infantry and cavalry passed through Middletown. But Adam Koogle, a farmer living one mile west of town, and the father-in-law of George C. Rhoderick, the editor of *The Valley Register* was not so lucky.

According to family tradition, Jeb Stuart made his headquarters, and planned his withdrawal from the Valley in the Koogle farmhouse late Saturday afternoon. And Stuart or someone ordered the destruction of the turnpike bridge. The fire spread to the Koogle barn, hay shed, blacksmith shop, wagon shed, and other outbuildings. They, along with their contents, were completely destroyed. The half-starved troopers also dug about 100 bushels of Mr. Koogle's potatoes and burned most of his fences.

Mr. Rhoderick looked upon it as an act of retaliation for Yankee acts in the South. However, it also made him angry.

> The destruction of this bridge was one of the most wanton and inexcusable outrages perpetrated during the war. Its destruction did not at all impede the progress of the Union army, for there is an excellent ford along side the bridge, where the water is not now five inches deep.

Some of the Confederates were very uneasy. They felt it would have been a simple matter for McClellan to have pushed the cavalry on to Turner's Gap while it was yet daylight, and thereby wreck the Confederate artillery and wagons. This might have caused a panic and the rout of the Army of Northern Virginia.

The Union troops not assigned to patrol duty or cavalry support, had a great treat in store for them, a great welcome in the streets of Frederick. David Strother, a member of McClellan's staff, writes a vivid description.

> We were welcomed with a spontaneous ovation that stirred every soul to its depths. The whole city was fluttering with national flags, while the streets through which we passed, from the sidewalks to the housetops, shone with happy human faces. It seemed as if the entire population had turned out, wild with joy. Handkerchiefs fluttered and flowers showered upon the moving troops; and when the commander and staff appeared the crowd became so demonstrative that we were forcibly brought to a halt. The officers of the staff received their due share of floral honors, but General McClellan and horse were absolutely

covered with wreaths and bouquets; while old men, women, and children gathered around anxious to touch his hand, as if by some word or act to testify to their enthusiasm for the leaders of the national powers.[11]

McClellan was deeply moved and wrote home to his wife:

> I can't describe for you for want of time the enthusiastic reception we met with...at Frederick. I was nearly overwhelmed and pulled to pieces. I enclose with this a little flag that some...lady thrust into Dan's bridle. As to the flowers—they came in crowds! In truth, I was seldom more affected by the scenes I saw...and the reception I met with....Men, women, and children crowded around us, weeping, shouting, and praying.[12]

David Strother was amazed at how well the Confederate soldiers had behaved towards "the country and citizens—better than ours will do, I fear...."[13]

McClellan made his headquarters a short distance west of Frederick in a field of clover.

Oliver Bobyshell and the 48th Pennsylvania Infantry spent the Friday night camped near Jug Bridge along the Monocacy River east of Frederick. The Johnnies had tried to blow up the bridge, but failed.

The 48th did not break camp until 3:30 p.m. "The tramp through Frederick was a perfect ovation. The Stars and Stripes were visible upon all sides. Old and young, ladies, men and boys waving it at every house. Cheering greeted the troops at every step. Cool water stood before every house, and good things in abundance were given the men."

Two young civilians of Frederick rode around carrying a huge American flag. The previous Saturday they kept the flag in hiding because of the Confederate occupation, but today they were in their glory.

The men of the 48th kept marching until 9:30 p.m. when camp was made near Middletown. Adam Hendley went looking for food and came back with a nice turkey. This he shared with Bobyshell. "A bright full moon lighted the boys to bed this night—the last night some of the poor fellows were to have on earth."[14]

During the gala festivities in the streets of Frederick, Jesse Lee Reno, commander of the Ninth Corps stopped for a while at the home of the aged Barbara Fritchie. He took a glass of wine and wrote a letter home. Mrs. Fritchie gave him a flag and her best wishes.

While Barbara Fritchie was hosting General Reno, Clara Barton was thinking about what to do next. She had been told to go to

Harpers Ferry as medical help was needed. But she learned that the place was virtually surrounded. With Lee in Maryland, there was going to be a big battle and she had to get to the scene of action. She would have her wagon prepared and in the morning follow the Army of the Potomac.

There was little sleep for the men of the Ninth New York. Shortly after returning from fighting the fire at the Frederick jail, reveille sounded. After a cup of hot coffee, they were ordered to Jefferson to support Rush's Lancers in an engagement with Confederate cavalry.

After Jefferson was cleared of the Rebels, the Ninth New York stacked arms in the streets of the village. Grateful citizens once again brought good food and drink to the men. Then the men grabbed a few moments of rest, lying by the side of the road. Cannon fire was heard coming from Harpers Ferry.

General Franklin arrived and took a hearty meal on the porch of a Jefferson home, but the troops were not dispatched to Harpers Ferry. Instead, at 6:00 p.m., they were marched back to Frederick. The men were tired because part of the march today was across plowed fields, and that for the infantryman is the hardest walking of all.

The Ninth New York started back to Frederick with a second wind. But then the colonel halted the column too soon for a break, and the men stiffened up. When the march was resumed, they thought they'd never reach Frederick. Silently and painfully they made their way back to Frederick and threw themselves on the hard ground to sleep.

The view from Jug Bridge Hill reminded the lads from New Hampshire of the hills and valleys of New England, and the rest of the regimental band arrived. They were formed in front of Colonel Fellows' tent and soon martial music was drifting over the Monocacy Valley.[15]

At four o'clock Nagle's Brigade of Sturgis's Division in the Ninth Corps was drawn up in brigade line. The Ninth New Hampshire possessed the only band in the brigade, so the men were to have the post of honor marching through Frederick.

None of the men ever forgot the welcome for the passing army from the local inhabitants. The town looked comfortable, and "all nature was in bloom." "All the pomp of war was present, glittering staffs and proud commanders...passed through the quaint and beautiful town, the streets resounded with applause, and from balcony and window fair faces smiled, and handkerchiefs and scarfs waved to greet the army of the Union....There were smiles and tears of gratitude and joy....That gracious scene of natural beauty and waving corps, that quaint and charming southern city, that friendly greeting, form a picture which can never pass out of the memory of any whose fortune it was to enter Frederick town that day.[16]

On through Frederick marched the men of the Ninth New Hampshire. The Catoctin Mountain loomed in front, and they started the climb. The sun began to sink in the west, the moon rises, and still they march, looking almost ghostly. In the moonlight a little town can be seen and marching columns. No pen can describe the scene. At midnight the men stumble into a field and fall to the ground to sleep. Three weeks had passed since they had left home and took up soldiering. Now they were on the eve of their first battle, and their baptism of fire.

Like the tempo of a ball game or of a political campaign, things were indeed picking up, excitement was in the air. And like all the others, the 35th Massachusetts would not forget this Saturday in Frederick.

Who that was present will ever forget the cheerful welcome received as the heavy columns of troops passed through Frederick City, flags and handkerchiefs waving, and friendly faces greeting the soldiers from all sides!

"Over the mountains winding down,

Horse and foot, into Frederick town."

At a corner of the streets General McClellan with his staff reviewed the troops and cheer after cheer rent the air as the regiments passed. The welcome from patriotic Marylanders made the soldiers feel as if they were to fight upon their own soil, and greatly inspired the army unused to such moral support. The song of "Maryland, My Maryland," was ever after a Union song. Our regiment sang together "Marching Along" and "Old John Brown," with grand effect, as we swung through the streets; but when we halted for a few moments in the outskirts, some of the cynical elders of the brigade suggested: "Save your breath, boys; you'll need it ahead there!" Too true! for we never sang together on the march afterwards, we had no heart for it, it seemed like tempting evil fortune.

Darkness gathered, but the march was continued. The road was ascending, passing over the Catoctin range of hills, outliers of the Blue Ridge. The scenery from these by daylight is described as surpassingly fine; but, as we stumbled along at a quick pace over the heaps of broken stone, dropped there for road mending—some of the men so tired as to be walking in their sleep—we minded little of the charm about us. The waning moon rose and was reaching the zenith, when, late at night, descending the hills we found ourselves in the valley of Middletown. Here a halt was called, arms stacked, packs un-slung, and a few moments found the tired men wrapped in sleep. Company D had the ill luck to be detailed for picket on this the night before our first battle.[17]

Although the Ninth Corps moved forward, the First Corps had an easy day. For most, including Patrick's brigade, there was but a short march from New Market to the Monocacy River east of Frederick. "The whole valley of the Monocacy was covered with our troops....We are to pursue (the Rebels) and give battle."

John Gibbon, a native of Baltimore, rode from his camp to see General McClellan. Headquarters were in a field in the suburbs of Frederick. Many old friends were there, including Dr. Jonathan Letterman, the Medical Director of the Army of the Potomac. Gib-bon was amazed at the transformation in terms of morale and spirit. There was a remarkable change from the days of Pope to the present. McClellan was talking about commanders, and expressed the hope of having John Sedgwick named as a corps commander.

McClellan then showed Gibbon a copy of Lee's Lost Order. He said he knew where Lee was, and if the men did their job, he'd pitch into the center, and Lee would have a most difficult time escaping. McClellan was full of confidence. He also promised Gib-bon the first new western regiment. John says, "I rode back to my camp...in better spirits than I had been in for a month, feeling confident that we had at our head, a General who knew his busi-ness and was bound to succeed."

Along the "Roads to Antietam" were two relatively new units, assigned to the Fifth Corps. They were the 118th Pennsylvania, Corn Exchange Regiment, raised largely through the efforts and finances of the Corn Exchange in Philadelphia, and the 20th Maine. The sun beat down relentlessly and the dust rose in thick, suffo-cating masses on the Maryland roads.

This was hard on the new soldiers and the men from Maine. After all, they were used to cooler weather. Sweat ran down over dusty faces. Blisters raised on sore feet. One by one, the men started to throw away everything they thought they would not need; blan-kets, jackets, and many other items.

Major General George Morell met a private from the 118th Pennsylvania, who was trying hard to keep up. The soldier inquired, "General, can you tell me where to find the 118th Pennsylvania?"

"Certainly, my man," replied the general. "Everywhere between here and Washington."

Some units reached campsites with no officers and just two or three men present and accounted for. The cool night air refreshed many of the men, and by morning they had found their outfits.

Sumner's Second Corps approached Frederick on the main road from Washington. Frank Sawyer, en route to Frederick with the Eighth Ohio, was somewhere between Frederick and the Monocacy when "Gen. McClellan and his staff and the McClellan Guards, a dashing body of some hundreds of lancers passed us."

McClellan had his advance man. A staff officer had preceded him saying the men would be permitted to cheer and no doubt urging cheers for the general. And the men cheered.

Soon General Ambrose Burnside came riding by on his bob-tailed horse. He had but one orderly with him. The men cheered again.[18]

Frank Sawyer enjoyed marching through Frederick, "a most beautiful town." Like the others he dwells on the welcome in his memoirs, but adds, "the men were almost wild with enthusiasm. We had not seen a woman's face that wore a smile in a year." The vinegar visaged Virginians' were the subjects of comparisons that were indeed 'odious.' However, the Virginians had not been happy to have Yankees on their soil. One of the Ohioans shouted, "We're in God's country again."

Jonathan P. Stowe, from Grafton, Massachusetts, was thirty years old in September of '62, and a member of the 15th Massachusetts Infantry. He noted that the day was very hot, and there was much suffering from the heat and thirst.

That morning he awakened at 3:00 a.m. and had some coffee. By daylight he and his comrades were on their way to Frederick. At 9:00 they apparently reached Monocacy Junction. An hour later, General McClellan passed amid deafening cheers. The Rebs had lived in the area for a week. "They slew lots of cattle." At noon, Jacob H. Cole, a member of the 57th New York also had a delightful experience on this pleasant Saturday in mid-September.

It was a welcome change also to be greeted with smiles instead of frowns. Probably no soldier who entered Frederick City on the morning of September 13th will ever forget the cordial welcome with which the rescuing army was received by the local inhabitants. For five months the Second corps had been upon the soil of Virginia where every native white face was with spite as the invaders passed, marching through or encamping in a region which to a northern eye was inconceivably desolate and forlorn, barren fields affording the only relief to the dreary continuity of tangled thickets and swampy bottoms. Here in the rich valley of the

Monocacy, shut in by low mountains of surprising grace of out-
line, all nature was in bloom. The signs of comfort and opulence
met the eye on every side, while as the full brigades of Sumner, in
perfect order and with all the pomp of war, with glittering staff
and proud commanders, old Sumner at the head, pressed through
the quaint and beautiful town, the streets resounded with applause and from balcony and windows fair faces smiled and handkerchiefs and scarfs waved to greet the army of the Union. Many
an honest and many a fair countennce of patriotic men and women
looked out upon the brave array of Sumner's corps with smiles
and tears of gratitude and joy. Amid all that was desolate and
gloomy, amid all that was harsh and terrible in the service, that
these soldiers of the Union were called to render that bright day
of September 13th, 1862, still that gracious scene of natural beauty
and waving crops that quaint and charming southern city, that
friendly greeting form a picture which can never pass out of the
memory of those whose fortune it was to enter Frederick town
that day.[19]

Josiah Favill says that Frederick presented the first real opportunity for the men to "show off for our countrywomen, and we
made the most of it." The folks were beside themselves with joy.
That night the 57th New York camped one mile west of town, but
Favill and the officers went back in to visit.[20]

H.R. Dunham and the 19th Massachusetts were roused at
the early hour of 3:00 a.m. By sunrise they were in line of march.
He was impressed with the pleasant little town of Urbana. "We
arrived at Frederick about noon...The people of the City were glad
to see us. The Stars and Stripes were flying from almost every house.
It made me think of Boston....Sum large number of Rebel prisoners here....Marched about two miles beyond the City and halted for
the night...General Orders read to every Regt. in regard to Straggling. Every man that straggles or flounders is to be shot down on
the spot...."[21]

The 14th Connecticut was also in good spirits as they passed
through Frederick. The men sang "John Brown's Body." On the
main street they received resounding cheers. Passing an old en-
gine house, now in use as a prison, the Rebels who were locked up
called, "What regiment is that?"

"The 14th Wooden Nutmeg," was the reply.

The Confederates shouted back, "You will soon get your heads
grated."[22]

The First Massachusetts cavalry spent the night near
Richardson's division of the Second Corps. One of the men found

part of a barrel of rye in a stable, this mixed with water comprised the evening meal.[23]

General A.S. Williams took time to write today. From near Frederick he states, "I have been so long without a clean shirt that I am rejoiced to be so near a town that I may reasonably hope to find a haberdasher....It is just a month that I have been without rest or sleep of a reasonable kind. Tonight I have straw under a blanket! Think of that....The enemy have gone towards Hagerstown."[24]

Men of the Twelfth Corps took time to think about their steps on the "Roads to Antietam." On the ninth they reached and camped at Middlebrook. The next day it was on to Damascus. On Thursday they rested. On Friday, the twelfth, they moved to Ijamsville, and on Saturday, they were within sight of Frederick.[25]

Julian Hinkley and members of the Third Wisconsin went into Frederick to visit old friends. Many of the fellows heard the story of Barbara Fritchie. The story was circulating through the town. So there must have been some truth to the episode.[26]

Colonel Andrews and Lt. Col. Wilder Dwight of the Second Massachusetts Infantry left their campgrounds, and about noon reached Frederick. Riding into the city, the officers were joyously welcomed by old friends from the preceding winter. Part of Saturday evening was spent with Dr. George Diehl.[27]

The 27th Indiana forded the Monocacy. The water was only knee deep and warm. It was no problem except for bringing additional damage to badly worn shoes. For the officers, it was worse. Some of them had just changed clothes and put on their best boots and pants. They were going into Frederick and they might have the chance to visit old friends. Water and dust are not the best for new clothes and boots.[28]

Emerging from the Monocacy, the men from Indiana heard the sounds of skirmishing in Frederick. But they were not engaged. They made camp in a field of clover south of Frederick.

The weather was beautiful. And as the soldiers talked and examined the ground on which the Confederates had previously occupied, three members of the 27th Indiana found "three cigars and a piece of paper."

There are still two major questions about the Lost Order: Who wrote it? And who found it?

The traditional theory is that shortly after the 27th Indiana complied with the order to make camp south of Frederick, Sergeant John M. Bloss and Private B.W. Mitchell approached Colonel Silas Colgrove with a piece of paper they had found wrapped around three cigars. This was a copy of Order No. 191 detailing the Confederate troop movements and the division of the Army of Northern Virginia.

The troops from the Hoosier State had occupied a campsite just vacated by soldiers under D.H. Hill. Lee had issued three copies of the order. One was given to Longstreet, one went to Jackson, and one to Daniel Harvey Hill. Jackson made a copy of the order and gave it to Hill. Who lost it? Longstreet memorized the contents, tore it up, and supposedly swallowed the bits of paper. Jackson, realizing the great danger of such a paper being found, memorized his copy and burned it. Hill kept Jackson's copy of the order until after the war. So, the document from Lee's headquarters is the one that was lost, and it bore the signature of Colonel Chilton. But who lost the order, and how it became wrapped around the cigars, "until the foraging Hoosier picked them up—God alone knoweth."

The next problem is who found the papers. Edmund Randolph Brown, a member of Company C in the 27th Indiana, writing the regimental history in 1899, says that he knows of nothing other than the account in *Battles and Leaders* which indicates men in the regiment found the order. Most accounts say the order was found by "a soldier" or "a member of an Indiana outfit." Brown tends to feel that his comrades have not been accorded a rightful place in history because they were not prominent men and just members of the rank and file.

Late in the afternoon, the Sixth New York cavalry marched about a mile north of Frederick and made camp. Company I was selected to guard the headquarters of General Ambrose Burnside.[29]

Ezra Simons and his friends in the 125th New York were placed on Bolivar Heights, over twenty miles away, to support the Sixth Illinois Battery. The men spent a very cold night. They had thrown away their coats and blankets during the hot, twenty-mile march on Friday. Now they regretted their actions.[30]

But others were faring better in Frederick and Jefferson. For George Washburn and the 108th New York the camp in Frederick was like "a grand spectacle, thousands of men bivouacking and the numerous campfires presented a grand scene....Officers were warmly welcomed and entertained by the loyal citizens in their homes."[31]

As the Sixth Corps advanced, Robert Westbrook and the 49th Pennsylvania departed from Sugar Loaf Mountain, heading for Buckeystown at sunrise. They crossed the Monocacy River on the covered bridge at the Monocacy flour mills, and reached the Thomas farm where they halted until 8:00 p.m. Then the tired men marched to "Jeffersontown." They made it in two hours.[32]

James N. Rigby was an officer in Battery A, First Maryland Artillery. He and his comrades arrived in Jefferson that evening. They were attached to Slocum's division of the Sixth Corps.

To James the village was lovely and made even more impressive by the smiling faces of the ladies and the cheers for the Union.

A Union camp was made on the farm of Harmon Culler, and Mr. Ahalt who lived there fed the soldiers homemade bread. One soldier, missing his own home and family very much, picked up the little Culler girl and gave her a big hug.

On September 6, Frederick County was occupied by the Army of Northern Virginia. Now the "Clustered Spires of Fredericktown" were surrounded by men in blue, troops of the Army of the Potomac.

Reno's Ninth Corps, with the exception of Rodman's division, was at Middletown. Joseph Hooker's First Corps was on the Monocacy, two miles from Frederick in the Jug Bridge area. Edwin Sumner's Second Corps was near Frederick, as was the Twelfth Corps. The Sixth Corps under Franklin was at Buckeystown, having come on the river road. One division of the Fifth Corps was near Frederick, the other at Licksville.

George McClellan wrote the orders for the troops to move early on Sunday. Joe Hooker and the First Corps was to move at daylight for Middletown. George Sykes and his division of the Fifth Corps was to move at 6:00 a.m., followed by the Artillery Reserve one hour later. Edwin Sumner was to move at 9:00 a.m., taking the Shookstown Road to Middletown.

CHAPTER VI

SUNDAY, SEPTEMBER 14, 1862

—ARMY OF NORTHERN VIRGINIA—

Things looked bad for the men in gray. Some were streaming to the rear. The line of defense was broken, and the commander of the immediate area was dead. The Ohio troops captured 200 Confederates from North Carolina.

Word of the critical situation was rushed back to D.H. Hill at the Mountain House. He was in charge of the defense of the two passes.

Garland's men had broken at Fox's Gap. No reserves were available at the moment and as Hill looked to the east, he was dismayed. Approaching from Middletown was a vast array of the enemy. "The marching columns extended back as far as the eye could see....It was a grand and glorious spectacle, and it was impossible for me to look at it without admiration. I had never seen so tremendous an army before...."[1]

The best Hill could do to stem the tide was to open fire with two guns from near the Mountain House, and form a line of battle with staff officers, couriers, teamsters, and cooks. He hoped this would make the Yankees think the Rebels had a solid line of defense. It was a big gamble, but it worked.

Harvey Hill felt so alone, "deserted by the rest of the world and mankind."

It was now about 10:00 a.m. Fairchild's Division of the Ninth Corps had left Frederick at 3:00 and was just now arriving in Middletown. No doubt it was part of the vast blue horde that Hill saw. But the division halted in Middletown, as did many other units arriving from Frederick. For some reason a lull developed in the battle, and this was the best stroke of luck the Confederates could hope for.

Not only was Lee's army scattered at Harpers Ferry, Loudoun Heights, Maryland Heights, Crampton's Gap and Hagerstown, but Hill's command was scattered. Originally Garland was at Fox's Gap with Colquitt at Turner's. Robert Rodes and Roswell Ripley were guarding the road from Boonsboro to Harpers Ferry (current Route 67). Hill ordered them up, but he could not expect them before 2:00 p.m. and perhaps not until 3:00 p.m. Hill was in a dilemma. And it was hard to tell when Pete Longstreet's command would arrive from Hagerstown.

Hill was just about helpless, but McClellan and his subordinates granted him the mercy of a lull. Both sides were now hurrying forward reinforcements.

As the Yankees headed for South Mountain from the east the Confederates marched to support their comrades from the west.

After a relaxing Saturday near Hagerstown, Longstreet's command was placed in line, headed back to South Mountain. A major action was expected. So at 9:30, John Dooley and his comrades marched through Hagerstown, just as the church bells were ringing and calling people to worship.

Soon the pace quickened, and the dust rose. The sounds of battle were heard. The Confederate rear guard was in great danger. About 2:00 p.m. Dooley's unit passed through Boonsboro. They saw the ambulance carrying the remains of General Garland, former commander of the Eleventh Virginia, one of the units of the brigade.[2]

Hurrying to the front, William Owen saw the ambulance bearing the body of General Garland going back to Boonsboro. The road was blocked with army wagons, and there was little progress. William saw General Lee and his staff pass, urging every man to move as quickly as possible.[3]

Dooley also saw General Lee riding in the ambulance. The sight of a dead general and a hurt leader, cast gloom over John. He did not feel it was a good omen.

About 5:00 p.m., Dooley and his comrades reached their position, one aimed to keep the Yankees from flanking the Rebel position. Union shells started to whistle and fall. John was scared. However, the Yankee infantry stopped, perhaps fearing a trick.[4]

Randolph Shotwell was among the shoeless Confederates and could not keep up with Longstreet's forces heading for South Mountain. In Funkstown, one compassionate soul took a look at Randolph's bleeding and blistered toes, and pulled off his own shoes, and offered them to the Confederate soldier. Sadly, they were four sizes too big, and would have caused even more blisters. Regretfully, Shotwell had to decline the gracious offer.

When Shotwell got under way again, he saw that the wagons had stopped. Asking the reason, a courier said, "Terrible fighting."

It was nearly 5:00 p.m. when Shotwell reached Boonsboro. A cloud of smoke, resembling fog, hung over the mountain. People were assembled on their porches and in the street. Each loud clash of battle brought fresh alarm to them.

Shotwell reached the summit and joined in the fray, describing the action as "Bushels of ball. Buckets of balls," with the action lasting until 10:00 p.m.[5]

Randolph Shotwell described the Union advance as looking like a horde of black ants, sweeping over the fields, skirting the timber, and climbing the hills, flags waving, bayonets gleaming, "Great long black centipedes, all aiming at the top of the Gap—and Coming! Coming!"

Dawn was just beginning to break when George Neese and Chew's battery broke camp, and climbed to the top of the mountain at Crampton's Gap. Before them stretched the lovely Middletown Valley, "with its wooded hills, pleasant fields, hamlets, and towns reposing in the quiet calm of a peaceful Sabbath morning. But with the first rays of the sun, came the booming of the cannon."[6]

The Yanks were coming.

Things were much better though for Jackson. Harpers Ferry was surrounded. Jed Hotchkiss could not understand why the general did not storm the town. At 3:00 p.m. Confederate artillery fired on the village, scattering the cavalry and forcing the infantry to take cover. The troops stood "to arms all day, presenting a very fine appearance."

At Crampton's Gap, George Neese felt as lonely as D.H. Hill the previous night at Turner's Gap. Apparently the Confederates did not look upon Crampton's Gap as being as important as Turner's Gap. Yet it was the shortest route to the relief of Harpers Ferry.

Several regiments of infantry, Munford's brigade of cavalry, and six pieces of artillery were all that stood in the way of the Union Sixth Corps. It was about ten o'clock when the blue infantry were first sighted. Then it seemed that "the whole country was full of bluecoats." They seemed to be coming out of the ground. George Neese felt helpless. Yet the Confederate small arms and artillery fire stopped the initial advance. George was sure the Northern writers would say that a little band of Union patriots cleared out a host of Confederates.

General Franklin brought up cannon, and in replying to their fire, Neese's gun was damaged. He had to leave it on the field. The mountainside had made it very difficult for recoil, and when the gun could not recoil, several bolts snapped.

George stood for a few moments to watch the scene. "I gazed at the magnificent splendor of the martial array that was slowly and steadily moving toward us across the plain below like a living panorama, the sheen of the glittering side-arms and thousands of bright, shining musket barrels looking like a silver spangled sea rippling and flashing in the light of a midday sun."[7]

Neese was amused at the caution of the Yankees. To him it seemed that they were like a lion, the king of the forest stalking a plunky little mouse.

When he left the mountain, George journeyed to Boonsboro, and then turned toward Shepherdstown. About four miles from Boonsboro, he made camp with the wagons.

James Rigby and his artillery were sent to assist the infantry fighting in Crampton's Gap. Shells from Confederate guns were falling on Burkettsville. But the Maryland gunners rode through the town at full gallop, while the ladies, unmindful of the shells, waved their scarves and cheered them on.

Among the fallen at Crampton's Gap was Benjamin Prather, the young man from Georgia who had been with General Lee on Friday. He was shot in the right knee and hip. And Dr. J. Garrett was to perform an operation amputating the leg four days later. Prather and other wounded in Burkittsville were visited by President Lincoln on October 4. Mr. Lincoln laid his hand on Prather's shoulder and prayed for him.

On the 9th of October, Prather wrote a farewell letter home. Somehow it never was mailed. And in 1976 after 114 years, it was found by Rev. Austin Cooper in an old hymn book in Burkittsville.[8]

Supposedly Lee talked with Hill and Longstreet about the situation on the mountain. When asked if he could hold out another day, Hill replied, "Not another hour—if pressed by the full weight of troops the enemy now has upon my flanks." So there was nothing to do but leave the field.

Lee said to Hill, "Proceed to bring off your men as quietly as possible. We will retire to Sharpsburg and make a stand there."

Things looked bad for Robert E. Lee. He was in a dilemma. Things were going against him and his army was divided.

Moxley Sorrel, one of Longstreet's staff officers, states, "We had a bad night on the mountain extracting D.H. Hill. He made a magnificent defense, but was terribly mauled and broken up....The mountain roads were filled with broken regiments and companies, and it was very late before they got to the foot of the mountain."

General Lee had gained a day by the fighting in the mountain passes, but he was still in a perilous position. The day had gone against the Confederates. Federal troops were swarming down the mountain at Crampton's Gap directly in McLaws' rear. McLaws was in danger of being cut off and McClellan now had a short and direct road to Sharpsburg, past which Lee hoped to move on his way back to Virginia soil. Later in the evening of the fourteenth, Lee received a report from Jackson, leading him to believe that Harpers Ferry would fall the next morning.[9]

After a careful analysis of the situation, Lee issued instructions as follows:

1. Longstreet and D.H. Hill, or the main part of the army, were to march to Keedysville, so as to be upon the flank and rear of McLaws and protect the road to Sharpsburg, where it was hoped the army could reunite.[10]

2. McLaws was to cross into Virginia, if he must, but was to seek a road over the mountains or follow the road up the river, and if he could march on Sharpsburg, was to notify headquarters which would be established at Keedysville.[11]

3. The cavalry under Munford that had fought at Crampton's Gap was to cover McLaws' rear, holding Rohrersville on the main road from Boonsboro to Maryland Heights.[12]

4. The commands of Walker and Jackson, after accomplishing the mission for which they had been detached were to rejoin the army.[13]

Before abandoning the position at South Mountain, Lee learned from a Union prisoner that a fresh Union corps, that of Edwin F. Sumner, was being put into position to renew the conflict on the morrow. This confirmed Lee in his determination to retreat. Accordingly, between midnight and 1:00 o'clock (the morning of September 15) Lee's army commenced its retreat. The dead and seriously wounded had to be left behind.

On the retreat, Lee sent another urgent message to McLaws, from whom he had heard nothing...telling him to move to Harpers Ferry if it had fallen by the time McLaws received his dispatch. Lee also decided not to halt at Keedysville, but to march on to Sharpsburg where he could take up a good defensive position, and where he would be closer to the Shepherdstown Ford, if Jackson could not rejoin him in time.

At 11:00 p.m., Dooley's unit was withdrawn. The retreat was completed in great silence.

The route was through Boonsboro where hundreds of Confederate wounded had been taken. Rebel soldiers knocked on the doors of houses, seeking aid, water, bandages, anything. But most of the citizens of Boonsboro did not come to the door. They raised their windows and asked who was there and what they wanted, and told the Confederates, "Please go on and don't bother us." Some said they feared ill treatment from the Union army or their neighbors if they helped the men in gray.

M.F. Rohrer was twelve years old in September of 1862. He and the family from their Keedysville home must have heard the sounds of battle during the day. No doubt they were excited. But more excitement was to come. During the night, Rohrer heard a rumbling sound like thunder. He arose and looked out. He saw the wagons of the Army of Northern Virginia heading for Sharpsburg.[14]

Randolph Shotwell of the Eighth Virginia describes the retreat from South Mountain.

"Go quietly to the rear—step easily—don't rattle your canteens—don't speak—follow your file leaders as closely as possible." So the retreat began.

Occasionally there was the dry, "Water, help me." But there was no time to go back and give aid. Shotwell would have been happy to stay. He was tired. There had been the trek from Hagerstown, a climb to the top of the mountain, and now more walking. Being shoeless, Randolph was soon alone among the boulders, the briars, and the thickets. Twice he fell and spent a long time looking for his musket and bayonet.

A worse experience was ahead. Reaching a clearing with a stonewall, he paused to rest and could see the lights of Boonsboro below. While leaning on the wall, it gave way, and either a sharp rock or his own musket cut a long deep gash across his bare instep. "The wound bled as freely as if an artery had been cut. I tore off strips of my blanket and bandaged it as well as I could, but I suffered extensively as I staggered along."

It was midnight when Randolph reached Boonsboro. Seeing a little straw rick by the side of the road, he threw himself down with his pain and fatigue. He got several hours of rest, although it seemed but a moment, when someone woke him and told him "The Yanks are comin'."

So there was nothing to do but to hobble to the Sharpsburg Road. By hiding and hobbling, Randolph finally made it to Sharpsburg and rejoined his command.[15]

Edward Porter Alexander was one of the foremost artillery officers in the Army of Northern Virginia. In September of 1862, he felt that neither Lincoln nor Stanton had much faith in McClellan but restored him to command as a last resort. Pope had proven incompetent, and Issac Stevens, whom Alexander thought would have been given top command, was dead.

However, Alexander had other things to think about this September Sabbath. He had taken his reserve ordnance trains with Lee and Longstreet to Hagerstown, then brought them back to Boonsboro as Longstreet hurried to aid Daniel Harvey Hill on the mountain. Now he was ordered to take his wagons to Williamsport, cross the Potomac and head for Shepherdstown. This seems foolish when the distance is but ten miles from Boonsboro to Shepherdstown. But the order was given to take the longer route.

The moon was rising when Alexander and the command started out. They forded the Potomac at daylight on the fifteenth, unaware of their narrow escape from Davis and the cavalry which had gotten away from Harpers Ferry.[16]

As the wagons of Lee's army were creaking toward Keedysville and Sharpsburg, a column of horsemen rode quietly through the night.

—ARMY OF THE POTOMAC—

On September 14, the Battle of South Mountain occurred. Fighting took place in the three mountain passes on the Frederick-Washington County border. The fighting on (Route 40,) the National Road, took place late in the day, both on, and north of the road.

Six miles south at Crampton's Gap, the Union Sixth Corps advanced from Jefferson and Burkittsville, and pushed aside the small Confederate defensive unit in Crampton's Gap.

The Battle of South Mountain actually started early Sunday morning at Fox's Gap on the Old Sharpsburg Road. This road was an early Indian trail, and many scholars feel it was one of the roads the settlers took into Washington County. Not only was it to be the scene of action that day, but the blue and gray traveled it during the Gettysburg Campaign and also during Early's invasion of Maryland in July of 1864.

At daybreak, General Alfred Pleasonton and his cavalry resumed their scouting and probing of the Confederate positions on South Mountain. The infantry support from the Ninth Corps did not arrive in time on Saturday to press matters, but the infantry was ready this Sunday morning.

No one can measure the effect of Buford's cavalry as it opened the fight at Gettysburg. To a degree, Pleasonton and his cavalry did the same at South Mountain. On Saturday Pleasonton had discovered the Old Sharpsburg Road south of the National Road, and another road leading to the right.

With the coming of daylight, Pleasonton directed Scammon's brigade of the Ninth Corps to move up South Mountain on the Old Sharpsburg Road, "gain the crest, and then move to the right to the turnpike in the enemy's rear."[17]

Pleasonton also placed Gibson's battery and some heavy artillery batteries in position on the left, covering the Old Sharpsburg Road and being in a position to fire on the Confederates in Fox's Gap. Heavy cannonading continued at intervals throughout the day.

It was 6:00 a.m. when Jacob Cox's division left the bivouac area near Middletown to move on Fox's Gap. Scammon's brigade was the first to go into action followed by that of George Crook.[18]

Sporadic shooting occurred until about 9:00 a.m. The Ninth Corps was encountering resistance from Garland's and Colquitt's Confederate troops, supported by Thomas Rosser and dismounted cavalry. Many of these troops were raw and inexperienced.

The 23rd Ohio, under Lt. Col. Rutherford B. Hayes, reached the crest of the mountain, advancing from the south side of the road, and obtained a position of the Confederate flank. Hayes, a future president, was severely wounded in the arm but refused to leave the field until compelled to do so by the loss of blood.

The 45th Pennsylvania writers tell us that on the "Roads to Antietam" "the weather was very warm, the roads dusty, and the water scarce."

The men of the 45th Pennsylvania heard the bells of churches in Frederick ringing this morning. Many of the men made plans to attend church. But their passes were canceled and they were told to "Fall in."

Dr. Ellis says the entrance into Frederick was one of great joy. The Army of the Potomac was looked upon as the agent to deliver the country, and at the same time drive the rebels from the area. Throughout the day, "long lines of men, horses, and artillery kept passing through the town, and it was not until midnight that the monster military procession had drawn to a close."[19]

A brief halt was made at the battery; then the order came to hurry up the old Sharpsburg road, at Fox's Gap, to the left. Away we went to the foot of the hills; the rear companies with difficulty closing up, so swift the advance. It was about half past three o'clock. The cheering and rattle of musketry were lively above us, and evidently our movement meant work. Half way up the hill we met a wounded man borne in a stretcher upon the shoulders of his friends. He shouted to us, as we breathlessly hurried by: "Forward, boys, forward! We're driving them! Don't let this scare you; give 'em hell! They can't stand cold steel!" We passed a low weather-stained house, and came into line of battle in its little cornfield, to the left, facing the woods just below the summit of the hill.

"Throw off your packs!" Away go our bundles, never to be seen again. "Fix bayonets!" The rattle of the steel replies. "Right face! Forward by file left! Double quick! Charge!" And Company A led off gallantly up into the thick woods in front, and through them into the open field upon the summit, the scene of the action.[20]

When darkness came, the night chill set in, and with it the chill of death. David Thompson and others walked over the fields at Fox's Gap and covered some of the Confederates with blankets they no longer needed. At 9:00 o'clock, the men covered themselves and laid down, "living Yankee and dead Confederate side by side."[21]

Some suggested that the battlefield of Fox's Gap be called Mr. Reno in honor of Jesse Lee Reno. But it never happened. Perhaps the general had a premonition of his death. As he was watching the action unfold before him an ambulance passed by going to the front to pick up the wounded. He remarked, "Wouldn't it be strange if that ambulance should bring me back from the battlefield?" According to local tradition, that same ambulance was used to bring General Reno's body back to Middletown.

The Civil War Centennial raised a question about Reno's death. Most scholars have always said that it occurred under the Reno Oak at the foot of South Mountain. However, Jonas Gross and another person living in the area at the time, (say) the general was placed under the oak, then carried to a nearby house where he expired.[22]

William Richard Todd of the 79th New York describes the cold night at Fox's Gap:

> All about us lay the dead and dying, while the groans and cries of the wounded sounded in our ears throughout the long hours of that weary night. Those in our immediate vicinity were relieved to the extent of our ability, but we were obliged to keep in line and under arms till daylight, and dared not wander far, even to give a drink of water to a tenth of those who moaned piteously for it. We expected that Longstreet, who commanded the enemy in our front would attempt to recover the lost ground during the night. The weather was cold and as we stood in line shivering and wishing for morning, we conversed in low tones with each other, congratulating ourselves on this our first victory

in the new campaign. Would the enemy now retrace his steps into Virginia? We hoped not, but that he would remain north of the Potomac long enough for us to annihilate him, horse, foot and artillery![23]

Among the units Hill may have seen streaming into Middletown Valley might have been those of the Union First and Second Corps.

Joe Hooker and the First Corps marched through the streets of Frederick. They too were greeted with flags, smiles, and handkerchiefs, and a great reception. John Gibbon, a Marylander, commanding a brigade in the First Corps was amazed to find so much Northern sentiment in Western Maryland, "the whole population seemed to turn out to welcome us." In a letter home he related that McClellan's welcome had not been equaled since the days of Washington. And all along the route, the welcome was repeated. "There is no question of the loyalty of this part of Maryland."

During a halt in the streets of Frederick, Gibbon urged his men to keep in step and refrain from straggling. If anyone dropped behind, the other men were to hoot and jeer at him. He also told the men that General McClellan had promised him the first western regiment, the reason, they were a good brigade. Gibbon told them he wanted nothing to happen that might cause McClellan to change his mind.

Then it was on to Middletown. En route the sounds of battle could be heard coming from South Mountain, and Gibbon's command was headed for the action and a new nickname.

Marsena Patrick has little to say about the day. However, his men tramped through Frederick, "the citizens waving their flags & giving us water & welcome....On arriving at Catoctin Creek we halted for lunch."

Rufus Dawes and the Sixth Wisconsin also broke camp near Frederick this September Sabbath. Rufus was impressed'with the scenery. "There are few fairer landscapes in our country than this valley affords from its eastern range of hills. The morning was bright, warm, and clear. The bells of the city of Frederick were all ringing. It was a rejoicing at the advance of the host for the deliverance of the Army of the Potomac. The spires of the city were glistening in the morning sunlight."

> Every soldier was stirred as he saw the vast swarm of blue coats. Confidence had returned. "We have a General now, and we will show the country what we can do."

The unit that was soon to be nicknamed the Iron Brigade formed at 8:00 a.m. near the Monocacy. The Sixth Wisconsin was the advance.

The entry into Frederick was triumphant. The Stars and
Stripes floated from every building and hung from every window. Little children offered cool drinks and baked goods.[24]

The reception was repeated in Middletown. However, there
was more alarm, as the sound of gunfire was heard, and blood-
stained men of the Ninth Corps were being returned to Middletown
hospitals.

Friday and Saturday had been difficult days for the Ninth
New York. Sunday was to be worse. Already fatigued from fighting
the jail fire, and marching to Jefferson and back on Saturday, the
men had barely rolled up in their blankets Saturday night, when
3:00 a.m. arrived. At that time they had to get up and start from
camp near the railroad depot toward Middletown. After a seven-
hour march, they were led into a field near Middletown for a rest.
The sounds of the cannonading in the South Mountain passes
grew louder and louder. The men slept though until about 2:00
p.m., when after coffee, they started to advance on Fox's Gap.

When David Thompson stopped to rest and looked back toward Braddock Heights he saw a sight he'd never forget, columns
coming over Catoctin Mountain like a mighty, swelling flood. As far
as he could see there were troops, supply wagons, and horses. War
had indeed come to the Middletown Valley.[25]

En route, Charles Johnson saw the lovely Middletown Valley.
He too was greatly impressed. But he saw the white puffs of smoke
on the mountain and heard the dull thud of the cannon. He knew
trouble was ahead.

When the men from New Hampshire wakened this morning,
they found themselves near Middletown and the Catoctin Creek.
They were impressed with the area. It looked like home. "Two
beeves on the hoof" comprised regimental ration. And soon there
were ten piles of fresh beef, one for each company in the Ninth
New Hampshire. "It wasn't quite up to 'mother's brown bread and
beans'...but cooked over fence rails and ramrods for toasting purposes," the meat with hardtack and coffee proved an acceptable
breakfast.[26]

Soon the men were placed under orders. They saw the puffs of
white smoke at Fox's Gap and saw the couriers coming and going.
As noon came and dinner was eaten, the sounds of battle drifted
northward from Crampton's Gap.

At last at 2:00 p.m. the 9th New Hampshire moved out and
through Middletown. Long lines of veteran troops were along the
roadside resting. They waded the Catoctin Creek and noticed the

timbers of the bridge and some nearby buildings still smoldering from the fires set on Saturday by the Confederates. Then it was on to the front and to combat.

David Strother says troops were all moving westward over the Catoctin Mountain and into the Middletown Valley. The headquarters staff rode rapidly toward Middletown and stopped at Burnside's headquarters in a field at the eastern edge of the village. McClellan wanted Strother to find a man to carry a message to General Miles at Harpers Ferry. Dr. Baer assisted in locating a courier.[27]

While there was a lull at South Mountain, things were happening down south at Harpers Ferry. The place was virtually surrounded by McLaws on Maryland Heights, Walker on Loudoun Heights, and Jackson pressing in from Halltown and Bolivar. The place was doomed. But there had to be a way out. At 2:00 p.m. an order, No. 120, was released to the cavalry units. At 8:00 p.m. they were to gather to Shenandoah Street without noise or loud commands. Cole's cavalry, the 12th Illinois, the 8th New York, the 7th Rhode Island, and the First Maryland were to meet without baggage, ambulances, or lead horses. They were to cross the river on the pontoon bridge and take the road for Sharpsburg. No other instruction was given. The men were to be guided by circumstances as they developed. They were on their own, commanded by Colonel Arno Voss, although Grimes Davis gets the credit for the escape. Cole's cavalrymen said they would never surrender. They offered to lead. So the cavalrymen prepared for their night escape attempt.

But Ezra Simon was sad.

> There remained now only one hope for our beleaguered troops, and that was in relief from the Army of the Potomac, only a few miles away. But the relief came not. General D.H. Hill exultingly attributes the failure to the "lost order," which ought to have insured success. But he overlooks that while General McClellan had been led to suppose that Longstreet, with ten thousand men, stood between him and Maryland Heights, yet sending, as McClellan did, 30,000 men towards the endangered point, only success should have been contemplated. But the forces moved with snail-like pace. No.! McClellan was not equal to the demand. He missed at once the opportunity to relieve the invested forces and to crash Lee's army in detail. He failed through an over-caution. He failed through that want of moral courage which consists of a greater confidence in your own men than fear of your enemy. McClellan's brilliant imagination played him false on the 13th of September....

It was a beautiful Sunday. But here we were—completely surrounded by one half of the rebel army: and the men were for the most part unconscious of the condition of things or of their danger. And away beyond Maryland Heights were sounding the guns of South Mountain, where the Union forces were victorious. There was no Sunday in the army—none if duty was to be done or danger to be met. The war laid its demoralizing hand upon a day of religious rest. On this particular Sunday effort was made for divine worship. On the open plain Chaplain Barlow was conducting a service when the rebel batteries on Loudon Heights sent their first shell at us. It came plunging and tumbling down in front of the Colonel's tent. Fortunately it did not explode or the hand writing these lines might have lost its "cunning."[28]

By 3:00 p.m. the bulk of the Ninth Corps was in position to resume heavy fighting and attack Fox's Gap. Reno and Burnside directed affairs from the base of the mountain. They were joined by General McClellan.

By then the Confederates had been reinforced by the arrival of the brigades of G.T. Anderson, Thomas F. Drayton, E.M. Law, and John B. Hood. These units clashed with the Ninth Corps from about 4:00 p.m. until dark.

Near sunset, Jesse Lee Reno rode forward to see in person how things were going. As he neared the front, there was a heavy exchange of musketry, and Reno fell mortally wounded about 7:00 p.m.

Samuel Sturgis, a division commander in the Ninth Corps, was with Reno when he was hit. The two had been friends and classmates at West Point. Sturgis immediately came to his aid, and said with deep emotion, "Jesse, are you badly hurt?" Reno replied, "Sam, I'm a dead man."

Then Reno, who was one of the most popular generals in the Union army, was tenderly carried down the mountain to a large oak tree where he died less than an hour later. General Burnside, in an official report, described Reno as "one of the country's best defenders."

About 6:00 p.m., Dr. Hastings ordered young Dr. Oliver to bring surgical dressings close to the front as the 21st Massachusetts was engaged in heavy fighting at Fox's Gap.

Earlier, Oliver had seen General McClellan sitting on his horse at the foot of the mountain watching the unfolding action. The general looked every bit a soldier. "He sat upon his horse with perfect grace....[Yet] his face indicated the responsibility that was upon him...Every feature of his fine face indicated anxiety, that the work before him was disagreeable."

But enough for reflections. Oliver was on his way to the front now and he saw another general. This time it was General Jesse Lee Reno being carried to the rear on a stretcher. Dr. Cutter was with him. Everyone aware of the general's loss was deeply upset. He was a good leader.

Darkness had fallen. The ground at Fox's Gap was covered with the dead and dying. Little could be done, but Dr. Oliver helped to amputate a leg by the light of a tallow candle. When morning broke, Oliver took the leg off a young Confederate.

It was a sad experience for the young man from Athol. "I never saw in my three years of service, so many dead bodies as lay on a few acres of ground on top of South Mountain. That hideous night, I shall always remember."[29]

From the pages of the 35th Massachusetts, we give a full account of what it was like this Sunday.

Walking stiff and sore to a beautiful Sunday morning (September 14), the first thought was breakfast. Some cattle were driven up and killed in the neighboring field, and we tried broiling collops of steaming fresh beef upon our ramrods. Some of the men visited the houses in the town in search of eatables, but with little success. The irrepressible Walsh returned with a tea-kettle and cabbage—of course he was a tailor as well as a marine—and set to work broiling the vegetable. While this was passing artillery firing commenced, and white puffs of smoke began to rise between us and the range of blue hills, called the South Mountain, about one hundred feet high, bounding our view on the west; to which, however, we gave little attention. Two o'clock in the afternoon came, and with it the order to "fall-in." The regiment was about eight hundred strong, with Colonel Wild in command. Walsh had not time to cook his cabbage; so he slung it, kettle and all, to his belt, in hopes of a chance to finish it.

We passed through the quiet town, houses and churches ominously silent and deserted, and out into the country, meeting the Twelfth and Thirteenth Massachusetts Regiments, with other troops, resting by the roadside; they laughed at our announcement that we, such raw troops, were going into battle. The wooden bridge over a small stream was destroyed, the timbers still smoking, but we found no difficulty in fording. We stopped there a moment to load our guns. As we proceeded ambulances met us, returning with wounded men. The sound of firing in front grew louder, and we could distinguish the rattle of musketry and see a line of smoke rising half way up the hills.

"Now, men, forward! right—shoulder-shift! quick time! double quick!" came the orders. We left the road, crossed the fields, jumping brooks, and were soon close upon our batteries, which were fuming like furnaces, and sending shells into Turner's Pass on the right and up into the woods on the left.

The 13th Massachusetts Regiment did not start to march until 1:00 p.m. on Saturday, and then covered twelve miles. Sunday they started at 5:00 a.m. and marched most of the day, allowing for frequent halts. Their path took them through Frederick and Middletown, and at last about 6:00 p.m. they went into action on the northwest side of Turner's Gap.

One of the men from Massachusetts got a real surprise. At Second Manassas many of them had lost their knapsacks, and felt they were lost forever. Along the path of advance up South Mountain, this soldier noticed a knapsack that looked much like his own on the back of a dead Georgian. He went over to get it, and found it was his very own. And to his surprise and delight he found the contents intact.[30]

George Noyes was awakened a little after daybreak. Preparations were made to move. As the officers were eating breakfast, "Little did we think of the danger, excitement, and death we were to pass before sunset. It was a fine marching day, everyone was in good spirits."

The march through Frederick was "a perfect ovation—one continuous fluttering of handkerchiefs, tossing of bouquets, and cheering by our men, who grew hoarse before they had passed through its main street."

With wagon trains in the rear, the division passed through Middletown, and General Rickets turned in his saddle and exclaimed, "What a view." Then it was on into action, and with the hail of bullets, Noyes wondered, "How is that any escape alive?"

Thomas Livermore of the Fifth New Hampshire says that the march to Frederick was "through green fields and camps by pleasant waters....We stacked arms and called rolls, and washed off the dust in cool streams." Then it seems they ate and ate rather well, at least the men from New Hampshire. Captain Cross detailed an Irishman by the name of Peter Brennan to look for food. He always came back with a pack horse laden down with good Maryland edibles. Before unloading, he built a fire, and then proceeded to produce legs of mutton, chickens with and without their heads, potatoes, turnips, and other items. Then from canteens he poured rich milk.

Sometime in Montgomery County, Livermore and his comrades were "fortunate enough as to find a still." Naturally they filled their canteens to the brim.

But the men from New Hampshire did not need any artificial stimulants to make them feel good when they reached Frederick.

> Our columns were aligned, our banners unfurled, and our bugles and drums played a soul-stirring march, and we marched proudly down the main street, while from every window the ladies smiled on us and waved...with patriotic joy. We passed General Burnside on the left, looking very gallant and warlike in his blue frock and side whiskers; alas, that so fine a looking man should be so poor a general![31]

While the first shots were being fired at Fox's Gap on the Old Sharpsburg Road, a wagon with white canvas top, drawn by eight long-eared mules pulled up in front of 488 1/2 Seventh Street in Washington. The wagon had been ordered to the residence of Miss Clara Barton by Major Rucker. Four men were to assist her in loading the wagon. To save space for vital medical supplies, Miss Barton took but a few personal articles tied up in a handkerchief.

To save time, the driver, Cornelius M. Welles, turned the wagon around in the middle of the street, and the group started its journey.

Early that morning the Eighth Ohio heard the sound of the cannon at South Mountain. They were anxious to move forward. When they reached the top of Braddock Mountain, "the whole panorama of the valley of Middletown lay before us, calm and beautiful" but beyond on the slopes of the mountain the artillery of the blue and the gray was belching forth volumes of smoke, death, and destruction. Yet the sounds of battle could not be heard now. "The tramp of 25,000 men, the rattle of our artillery along the stony roads, and the hum of subdued tones of voice among our troops completely shut out any sound from beyond.[32]

For Frank Sawyer, the scene "was grand beyond description." He and his Ohio comrades witnessed batteries galloping across open fields and going into action. "Skirmish lines appeared and disappeared along the ridges and crests." Clouds of smoke broke forth from the woods.

But the Eighth Ohio did not get into action. They halted about two miles from the Gap, and watched the continual stream of ambulances and litter bearers as they took the wounded back to Middletown. Frank Sawyer got little sleep that Sunday night for the ground was dirty and damp, and all through the night, the procession of ambulances and litters continued.

Charles Page and his comrades in the 14th Connecticut spent the night about two miles from Frederick near the reservoir. They were awakened at 2:00 a.m. and told to draw rations of hardtack, salt, pork, sugar, and coffee. Then in typical military fashion, the men were permitted to rest until 8:00 a.m. At that time they were told to "Fall in," and the march resumed.[33]

The congestion of men and wagons made slow progress through the streets of Frederick. The church bells were ringing, regimental flags flying, while division after division, train after train, and battery after battery went through Frederick.

Full of hope, and confidence in George B. McClellan, the Fifth New Hampshire set out with other units in the Second Corps to "drive Lee out of Maryland." The regiment passed "through Frederick in fine style; the Fifth with bugles blowing, drums beating and our faded and tattered colors flaunting bravely....It was a stately and gallant sight."[34]

As the conflict raged on South Mountain, old General Sumner rode through the columns of the Second Corps, "all afire to reach the field" of action. His long white beard was streaming in the breeze. He stopped and berated an officer who was tearing down a fence piece by piece. He wanted it torn down at once so the men could advance to the front. Now was not the time to respect public property.

H.R. Dunham was a little tired. He had spent Saturday night on guard duty. "It was rather cool much like our fall weather at home. We had roll-call at 5 a.m. Were ordered to start at 7 a.m. Which way or where we are going none of us knows. Yesterday we heard heavy firing just over the mountain on our left. It began at daylight this morning. Nothing to remind one that it is Sunday. No Sunday it was....We marched until about 5 p.m."[35]

The Fifth Connecticut spent Saturday night one mile from Frederick, then they were assigned to provost duty in the town. Throughout the day the men heard the sounds of battle from South Mountain.[36]

The Irish Brigade arrived too late in the day to take any part in the fighting at South Mountain, but the smell of combat was in the air, and men knew that very soon they too would be in action.

The stakes were high. If they lost, then the North would be at the mercy of Lee and Jackson. The Army of Northern Virginia could march through Maryland and Pennsylvania at will, with nothing but a few home guards comprised of boys or old men to oppose them. The government in Washington might fall, and the South might just become an independent nation.[37]

As the Second Corps tramped from Frederick toward South Mountain, some of the lads amused themselves by counting the intervals between the puffs of smoke on the mountain and the time they heard the sound..."thus calculating the distance between themselves and the battlefield."[38]

Andrew Ford of the 15th Massachusetts summarizes the day.

The brightness of the day, the natural beauty of the region, the charm of the quaint old town and the cordial greetings of the inhabitants combined to fill the hearts of the soldiers with cheer. At four p.m. of this day, Richard Derby wrote: "We have just marched through the city, and are bivouacking in the clover-fields near by. There has been a running fight between our advance of cavalry and flying artillery all day, but several miles from us. We could see the smoke of the cannonading on the mountains across the valley as we came down into Frederick; but it has gone over to the west side now. What the rebels mean by their movements, is a mystery; and of course our movements depend upon theirs; and I cannot tell where we shall go next."[39]

William Pickerall says, the lines answered each other with volleys and yells. "The thunder of all the artillery of both armies echoed and re-echoed down this lovely Middletown Valley, interspersed with rolling volleys of musketry and the fierce yells of men engaged in a death struggle."

It was a rough day for the men of the Second Massachusetts; they did not see combat, but due to the congested roads, they moved a little, then halted, and repeated the process. It was nearly midnight when Colonel Dwight and others reached the slope of South Mountain, and laid down cold, and supperless.[40]

The Sixth Wisconsin halted for a time in Middletown. George Miles was very quiet. Asked why, he replied, "You would be too, if you knew you would be killed tonight."

George knew time was running out. Sadly, a few hours later he was killed at South Mountain.

In Middletown, Rufus Dawes heard that a colonel from an Ohio regiment was being treated for wounds received at Fox's Gap. Making an inquiry, he found that it was Lieutenant Colonel Rutherford B. Hayes of the 23rd Ohio. The Sixth Wisconsin marched about a mile and a half beyond Middletown and turned into a field. There was no time to make a cup of coffee because General Hooker said, "The crest of that mountain must be carried tonight."

Hatch's division turned to the right, but Gibbon's brigade was countermarched to the National Pike, then up the road, and then to a field left of the road. The 7th Wisconsin and 19th Indiana were in front, with the 6th Wisconsin along with the 2nd in the second line. Simmon's Ohio Battery was with them and started to shell the Confederate positions. Ahead of Gibbon's brigade was the top of the mountain, almost two miles away up a steep, and stony slope.

Two miles away to the right, Dawes could see the rest of Hatch's Division advancing with the sinking sun gleaming on their bayonets. The flags were flying. It was a picturesque scene.

Off to the left the battle was heating up at Fox's Gap. "There was a crash of musketry, and the roll of cannon, and a white cloud of battle smoke rose above the trees. Then came the sounds of the cannon fire from the right. The Rebels had commenced firing on Hatch's division as it threatened turning the flank. For nearly an hour Dawes and his men laid, listened, and watched. But their turn was coming. The sun was going down, when the order came to move forward.

The men from the midwest started to climb the mountain. At first it was easy, but then the route lay through patches of stone, orchards, and thick woods. Companies B and K advanced a line of skirmishers, and the men ran from tree to stone to log, and got off their shots, fighting for every inch of ground. This went on for half a mile.[41]

Two pieces of artillery under Lt. James Stewart, part of Battery B, were brought up on the National Road, and every chance they got, they wheeled and lobbed shells at the Confederates. The enemy in return started firing with artillery from Turner's Gap. But the shells flew over the heads of the men from Wisconsin and Indiana.

General Gibbon came riding to the scene, riding on high ground where all in his command could see him. Loudly and clearly he shouted, "Forward! Forward!" So the advance continued as the darkness fell, into trees and underbrush. The fire of the muskets looked like tongues of flame spitting out into the twilight. South Mountain had never witnessed such a show.[42]

As darkness fell, men shot at each other from the sight of the musket flash. The Yankees were tired, thirsty, and many were about out of ammunition. The Confederates unleashed a heavy volley of fire, and then fell back. The exhausted men of Gibbon's command lay among "thick bushes on the steep rough slope of a mountain in almost total darkness."

General McClellan had watched most of the advance while mounted on his horse in the same field with Simmon's Ohio Battery. He was so moved that he wrote to the Governor of Wisconsin, saying, "I beg to add my great admiration of the conduct of the three Wisconsin regiments in General Gibbon's Brigade. I have seen them under fire acting in a manner that reflects the greatest possible credit and honor upon themselves and their state. They are equal to the best troops in any army in the world." They were like an "Iron Brigade."

The advance had been rough. Canteens were empty, and tongues swollen from biting the ends off cartridges. After 10:00 p.m. the men of the First Corps were told that General Reno had been killed.

But there was to be no relief for Gibbon's Brigade. They were out of ammunition and told to hold the mountain with "every inch of their bayonets." Rufus Dawes described the Sunday night.

> The night was chilly, and in the woods intensely dark. Our wounded were scattered over a great distance up and down the mountain, and were suffering untold agonies. Owing to the difficulties of the ground and the night, no stretcher bearers had come upon the field. Several dying men were pleading piteously for water, of which there was not a drop in the regiment, nor was there any liquor. Captain Kellogg and I searched in vain for a swallow for one noble fellow who was dying in great agony from a wound in his bowels. He recognized us and appreciated our efforts, but was unable to speak.

> The dread reality of war was before us in this frightful death, upon the cold, hard stones. The mortal suffering, the fruitless struggle to send a parting message to the far-off home, and the final release by death, all enacted in the darkness; were felt even more deeply than if the scene had been relieved by the light of day. After a long interval of this horror, our stretcher bearers came, and the poor suffering heroes were carried back to houses and barns. At last word came that General Sumner's troops were marching up the mountain to relieve us. How glad we were to hear it, they only can know who have experienced the feeling of prostration produced by such scenes and surroundings, after the excitement of a bloody battle. It was after midnight, and it seemed to us bitterly cold.[43]

William Pickerall of the Third Indiana remembered the night all too well.

> Lanterns carried by stretcher bearers flashed here and there amid the mountainside forest where the battle had been fiercest, as these messengers of mercy pursued their quest among the wounded and dying. Otherwise the stillness of night and death was upon the scene, as the stars twinkled from the sky of azure blue....From our elevation we heard the bey of the

farm dog and the tinkling cowbell in the valley far below, while from distant hills flashed the lights of the signal corps.[44]

The Eighth Illinois cavalry watched the unfolding drama on South Mountain. "The rattle of musketry was terrific." There were repeated cheers. Sometimes they came from the Union as they gained an advantage, and at times they came from the Rebels.

There were a lot of rocks near the cavalrymen. And the echo of the cannon sounded like thunder. It was almost deafening. After dark the flashes of the muskets looked like lightning on the mountain. And the men from Illinois saw men carrying a litter on their shoulders. It was the remains of General Reno.

"Many of the wounded were brought to a farmhouse on the Boonsboro Road. Straw was scattered in the yard....The surgeons worked (wearily) all night to relieve their distress."

Then a voice called out in the darkness, "Dr. Hard, is that you?" The physician answered the summons and found it to be Lt. Arthur Ellis of the sixth Wisconsin, severely wounded in the leg. Ellis and Hard had been childhood friends. And in the darkness at the farmhouse hospital, he had recognized Hard's voice.[45]

Hillman Hall of the Sixth New York Cavalry describes the action where so many fell "as an interesting and impressive scene."[46]

And in the meantime, down the mountain, the Sixth Corps, the unit of the Army of the Potomac nearest Harpers Ferry was moving from Jefferson toward Burkittsville and Crampton's Gap.

Dr. Ellis says that after the action in Crampton's Gap, the road was "filled with long and winding lines of ambulances, going and returning." The wounded were taken to large, private homes in Burkittsville. There the men received great treatment from the townspeople. "The surgeons were busy all night, and many painful operations took place....The rebel wounded were nearly all taken to the Baptist Church in Burkittsville."[47]

Newton Curtis was hospitalized at Harrison's Landing on August 11 and two days later sent to Point Lookout. Remaining there until after the 16th New York had started after Lee, Curtis left the hospital against doctor's orders. He and some friends who had shared the hospitalization traveled via the Baltimore and Ohio Railroad to Frederick. Here they were able to hire a horse-drawn vehicle to take them to Jefferson, the location of the Sixth Corps on Saturday. The sounds of battle could be heard coming from Crampton's Gap, and no amount of money or persuasion could lead the driver to take them any farther.

Curtis and his friends had to walk with their baggage, and arrived too late to take part in the battle. Their next task probably

made them wish they had stayed in the hospital. They were assigned to the care of the wounded and the burial of the dead. Most
of the losses were halfway up the mountain, victims of Confederate
firing from a stone wall.

The ambulance corps was very busy, and the streets of
Burkittsville were filled with ambulances coming and going. A second lieutenant was in charge of brigade and ambulances. There
were three ambulances with drivers, two stretcher bearers for each
ambulance, and a non-com and nine men detailed from each regiment to assist.

First Lieutenant Wilson Hopkins of the 16th New York was in
command of the ambulance corps of General Slocum's division. He
tells about Sunday afternoon and night at Crampton's Gap and
Burkittsville.

> Most of our badly wounded were brought to the hospital
> by dark. We then began to collect the wounded Confederates,
> who were found from the base of the mountain, increasing in
> numbers as we ascended, to the very top. We carried them to
> the field hospital until midnight, when the surgeons, overcome
> by exhaustion, were unable to care for more. We then collected
> all we could find and placed them in a group, near the top of the
> mountain, gave them food and water, built fires to warm them,
> and I directed two Confederates, found hiding behind the rocks
> and uninjured, to remain with their wounded comrades, attend
> to their wants and keep the fires burning. At sunrise the next
> morning, I went with my stretcher-bearers to the camp I had
> made for the wounded Confederates, and found the fires burned
> out, six of the forty dead, and learned that the two men I had
> placed in charge of them with directions to keep the fires burn-
> ing, had, soon after I left them the night before, abandoned their
> charge and rejoined the Confederate army encamped in the val-
> ley beyond. We carried the survivors to the hospital, leaving a
> detail to bury the dead.
>
> This was my first experience in gathering the wounded
> from a battlefield after it was won. Many have visited such places
> and reported the sickening sights, but I cannot describe their
> ghastly realities. Later I became more familiar with such scenes,
> yet I can never forget that dreadful night; its horrors overshadow
> all spectacles I witnessed on other battlefields, and the memory
> of what I there say will remain with me to the end.[48]

Apparently a lot of musket shots had been ineffective in the
earlier battles of the war, because of shooting high. However, at

Crampton's Gap, the Confederates were firing down hill, and the percentage of effective shots was appalling. Many Union soldiers were hit in the head, chest, or lungs, producing many outright deaths, and a high mortality rate among those who lingered.

Curtis spent Sunday night and Monday burying the dead and assisting in the care of the wounded.

Charles Coffin arrived in Greencastle on Sunday morning. He writes, "This usually quiet little Pennsylvania village is all commotion. The rebels are at Hagerstown, eleven miles distant....Their pickets extend to State Line."

Later Charles Coffin heard some great news. A "dispatch came over the wire that McClellan had an engagement with the enemy, and that they are running toward Sharpsburg in perfect panic."

This was not quite true, but Lee had been in better situations, and now all depended on how quickly things were terminated at Harpers Ferry.[49]

Sunday morning eight new regiments of Pennsylvania troops started forward. They numbered 8,000 and took the shortest route from Washington to join McClellan's army in Western Maryland. "The troops, though heavily burdened, marched all day in the great heat and dusty roads, making over fifteen miles, which was regarded as a most satisfactory feat for fresh troops but a little over a week from home." Late in the afternoon, the Pennsylvanians reached the outskirts of the beautiful little village of Rockville. Private Robert Hill went looking for additional food in a peach orchard and was shot in the foot by a so-called "overzealous guard."

Andrew Atkinson Humphreys, son of a prominent Philadelphia family, and a West Point graduate, was in command of the new Pennsylvania regiments traveling the "Roads to Antietam." On that September Sunday, he was constantly seen as he rode from the head of the column to the rear, several times, urging the men to hurry. He looked to be about forty-five years of age, a natural soldier, and a very serious and determined man. He wore a military cape and a slouch hat, with field glasses dangling from his neck.[50]

While the Union army was moving on South Mountain, the 118th Pennsylvania left the hamlet of Rockville. "Through sultry, suffocating heat and clouds of...choking dust, the column bowled along...from seven in the morning until six in the evening", the wearisome journey concluded on the banks of the Monocacy. During the morning hours the men heard the booming of the cannon in the South Mountain passes. The sound intensified as they neared Frederick.

As twilight fell the men noticed objects moving in a nearby woods. Some hogs had escaped their pens and were roaming at will. The 118th was glad to round them up, making sure they would roam no more. Shots rang out along the banks of the Monocacy. Soon the aroma of fresh pork floated on the breeze. Many a tired soldier had fried pork for supper prepared over their campfires by the river.[51]

By nightfall, a wagon loaded with medical supplies reached the edge of Frederick. It was Clara Barton's wagon. Her aides made a campfire and prepared supper, and then rolled up in their blankets. Miss Clara slept curled up in the wagon.

At 8:00 p.m. Union cavalry units formed on Shenandoah Street in Harpers Ferry with the Potomac Home Brigade in the van. While they waited to hit the pontoon bridge, they received a pleasant surprise. The sutlers, not wishing their wares to fall into the hands of the Confederates, moved among the troopers and gave packets of tobacco and other little items.

Major Augustus Corliss of the 7th Rhode Island told his troopers, "Tomorrow morning we'll be in Pennsylvania, on the way to Richmond, or in hell."

The 7th Rhode Island was a young outfit, mostly college men from Dartmouth and Norwich.

Lieutenant Hanson Green of the 1st Maryland and Tom Nokes led the troopers across the river, traveling in a column of twos. Once across the river they turned to the left and took the road leading to Sharpsburg. The road is still narrow and dangerous, but picturesque, especially in the autumn. It led right under Maryland Heights.

It was an eerie night. The sounds of autumn were in the air, but they could not be heard for the clatter of the hooves, and the noise of men moving through the darkness.

Late that night they reached Sharpsburg. And some of the men got water at the town spring. They also ran into a Confederate outpost and received a scattering of fire. Then it was on to the College of St. James, an Episcopal Boys School where the troopers stopped to rest their horses.

John Shay lived at the edge of Sharpsburg. The first of the escaped cavalrymen reached his home shortly after 10:00 p.m. For the next several hours, John pumped bucket after bucket of water for the thirsty horses. The next morning his bucket was found at the square in Sharpsburg.

Remounting, the troopers headed for Williamsport. They narrowly missed capturing the trains of William Nelson Pendleton and the Artillery Reserve of the Army of Northern Virginia. They heard sounds of other wagons, those belonging to James Longstreet.

Escape from Harpers Ferry

The Middle Bridge at Antietam

Colonel Davis was born in Alabama, and entered West Point from Mississippi. So there was no problem when he gave orders changing the route of travel. Many were unaware of what was happening. The darkness was a real blessing for the Yanks. When the Confederates discovered their predicament, they were told that anyone attempting to escape would be shot.

Captain Frisbie led the sixty Confederate wagons to Greencastle. About 9:00 a.m. they arrived, covering over fifty miles in thirteen hours. Quite an achievement. The folks in the little Pennsylvania town brought food and drink to the exhausted troopers. The Yanks were happy, but the Rebels were dejected.

Charles Dawson never quite made it to Antietam. He had been with the wagon trains of Longstreet's Corps. After the battle of South Mountain, he was preparing supper at the late hour of ten. But before he could finish, an order came from Longstreet to take the ordnance trains to Williamsport. The order was urgent, and Dawson was to move at once. He tells his own story.

At about ten o'clock at night I started. It was intensely dark and the roads were rough. Towards morning I entered the Hagerstown and Williamsport Turnpike, where I found a cavalry picket. The officer in charge asked me to move the column as quickly as I could, and to keep the trains well closed up. I asked him if the enemy were on the road, and he told me that it was entirely clear, and that he had pickets out in every direction. It was only a few miles now to Williamsport, and I could see the camp-fires of our troops across the river. I was hungry, sleepy and tired, and the prospect of camp and supper in an hour seemed the summit of bliss. I was forty or fifty yards ahead of the column, when a voice from the roadside called out "halt!" The gloss was not yet off my uniform, and I could not suppose that such a command, shotted with a big oath, was intended for me. In a moment it was repeated. I quickly rode to the side of the road in the direction of the voice, and found myself at the entrance of a narrow lane, and there adown it were horses and men in a line that stretched out far beyone my vision. To the trooper who was nearest to me I said indignantly: "How dare you halt an officer in this manner." The reply was to the point: "Surrender, and dismount! You are my prisoner!" Almost before the words were uttered I was surrounded, and found that I had ridden right into the midst of a body of Yankee cavalry, numbering about two thousand, who had escaped from Harpers Ferry that night to avoid the surrender which was to take place in the morning. I was placed under guard on the roadside, and as the trains came up they were halted, and the men who were with them were quietly captured. In a short time the column moved off in the direction of the Pennsylvania line. I was allowed to ride my own horse. By the side of each team a Federal soldier rode, and, by dint of cursing the negro drivers and beating the mules with their swords, the cavalrymen contrived to get the jaded animals along at a gallop. While we were halted, one of my sergeants had knocked the linchpins out of the wheels of the leading wagons, in the hope that this would delay the march. The wheels came off and the wagons were upset, but a squad of men dismounted instantly, threw the wagons out of the road, and set fire to them, so that there was no halt of consequence. I had a cavalryman on each side of me, and tried vainly to get an opportunity to slip off into the woods.

Soon after daylight we reached the little village of Greencastle, Pennsylvania, where the citizens came out to look at the "Rebel" prisoners. They hurrahed for their own men and cursed at us. Even the women joined in the game. Several of them brought their children to the roadside and told them to shake their fists at the "D—d Rebels." Still there were some kind people in Greencastle. Three or four ladies came to us, and, without pretending to have any liking for Confederates, showed their charitable disposition by giving us some bread and a cup of cold water. My horse was taken from me at Greencastle and ridden off by a dirty-looking cavalryman. Then the Confederates, numbering a hundred or more, were packed into the cars, and sent by the railway to Chambersburg.[52]

One of Dawson's men had fallen asleep in one of the wagons, slept through all the commotion, and all the traveling, and never woke up until the column reached Chambersburg. He must have been tired, and what a surprise awakened him.

Once in the Pennsylvania city, the Confederates were placed in the open yard of the prison. The little boys of Chambersburg played a game with them. They threw stones over the fence, with the objective of hitting one of the men in gray. This they could do at no risk to themselves.

Private Louck of Company I, 8th New York, was very happy to be in Greencastle. He had used three of his nine lives during the thirteen-hour ride. Shortly after crossing the Potomac, Louck's horse fell into the canal or disappeared by the side of the road. Extra mounts were not available, so Louck was told to go to a farmhouse and surrender next morning.

However, Louck started walking, and apparently kept up. He was found sinking in the mud at a ford. He was rescued and again left behind. On down the road he was pulled from another stream and saved from drowning.

Then he apparently used his head and hitched a ride. When the wagons were captured, he had the answer, crawl into one. But the wagons that could not keep up were burned. One exploded and a body came flying out. The men were sure it was Louck, his number was finally up. However, Louck survived the explosion although his clothing was burned and he was singed. He was taken to a nearby farmhouse to breathe his last.

Louck was not ready to give up. While the troopers rested in Greencastle, they heard a familiar voice saying, "I was killed once tonight by being thrown over a mountain, drowned twice, blown up and killed, but here I am, ready for all the rations I can get."

CHAPTER VII

MONDAY, SEPTEMBER 15, 1862

—*ARMY OF NORTHERN VIRGINIA*—

Fitz Lee deployed his cavalry and artillery at the east end of Boonsboro to hinder the Yankee advance. As Pleasonton and Richardson's Infantry advanced, Lee fired and then fell back, and kept repeating the procedure.

But then the blue horde increased and spread out, and Lee knew he was in danger of being outflanked. So he prepared to withdraw. At that moment the ranks of the Union infantry parted to let the blue cavalry charge.

Fitz Lee had to commit the Ninth Virginia Cavalry under Lee's son, Colonel W.H.F. Lee. Otherwise he was going to be cut off. Union sympathizers aided the troopers by shooting at random from the windows of their homes, unaware of the great danger, or uncaring. "Rooney" Lee was thrown from his horse and stunned, but not badly hurt. By hiding and crawling, he was able to get to Sharpsburg. This action caused enough delay as to permit the Confederate infantry to reach the hills of Sharpsburg.

About daylight, the weary troops of Daniel Harvey Hill crossed the Antietam and took position on the hills overlooking the west bank of the creek and the approaches from Boonsboro. Robert Rodes, along with Colquitt's brigade, marched through the town to secure the area from an attack from the Potomac. Apparently the high command had heard of the escape of the Union cavalry.

D.R. Jones spread his thin gray line from the hill now occupied by the National Cemetery to a point opposite the lower or Rohrback Bridge.

John Hood's men assumed positions from the Hagerstown Road to the Dunkard Church and West Woods, while Nathan Evans took care of the center and the immediate area occupied now by the town and the National Cemeteries. Stuart's cavalry and horse artillery went to the left and the hills of Nicodemus Heights, guarding that flank, while Munford's men protected the Harpers Ferry Road and Antietam Furnace area.

The steeple, or cupola, of the Lutheran Church was turned into a signal station and observation tower.

At 1:00 a.m. George Neese was awakened from his sleep near Keedysville, and ordered to move toward Martinsburg. So the command journeyed to Williamsport. Here the troops forded the Potomac. George found it "about two feet deep, with a gentle current and smooth gravely bottom."[1]

Meanwhile, the end had come at Harpers Ferry. The town was sealed in. A heavy mist covered the area. Jackson was up at 3:00 a.m. The gunners had zeroed in during the clear weather, so the mist was no problem. The bombardment was terrible. There was no safe place.

Within an hour, the Union guns had ceased firing, and Jackson had A.P. Hill's infantry ready to advance on Bolivar Heights. As they did so, the Union guns opened fire again. Confederate guns moved forward and opened a heavier fire. Colonel Miles was killed and General White surrendered Harpers Ferry. A.P. Hill and Henry Kyd Douglas met the Union representatives. In a few moments it was all over.

Jackson rode into Harpers Ferry to inspect the town and to see the Union troops. A.P. Hill handled the surrender and paroled the 11,000 Union soldiers. Messages were sent to Walker and McLaws to start for Sharpsburg as soon as possible.

The Confederates were most happy to get the large stores of food and ammunition. They were distressed to find the cavalry and good horses gone. It was such a shame. Jackson would rather have had the horses than anything else, while the men wished for the carbines.

Franklin's men in Pleasant Valley heard the guns cease. It meant one thing. The end had come at Harpers Ferry. Cheers filled the air on the Confederate side. But McLaws had to be careful. Franklin was close, and he had to cross the Potomac and take the long way around to Sharpsburg. He must watch his step, or the Yanks would have him.

Jed Hotchkiss says, "Our soldiers are as dirty as the ground itself and are nearly of the same color. The enemy looked at them in amazement, especially when they cheered General Jackson as he rode by..."[2]

Jackson and his men were headed for Shepherdstown, making haste to join Lee north of the Potomac. McLaws and his division came over from Maryland Heights. There was no way they could move up Pleasant Valley to Sharpsburg. They spent the night near Halltown.

In the Valley of the Antietam, Robert E. Lee was personally involved in placing his 18,000 men in defensive positions.[3]

About noon, a courier galloped up from the Shepherdstown Ford with a great message from T.J. Jackson.[4] It read:

> Near 8 a.m. September 15, 1862
>
> General: Through God's blessing Harper's Ferry and it's garrison are to be surrendered.[5]

"That is indeed good news," said Lee, "let it be announced to the troops."[6]

> Quickly the word was passed; the men seemed charged with new courage when they heard it. The worst danger from the division of the army would soon be over.[7]

After the guns of the Washington Artillery were posted on the ridges in front of Sharpsburg, they too were inspired by news of the fall of Harpers Ferry. The commander of the unit and William Owen were in a house at the edge of Sharpsburg. After the news was announced Lee and Longstreet held a discussion in a house across the street.

When Randolph Shotwell reached the Antietam Creek, General Longstreet was off his horse training Confederate guns to the right of the Boonsboro Road. The baggage and supply wagons of the Army of Northern Virginia were entering Sharpsburg and heading north on the Hagerstown Road. There were alarming intervals between brigades and gaps in the line of defense. This was caused by the lack of men Lee had available.

The troops were very hungry. Finally the order was given for details from each company to enter the fields of the farmers in the Valley of the Antietam. Eight ears of corn were to be gathered for each man.[8]

Some of the Confederates urged the Mumma family, living north of Sharpsburg, to leave the farm before the bullets and shells started to fly. One gallant Rebel officer even offered to assist Lizzie and Allie Mumma over the fence. But the girls were angry over the invasion of their farm and their privacy and would have nothing to do with the lad. When evening came they went to the Hoffman farm, and made plans to join many of the Dunkards the next morning at Manor Church. There they would take shelter and await developments.

On the hills of Sharpsburg, overlooking the Antietam Creek, James Longstreet watched the build-up of the Army of the Potomac. It was almost 3:00 p.m. Harpers Ferry had been good news, but the sight before Longstreet's eyes was bad news.

> The number increased, and larger and larger grew the field of blue until it seemed to stretch as far as the eye could see, and from the tops of the mountains down to the edges of the stream gathered the great army of McClellan. It was an awe inspiring spectacle as this grand force settled down in sight of the Confederates.[9]

Late in the afternoon, "Stonewall" Jackson ordered General Lawton to move his division on the road to Boteler's Ford on the Potomac. Jubal Early did not get started until after night. Early did not meet his commander until daylight the next morning, four miles from the ford.

Across the Antietam, Jeb Stuart was arriving, bringing a personal description of the capture of Harpers Ferry. Lee and McClellan both were to receive criticism for the day. Lee, for making a stand against great odds, and McClellan for moving so slowly. After all, he had just about eight miles to cover and a great advantage, but he frittered away the day. With a handful of men, Lee stood in front of Sharpsburg, while with an entire army, McClellan crawled to Antietam.

—ARMY OF THE POTOMAC—

It was a chilly, damp night on South Mountain. It was also a scary night as the living and the dead slept side by side. For others it was a night of fatigue as they searched for the wounded at Turner's, Fox's, and Crampton's Gap, or assisted in their treatment.

During the night, McClellan gave orders to the corps commanders "to press forward the pickets at early dawn. This advance revealed the fact that the enemy had left his positions."[10]

McClellan then ordered an immediate pursuit. Sumner's Second Corps, followed by Hooker and the First, and Mansfield with the Twelfth were to advance behind the cavalry from Turner's Gap. Burnside and Sykes's division of the Fifth Corps were to move via Fox's Gap and the Old Sharpsburg Road into the Antietam Valley, while Franklin and the Sixth Corps was to move through Crampton's Gap, move into Pleasant Valley, and hopefully relieve Harpers Ferry.

William Pickerall from a point northwest of Middletown watched the sun creep over the Catoctin Mountain and strike the National Road, making "it look like a thread of silver."

At our feet lay the Army of the Potomac, and the smoke curled upwards from a thousand campfires....From our mountain eyrie we now had our fairest vision of the beautiful Middletown Valley, as it lay spread out before us....(Pickerall could also see) the old country frame schoolhouse with its playgrounds, which had been our battlefield on the afternoon of the thirteenth, and where we had given up a comrade, who himself had been a country school teacher. Scattered over the fertile plain and stretching up the mountain-side into the timber were the camps of fifty thousand soldiers whose stacked muskets, with fixed bayonets, glistened in the sunlight of the early morning. Parks of army wagons with their braying mules and batteries of artillery trained on every approach to the Valley, hospital tents interspersed among the cottage homes...all made up a grim and unique scene for the beholder perched upon the mountain top.

This was Monday morning, September 15, on the eastern slope of South Mountain.

Alfred Pleasonton, the cavalry commander says, "At daylight....I started in pursuit of the enemy with a part of the Eighth Illinois Cavalry."[11]

The Eighth Illinois was divided this morning. Six companies under Colonel Elon Farnsworth were sent on the main road toward Boonsboro, while another party went over the mountain to the left. Dr. Hard must mean that they went to Fox's Gap.

Descending into the valley, the men from Illinois found almost every house and barn contained wounded Confederates. But there was no time to treat them.

Colonel Farnsworth ordered a charge into the rear guard of Fitz Lee's cavalry. The Rebels broke, followed closely by the men in blue. Some took to the fields, making pursuit difficult. There were many contests involving individual hand to hand combat.

In one of these Colonel Farnsworth shot a Rebel from his horse, and was chasing the man, unaware that another man in gray was ready to strike him a deadly blow with his saber. At that time a shot rang out, and a man in Company B shot Farnsworth's assailant.

The Eighth Illinois also captured Fitz Lee's horse and equipment, while the Confederate officer made his escape through a Maryland cornfield.

Dr. Hard felt that the fight and the conduct of the Eighth Illinois was one of the most daring and best executed of the war.[12]

Folks along the way told the troopers that Lee's army was "disordered" and "retreating in the greatest haste." This was stretching the truth a bit, but McClellan believed it.

Henry Neikirk, a former County Commissioner and a farmer neighbor of the Mummas, had a narrow escape. Like other farmers, he made an effort to hide his horses. Somehow the Confederates learned about this and came to get the animals. They were safely hidden among the rocks along the Antietam, and Henry was not about to divulge his secret. In a rare display of temper, the Confederates threatened to burn Neikirk's house; took some money, and strung Henry up by a leather halter. Then they rode off. Henry's son George arrived just in time to cut him down.

Henry Piper and his family lived nearer town. Mary Ellen, his daughter, writes, "On Monday, prior to the battle, we all went away from our house to my uncle's, Samuel J. Piper, who resided...on the Potomac River about three miles west of my father's house. We left everything as it was on the farm, taking only the horses with us and one carriage."

Jonathan Stowe and some of his mates crossed Catoctin Mountain on Sunday via a rough, narrow path. They were glad the sun was under the clouds. Before daybreak that morning, some of his comrades ransacked nearby farmhouses and took all the fruit and vegetables they could carry. They felt justified in this as the government was not keeping them supplied.

Stowe's outfit did not move until 9:00 a.m. They had the chance to rest, stretch, and fix coffee. Stowe was fearful the Rebs would cross the river without a fight.

As midday approached, the sun became quite warm, and Stowe says that "at $12^1/2$ (we went) forward thru Booneville."

Cheering citizens met the men from Massachusetts with pails of water. They saw many squads of captured Rebels being herded to the rear. "General Mac" passed and was cheered. Then came the tramp through Keatiesville (Keedysville) and finally camp about 9:00 p.m. in a field to the right of the road.

The men in Tom Livermore's New Hampshire outfit cooked and drank their coffee in the dark that morning, and started to climb South Mountain just at daybreak. At the beginning they passed some Rebel prisoners being escorted to the rear. Then the men from New Hampshire left the road and formed a line of battle. They expected to be in combat any moment. Much to their surprise, they found the enemy gone, and no action forthcoming.[13]

Leaving the steep mountain, the men hit the road once again, and were ordered to "double-quick" so they could pass the head of their particular column. The canteens and other equipment rattled so much that others thought it was a mule train coming. The Irish Brigade hooted and shouted, chagrined because they had not been given the honor of being first in line.

The New Hampshire lads entered town in skirmish line, expecting their advance to be contested, but it was not. They rounded up some stragglers and pillagers, but that's all. Tom Livermore captured some men from Wade Hampton's Legion. Needless to say they were very upset to be captured by Yankee infantry.

Between Boonsboro and the Antietam Creek, Tom found the evidence of a substantial Confederate encampment from the previous night. "There were embers of camp-fires, scattered ammunition boxes, and other traces of a bivouac."[14]

Livermore describes what it was like from a spot near the Middle Bridge over the Antietam.

> The turnpike which we had followed from Boonsboro crossed the creek by a bridge a stone's throw in advance of us and then ascended a gentle slope for a mile (northwest) toward Sharpsburg and was lost to sight in the undulations of the country. The slope presented a broad surface extending up and down the stream, diversified by gentle hills, shallow valleys, cornfields, pastures, patches of woods, and houses then in sight, and other features which became apparent afterwards when we marched over it. The enemy's skirmishers had retreated across the creek and were concealed behind some houses and other obstructions. From there on for a mile nothing but a few, some mounted and some on foot, could be seen; but at that distance, perhaps, from the creek a vision which I never shall forget opened to our view.
>
> The last of the gray masses of the rebel army were moving up the turnpike in orderly array to a point on the crest of the slope, and here they followed the thousands who had gone before and deployed on either side and faced us in line of battle, whose front spreading far out on either side in some places stood boldly out in view and in others was concealed by the unevenness of the ground, or only was made known by a standard or an occasional straggler. The dull color of the line was relieved by gay flags and guidons, and the brass guns of the artillery brilliantly reflected the rays of the September sun; horsemen galloped along the lines and the serried ranks deliberately moved to their positions and formed line of battle, and everything betokened at least a contest with the rear guard.[15]

Soon musket and artillery fire greeted Tom and his comrades, and the young officer dove for cover, and then fired a few shots in return. General Richardson arrived and said he had no artillery with him. He also stated that no demonstration was to be made against the Rebels. Tom could not understand this. The Second Corps had marched but twelve miles and was relatively fresh. 30,000 men were on hand, why not hit the Confederate positions now? But McClellan said no, and waited and watched.

Later in the day a Regular Army unit relieved the Fifth New Hampshire, and the men took shelter in a ravine near the Sharpsburg-Boonsboro Road.

Livermore and his unit remained here until Tuesday evening. A few rounds of artillery were showered upon them by the Confederates. However, the ravine offered good protection. Sadly, the favorite horse of Lieutenant Colonel Nelson Miles was killed by a stray shot. Miles was with the 61st New York at Antietam and later became commanding General of the Armies of the United States.

Toward evening the 5th New Hampshire was sent to a point near the Pry House to guard army headquarters.

About 10:00 a.m. the 14th Connecticut crossed South Mountain.

The 14th Connecticut reached Boonsboro about 3:00 p.m. and then continued to Keedysville. "On the line of march acres of soldiers were camped upon each side of the road. The scene was at once weird and impressive. Hundreds of campfires were blazing as far as the eye could reach." Finally, the men from Connecticut were told to "Fall out." Camp was made in one of Philip Pry's fields, just to the rear of army headquarters.[16]

William Child of the Fifth New Hampshire describes the chase:

> Early in the morning we formed in line of battle and started over the mountain where the rebels had been stationed the day before. We passed over the dead and some wounded. I saw seventeen dead in one awful group—all from an Alabama regiment. The rebels had a very strong position on the slope of a rocky, wooded mountain, commanding the gorges and hollows in every direction. The struggle appeared to have been fierce and bloody; but our brave troops finally drove the rebels over the crest and down the hill, giving them a tremendous defeat. The road was strewn with clothing, equipments, and the wounded.
>
> Expecting a fight every moment, and full of confidence, we hastened along, General Richardson's Division in the advance, the Fifth forming the rear guard. About half a mile from the village of Boonsborough, the division suddenly halted, and orders came for the Fifth regiment to get to the front double-quick. With a cheer the boys started off, all the other troops breaking to

the right to let us pass. 'There goes the Fighting Fifth.' "Give 'em h—l, boys." "Hurrah for Richardson's Cavalry!" was shouted on all sides by the German and Irish troops of the division. As I rode up to General Richardson to report, he said, "We have no cavalry nor artillery; your regiment must act as both. Deploy and sweep both sides of the road"....

In this manner the regiment marched at least two miles.

We swept quickly through the town and captured several prisoners. The Eighth Illinois Cavalry coming up, pursued the enemy on the Williamsport road, while Richardson's Division took the Sharpsburg turnpike. The cavalry of the enemy had just left. One little bridge was in flames, but we put out the fire. The wounded of the enemy came out from the fields and houses to meet us. We kept on for a couple of miles, passing the little village of Keedysville, my skirmish line constantly exchanging shots with the cavalry of the enemy. About noon my picket line came in full view of the enemy, drawn up in line of battle, their line appearing about a mile long with plenty of artillery. They did not keep us long in suspense, but opened with shell and solid shot. That afternoon was when the enemy should have been attacked.[17]

Josiah Favill whose regiment was in the Brigade of Richardson's Division leading the Second Corps to Antietam, describes the action near the Antietam Creek.

Passing through Keedysville we marched along the Sharpsburg pike towards the Antietam, our brigade leading the corps and the Fifty-seventh the brigade; we were marching at the route step in column of fours, taking it leisurely, Colonel Parisen and I some distance in advance, when all at once we noticed the dust flying suspiciously in many places around us. We halted the column, took out our glasses, and there, directly in front of us, saw the rebel army drawn up in battle array about half a mile in front. To get a better view, I rode up to a fence a short distance ahead, and standing on the top rail, easily made out the long gray lines, extending from left to right, as far as I could see. My further observation from this position was interrupted by a round shot which struck the fence and sent some of the rails spinning out of sight and me to the ground, sans ceremonie; after some delay, General Richardson came up and ordered line of battle formed parallel to the river, which brought our regiment just under the crest of a considerable hill, overlooking the whole country, and from which we subsequently examined the enemy's lines at leisure. They were admirably posted in rear of the Antietam upon a long line of low hills, commanding the entire valley. The left of our division rested on the Sharpsburg road; Sykes's division formed the other side of it as soon as it came up, extending the line well towards the left. During the formation the enemy, who could distinctly see us, shelled us and for a while made things lively. One of our batteries of three inch guns in position on the hill in front of our brigade, replied, but was immediately stopped by General Hooker, who just then came along and directed all offensive operations to cease until more troops came up, as the whole rebel army was in front of us, he said, while the greater part of ours was yet many miles in rear. Fresh columns of troops arrived on the ground continuously and went into position on either side of us, the reserve artillery as it came up occupying all the commanding positions with heavy guns. A battery of twenty powder Parrots replaced the three inch guns on the hill, just in front of the Fifty-seventh. During the evening, many of the natives came from the other side and told us what they knew of the enemy's movements. It seems they only came on the ground about an hour before our division, and were in fact selecting their positions, when the head of our column came in sight. These countrymen say only a part of the rebel army is in front, a considerable force having been detached to capture Harper's Ferry, which is held by a garrison of ten thousand men under Colonel Miles. We understood this however, several days since, and also that Franklin corps had been detached to try and cut them off, or at least detain them long enough for us to thrash these fellows now in front of us. We slept on the side of the hill, rolled in our blankets, expecting to open the ball at daylight."[18]

Because the First Corps had been engaged on South Mountain, they were given a break while the Second Corps moved up. Then while the Second Corps took a break near the Mountain House, the First Corps moved through their ranks and down the mountain. General Sumner's adjutant told Gibbon he was sorry he had arrived so soon. Sumner sent word to his men to cheer Gibbon's brigade as a testimony to the gallantry exhibited Sunday afternoon and evening during the action. This made Gibbon very happy. Then it was on to Boonsboro and Keedysville.[19]

The folks in Boonsboro and Keedysville made the lads in the 13th Massachusetts feel right at home. Union flags were flying in both towns. The residents seemed like those in New England and gave encouraging words along with a pat on the back.

As the Sixth Wisconsin neared Boonsboro, the folks were frantic with joy, laughing and crying. One elderly man said, "We have watched and waited for you. We have prayed for you, and now thank God you have come." The old man cheered the boys in blue, and the 19th Indiana returned the cheer.[20]

The welcome received in Frederick was repeated in Keedysville. Everybody was in the street, many complaining that the rebels had taken their provisions and their horses.

H.R. Dunham spent a quiet night on the slopes of South Mountain. Roll call was at daylight, and about 9:00 a.m. his regiment started after the retreating Rebs. "We pushed through the town of Boonsborough a very pretty little place....Think they are almost all Union here. Our troops had a skirmish here. Saw many wounded Rebs left behind. Our company was consistently bringing in prisoners during the day. About 7 p.m. we passed through the town of Keedysville. Halted about 9 p.m."

Dunham had seen General McClellan earlier in the day. Riding through the ranks to the front, Dunham says "the welcome that he received from his ole Army of the Potomac must have done his heart good. God bless General McClellan. Long may he lead...!"

Like many others, Dunham lamented the food. "Our rations for the last five weeks have been nothing but salt pork & hard bread & coffee."[21]

When the 19th Massachusetts reached the top of South Mountain, the view was so impressive that Jack Adams started a song. The men heard the generals were meeting in the Mountain House, planning strategy.

The men from the Bay State noticed dead Confederates all around. The ground was also littered with items purchased or lifted from stores in Frederick during the recent Southern occupation. The 19th also found a little church in Boonsboro full of wounded Rebels. The folks in Boonsboro were ministering to the men from the South, but there was no question that their loyalty was to the North. The men in blue were warmly welcomed and met with pails of ice water and cold milk.[22]

Jonathan Stowe complained that the weather was very hot. The 15th Massachusetts halted on top of South Mountain in Turner's Gap near the Mountain House and visited with comrades from the 12th and 13th Massachusetts. They had a "jolly bully time." The local people told them they'd never catch the Rebs because they were headed for the river as fast as they could. When the column got under way again, headed for Boonsboro, Stowe found it "exceedingly hot." The townspeople came to the roadside with buckets of water to "refresh us." They also urged the Yanks to "Catch the Rebs."

Prisoners captured by the cavalry were marched by, headed for the rear. Toward evening the men halted to make coffee. Nearby was a great spring. Stowe got a pitcher of ice cold water. Then "Gen Mack passes us, how they cheer him. Forward at sundown thru Keatiesville (Keedysville)....Finally file into field to right and camp for the night." This was on the farm of Philip Pry. Before hitting the sack, Stowe heard rumors that the Rebs had already crossed the Potomac.[23]

Oliver O. Howard was rather critical of operations at Harpers Ferry. Once again he voices the feelings of many.

> At sunset of the 13th Mile's garrison was completely invested. The whole story of the defense is a sad one—more than 13,000 of as good troops as we had forced to surrender.

> One would have thought that any army officer, one even as feeble as Dixons Miles, would have placed his strongest garrison on Maryland Heights and defended it to the last extremity; and, indeed, while he ventured to remain at Harper's Ferry, how could he have failed to fortify Loudon Mountain and hold its summit and nearer base? Had this been done there would have been some reason for facing Jackson along the Bolivar Ridge.[24]

Hillman Hall of the 6th New York crossed the battlefield at 11:00. He omitted a description of what he saw because it was "futile. It is beyond the power of my pen...(and) it is just as well that our children should not look upon it."

The First Massachusetts cavalry crossed South Mountain at a trot today. The National Pike was strewn with the debris of Lee's army; "abandoned wagons, some broken artillery, prisoners and wounded. The road was very dusty."

Camp was finally made at Keedysville. The men and horses were tired. Very little in the way of rations had been given to them. The limestone roads played havoc with the horses' hoofs. And subsisting on green corn had sown the seeds of a terrible epidemic called "greased hell." Within two weeks, "nearly half of the horses of the Army of the Potomac were rendered unserviceable, and vast numbers died. The same disease raged in the horses of the Confederate army."[25]

Company G of the First Maine Cavalry had been assigned to escort duty with General Reno on September 7. They had watched the battle on the fourteenth, kept stragglers from going to the rear, and acted as orderlies. After Reno's death they escorted the body back to Middletown, and on Monday the troopers were assigned as orderlies and guards at Burnside's headquarters.[26]

North of the Potomac, near Boonsboro, the Yankees were advancing. The Second Corps was in front, and the First Corps getting under way.

Marsena Patrick spent Sunday night sleeping in an ambulance on the eastern slope of South Mountain. His command was delayed in moving toward Sharpsburg due to the passage of the Second Corps, and the tremendous army traffic jam between Boonsboro and the Antietam. On the way he saw General McClellan pass by and listened to the cheers of the troops.

Patrick turned his brigade into a field at the edge of Boonsboro. One with woods at the edge and a nice little stream running through it. He rode on then and reported to General Doubleday. After a conference, it was decided to let the brigade stay where it was, and move on to Sharpsburg on Tuesday morning.[27]

George Noyes saw that the National Road was very much congested as the Army of the Potomac was moving forward. His comrades believed they had the Rebs on the run and were singing "My Maryland." They were in hot pursuit. When Noyes reached the Mountain House he found the eats and drinks had been consumed by D.H. Hill's men, and the house itself ransacked.[28]

Noyes headed for the spacious barn which lasted until recent years, and found some hay for his mare, her first meal in over twenty-four hours. General Rickets and other officers were in the Mountain House. The division itself was resting in the fields alongside the road. Noyes sat down on the porch and watched the continual procession of troops and wagons going by.

Some Confederate prisoners were being taken to the rear. They were permitted to get a drink at the pump at the Mountain House. One man was friendly, but assured all the men in blue, that the "South would fight to the end."

Next came a Confederate doctor with a blood-stained stretcher and a flag of truce. He was seeking a ranking general in an effort to recover the body of Colonel Strange.[29]

Moments later, Noyes saw Edwin Sumner, the old cavalry officer now in command of the Second Corps. Sumner reminded George of the "best days of the Roman Republic."

By now it was 4:00 p.m. and Noyes felt that half of the Army of the Potomac had passed by as he watched and waited. Hard to tell where his supply wagons were. He'd just have to wait. But he was getting hungry and he thought he'd better look for a place to sleep. He struck off on a road to the right, when whom should he encounter but "General McClellan, followed by a brilliant cavalcade and body guard," proceeding rapidly to the front.

Riding down a narrow country road, Noyes came to a pretty farm halfway down the western slope of South Mountain. It belonged to a German family by the name of Van Snuff. Some women came out and told them all their troubles and how the cannon balls had flown overhead. There was nothing to do but listen. Finally the officers were invited in, and a little later shared a fine dutch meal with "a fair cup of coffee."[30]

George was impressed with the beauty of the mountain glen. He envied the people who lived here, and was sorry for the disturbance created by the battle. "Strange indeed to these secluded homes must have been the roar of artillery, the rattle of musketry, the shrieking shot and shell, and the squads of half crazed men, the drift-wood of the receding rebel tide—who rested awhile in their porches...."

Noyes finally bade Godspeed to his German friends, and left them with a story to tell their children and children's children.

Going down the mountain, Noyes was impressed with the rich view and the lovely landscape before him. The scene was one of peaceful habitations, and pleasant homes. "Few districts in America are more lovely to look upon...."[31]

The road to Keedysville was congested. The inns and the shops were full. Wounded Confederates were in the halls and churches. George finally found a strong Union sympathizer who gave him a nice room and took good care of his horse.

The 49th Pennsylvania assisted in bringing up the sick of the brigade as the column left Burkittsville. They discovered the Rebels were good at camouflage. On the slope of the mountain they found a cannon. But it was made of old car wheels with a stove pipe as a barrel, and had been used to trick the Yankees.

This was a day of mixed emotions for the Ninth Corps. They felt they had been successful. The enemy had been pushed off the mountain; their objective had been gained. But they had suffered losses too. So the morning was spent in regrouping, caring for the wounded, collecting arms scattered on the field of battle, and in burying the dead.

General Burnside was sad. His long and intimate friendship with Jesse Lee Reno had ended at sunset. He could not put into words "the deep sorrow which the death of the gallant Reno had caused me....Reno's noble character had endeared him to all with whom he served. No more valuable life than his has been lost during this contest for our country's preservation."[32]

A few days later, Burnside issued a formal note of sympathy to the command.

General Orders   Headquarters Ninth Army Corps No. 17

Mouth of Antietam, Md., September 20, 1862

The Commanding General announces to the corps the loss of their late leader, Maj. Gen. Jesse L. Reno.

By the death of that distinguished officer the country loses one of its most devoted patriots, the army one of its most thorough soldiers. In the long list of battles in which General Reno has fought in this country's service, his name always appears with the brightest luster, and he has now bravely met a soldier's death while gallantly leading his men at the battle of South Mountain.

For his high character and the kindly qualities of his heart in private life, as well as the for the military genius and personal daring which marked him as a soldier, his loss will be deplored by all who knew him, and the commanding general desired to add the tribute of a friend to the public mourning for the death of one of the country's best defenders.

By the command of Major-General Burnside:

William Todd was another who waited for the dawn, and then was almost sorry to see it.

Morning of the 15th dawned at last, and on such a sight as none of us ever wished to look upon again. Behind and in front of us, but especially in the angles of the stone walls, the dead bodies of the enemy lay thick: near the gaps in the fences they were piled on top of each other like cordwood dumped from a cart. The living had retreated during the night and none but the dead and severely wounded remained. As soon as the retreat of the enemy was confirmed at other points along the line, we set about getting breakfast, for we had had neither dinner nor supper the previous day, save perhaps a dry cracker or two, and were in a fit condition to enjoy a cup of coffee, even amidst such ghastly surroundings. Shortly before noon Sykes' brigade of regulars passed us, in the Fourteenth regiment of which were several New York boys known to some of us. They said they had not been engaged during the battle, but were held as a reserve, which led some of us to wish that we were regulars too. About noon we moved off the field, and on our way saw many more evidences of the battle. At one angle of the stone walls fourteen bodies of the enemy were counted lying in a heap, just as they had fallen, apparently. We referred afterwards to that spot as "Dead Man's Corner." A curious sight presented itself in the body of a rebel straddling a stone wall; he must have been killed while in the act of climbing over, for with a leg on either side, the body was thrown slightly forward stiff in death, We were glad to leave these scenes behind us.[33]

Dr. Ellis was appalled at the heavy casualties at the intersection of the Fox's Gap Road and the road running across the top of the mountain to Turner's Gap. He was saddened that in the Confederate ranks there were so many young boys, lads who would never see home and family again. They had given their all, "for what?"

Details were selected to clear the way and bury the dead. While this was occurring, "General Burnside rode by...welcomed by shouts of delight." It was expected that the rebels would try to cross the Potomac, but the men hoped McClellan would attack and cut off their line of retreat.

David Strother and part of the staff rode up the Old Sharpsburg or Fox's Gap Road. At the summit "we came upon their dead lying scattered through the woods and...in a stone fence lane....The dead lay so thick that the lane was choken with them. General Samuel Sturgis had them thrown aside so he could move his artillery through. It was a sad scene. Some of the dead Confederates were grasping sticks and leaves. One had a pleasant smile on his face."[34]

The men were glad to see morning come. The night had been chilly and foggy, and most difficult. But when morning broke, the men almost wished for darkness. The night had veiled the scene of carnage. All around were grim pieces of evidence from the battle of Sunday afternoon and evening. The trees were all shattered and torn, and "ghastly corpses were all over fields. Eighteen Confederates were grouped together. Most of them were very dirty, ragged, and shoeless." Such are the horrors of Maryland, and pictures at one of the prettiest spots in Maryland.[35]

The work of the grave details was "made extremely difficult by the stony character of the ground. It was a gruesome task." Guns, blankets, and haversacks littered the ground.

Several members of the Ninth Corps, including those in Durell's Battery, say that about midday Burnside and McClellan rode up Fox's Gap together, and were cheered by the troops. The generals rode through the ranks and on to the front.

This again raises a question about McClellan's route to Antietam. From the accounts of the Second and Twelfth Corps, he must have gone into Boonsboro and then out the Boonsboro-Sharpsburg Road.

Apparently Burnside parted company with him at the western side of Fox's Gap and came back to the Ninth Corps.[36]

This morning men from the 45th Pennsylvania were assigned to burial details and went about the sad, unpleasant task, wrapping the dead in their own blankets, and burying them above a little log house near the Old Sharpsburg Road. Among the dead was George Brenton with whom the regimental historian had eaten breakfast on Sunday morning. It was a "sinking sight" to see the dead Confederates too. Many hearts went out to them, and to their families. Those in the burial detail were "gratified they had escaped."

It was afternoon when the Ninth Corps left Fox's Gap. Once down the mountain, their exact steps are hard to follow. Jacob Cox says that his command marched to the Boonsboro-Sharpsburg Pike. It is unlikely that they turned north after striking what is now Maryland 67 leading to Pleasant Valley.[37]

No doubt they took the Old Sharpsburg Road to Mount Hebron Road and crossed to Keedysville or Centreville as it was known then. Cox speaks of coming up in the rear of Sumner's Corps on the Boonsboro Pike. Then Cox's command turned to the left and rested momentarily in the field. It was about 3:00 p.m. General McClellan rode up accompanied by a large staff. Cox rode to meet him along with General Burnside. Although Cox had never met "Little Mac," he was received most cordially.

The group of officers walked up the slope and looked out over the valley and the ridges beyond the creek where the Confederates had gone into position. It was a large group and rather conspicuous. About that time there was a puff of smoke from a knoll on the right of the Sharpsburg Road, and a shell came screaming overhead. McClellan gave orders for the group to disperse, and continued to reconnoiter with one or two aides. He was very cool and business-like, even under fire. Soon the Union artillery replied to that of the Confederates and the hills shook.

Orders were then given for the Ninth Corps to move to the left, keeping out of the fields occupied by Sumner's command. They tramped overland until dusk. Cox's division went into bivouac about a mile south of the bridge, in the rear of the hills bordering the Antietam Creek.

Charles Johnson felt very uneasy marching from Fox's Gap to Red Hill. He saw the visitation of death. He saw their bodies and uniforms covered with dust and large spots of dark red blood. It wasn't pretty to look at, and it is unpleasant to read about. One large Confederate with a beard and mustache made a special impression on Charles. As Johnson looked on his lifeless form, he wondered how soon he might be lying cold on some battlefield. Charles looked to the sky, and hoped the dead man's soul was up there, free from war and strife.[38]

Edwin Lord and his comrades were tired and hungry. They tramped but eight miles, but the short march did not help the fatigue.[39]

The Rebels weren't the only ones with food and supply problems. Somewhere near Keedysville, Dr. Ted Dimon, attached to the Second Maryland, sent his black helper to look for food. However, he had no luck. Then the physician found a lady who was baking bread. He bought "a loaf of splendid bread and a pound of glorious butter," wrapped it in a cabbage leaf and rode off. This was Monday afternoon.

The next day, Captain Wilson found two stray bulls and butchered them. These were shared with the Sixth New Hampshire. Every man had roast beef for breakfast, using sticks to roast the meat over the fire.

The Ninth New York was relieved today and put into reserve for rest. However, no food was available. The wagons had not arrived. This was because troops chasing Lee's army had priority over supplies. The men therefore went foraging in the potato patches and cornfields near Fox's Gap. But they faced slim pickings as the Rebels had earlier gotten the best. About 5:00 p.m., the Ninth New York was ordered to cross South Mountain and proceed down the western slope. It was almost 11:00 p.m. when the column, after fording the Little Antietam and another stream near Locust Spring, reached the foot of Red Hill. Too exhausted to fix their shelter halves, and without food, the men stretched out to sleep under the stars.[40]

David Strother stopped at a white house at the east end of Boonsboro. He was ordered to send a message to General Mansfield, commander of the Twelfth Corps, telling him to take the Porterstown Road in an effort to flank the Rebels.

Then it was on to Keedysville. "The whole road was through masses of troops and our movement was escorted by one continuous cheering."[41]

Today large numbers of Confederate prisoners, taken in the fighting at South Mountain, arrived in Frederick, along with the body of General Jesse L. Reno.

Jonathan Letterman, the father of the U.S. Army Medical Corps, was a busy man today. He had established hospitals in Middletown and Burkittsville to care for the wounded, his own, and those left behind by the Confederates. Now as the realization of an even bigger battle loomed on the horizon, he had a lot of work to do.

> In addition to our own wounded, we had upon our hands from the battles of South Mountain, Crampton's Gap, and Antietam in all about 2,500 Confederate wounded. Those taken at South Mountain were taken to Middletown, and those at Crampton's Gap to Burkittsville.

Immediately after the retreat of the enemy from the field of Antietam, measures were taken to have all the Confederate wounded gathered in from the field, over which they laid scattered in all directions, and from the houses and barns in the rear of their lines, and placed under circumstances as would permit of their being properly attended to, and at such points as would enable their removal to be effected to Frederick and thence to Baltimore and Fortress Monroe to their own lines. They were removed as rapidly as their recovery would permit. The duty of attending to these men was assigned to Surgeon Raunch, U.S. Volunteers.

Passing through the village of Boonsborough, (on Sept. 15) it was examined to ascertain what accomodation it afforded for hospital purposes in the event they should be required there. Later in the evening we passed through the village of Keedysville...which was also subjected to a similar examination. Passing beyond this village, we came in sight, late in the evening, of what afterward proved to be the battlefield of Antietam.

As soon as the nature of the country and its resources for hospital purposes could be ascertained, and when an idea of the nature of the anticipated battle and position to be occupied by our troops, directions were given to the medical directors of our corps to form their hospitals as far as possible by divisions, and at such a distance in the rear of the line of battle as to be secure from the shot and shell of the enemy; to select the houses and barns most easy of access, and such as were well supplied with hay or straw and water.

Barns Preferred

When circumstances would permit barns were to be designated as preferrable in all cases to houses, as being in that season of the year well provided with straw, better ventilated, and enabling the medical officers with more facility to attend to a greater number of wounded....Hospital supplies were to be taken to all points selected.[42]

Among the places examined by Dr. Letterman were the farms of Bishop John Russell at the base of Red Hill, the Hoffman farm near the Upper Bridge, and Samuel Pry's big mill along the Little Antietam.

The 27th Indiana found itself among the wreckage of battle when Monday morning dawned, and in the midst of traffic congestion as troops were constantly moving to the front. After breakfast, the men from Indiana crossed Turner's Gap. On the way, "we saw a large number of dead rebels, dead horses, disabled caissons, broken wheels, muskets, cartridge boxes, and other articles, always found upon a battlefield."

Boonsboro was so full of wounded Confederates and gray clad medical staff, that Edmund Brown's first thought was that the Rebels were in possession of the town.

Just beyond the town, to the north of the Sharpsburg Road, the men from Indiana took a break. The fields were full of Yankee troops. The soldiers were in great spirits and the air was rent with repeated cheers. A victory had been won on South Mountain and the troops were happy.

They were also cheering the presence of Generals McClellan and Burnside. The generals with their staffs, orderlies, clerks, and escorts had passed the 27th Indiana on the mountain. It was the rule at this stage of the war to cheer whenever a high-ranking officer appeared. But Edmund Brown says that McClellan had an advance man who rode in front and instructed the troops to cheer. In fact, this September Monday, McClellan rode by twice, drinking in the cheers of his men. The cheers were loud and long. The soldiers were glad to see the officers, and the generals relished the cheers. Everything stopped. For a moment time stood still, and no one seemed to realize there was a war on and that the Army of Northern Virginia was the objective.[43]

Later in the day, the 27th Indiana went into camp east of the Pry house, the farm spring furnishing refreshing water for the Hooisers until Tuesday night when they moved on. Brown did not like McClellan's pompous activities. He felt 'Little Mac' should be chasing the rebs."

As the Union cavalry started after the Confederates, Clara Barton and her aides broke camp near Frederick and started after the army. Before long the debris of the Battle of South Mountain was seen. Dead horses and abandoned equipment littered the roadside.

Late Monday evening, Philip Pry, living in a lovely brick farmhouse, just eighteen years old, was startled to see a cloud of dust coming down his farm lane. It was caused by a column of horsemen.

A dashing young officer ran up to the door and said, "General McClellan, the commander-in-chief of the Army of the Potomac desires to make his headquarters here."

Mr. Pry thought the officer's name was Custer. It might have been. George, who was a favorite of both Alfred Pleasonton and General McClellan, was on the staff.

This brought a whirlwind of activity. Tents were erected, flags unfurled, and stakes driven to support telescopes. McClellan was in good spirits. He told Mr. Pry he expected a big battle, and hoped to give "Bobby Lee the whipping of his life." He also told Mr. Pry he had nothing to fear. The soldiers would protect the family and give them transportation to the rear if necessary.

After dark, Dr. Hard was informed that two wounded members of the 8th Illinois were at the home of a doctor in a little village called Mount Pleasant. At 10:00 p.m. Dr. Hard took an ambulance and went searching for his comrades. It was midnight, but everybody in the village was up. The events of the weekend had been too much. No one could sleep. Besides, they did not know what was ahead.

No members of the Eighth Illinois were there, but two wounded Confederates were present. Hard was about ready to return to Boonsboro, when a young man, pretty well drunk, came and told him a wounded Confederate was in a nearby home, being hidden by the women.

The doctor went, and entered without knocking. He found the Rebel in an elegant parlor, with "a plate of cake and pie." By his side was his revolver, and around him were three young ladies, and smiles.

Hard pulled a gun and demanded his surrender. The lad made no fuss. But the three young women heaped all kinds of abuse on the doctor, calling him every name in the book, and telling him he had no right to enter their home.

But their words had no effect, and the Confederate who was having such a fine time was taken back to Boonsboro. Writing later, Hard said that his regiment would be forever grateful for the untiring devotion of the citizens of Boonsboro to the wounded. In a few days, the physician would have the pleasure of meeting Clara Barton at a farmhouse hospital.[44]

That morning Andrew Humphreys and his new recruits from Pennsylvania hit the road early and continued the march until 3:00 p.m. All along the way were knapsacks, overcoats, and other articles of war, discarded by the soldiers who had traveled the route earlier. Some of the teamsters were slick. If they got a chance, they stopped their wagons, and gathered up the coats and blankets. Then when an opportunity arose, they sold them to citizens. The 155th Pennsylvania reached Clarksburg, "tired and worn out by the severe marching in hot weather."[45]

It was a difficult day for the 155th Pennsylvania. The weather was hot, and as they marched from Clarksburg to Urbana, they too unloaded blankets and overcoats by the side of the road. The heat and dust started to take its toll on these new men. They became a little upset with General Humphreys and two colonels, who were superbly mounted but continually urged the men to make haste. This seems to have been a characteristic of Humphreys. A year later in the Gettysburg campaign, soldiers in the Third Corps would remember forever how the general forced them to march at night in the rain and mud.

At the end of the trek was Urbana and the Young Ladies Seminary building where just a week earlier Jeb Stuart and the Confederate cavalry had held a ball. There were nice rooms in the building, and the structure was surrounded by fine apple and peach orchards. It almost seemed like an oasis in the desert.

As the men took to the rooms, they found inscriptions and cartoons scrawled on the walls by the Rebel cavalry and some of Longstreet's infantry. There were also many Confederate signatures on the wall, along with the names of many regiments.

Alas for the poor owner. The Yanks would not be outdone. They had to have their art show too. So they scrawled their names, and slogans about their regiments, and as the Rebels had made fun of Washington and Lincoln, they fixed several for Jefferson Davis. For years people could see the names of John Lancaster, Hugh Leonard, Thomas Tomer, and others belonging to the 155th inscribed on the walls of the hall in Urbana.[46]

After Second Bull Run, Oliver Norton, a member of the Fifth Corps, had marched forty-six miles on nothing but raw beef and drinking water obtained from a ditch. But life in Maryland was different.

> I shall always remember the march through Maryland as among the most pleasant of my experience as a soldier. The roads were splendid and the country as beautiful...as I ever saw....Everywhere landscapes of exquisite beauty meet the eye. Pretty villages are frequent, and pretty girls more so, and instead of gazing at passing soldiers with scorn and contempt, they were always ready with a pleasant word and a glass of water I almost forgot the war and the fact that I was a soldier as I gained the summit of the first range of mountains....The brightest, warmest, richest landscape I ever saw lay sleeping in the mellow sunlight of a September afternoon.[47]

As night fell, Hooker's corps was between the Upper or Hitt Bridge over the Antietam, on the road to Keedysville and the Hagerstown pike. The Twelfth Corps was near Keedysville. Sumner's Second Corps was astride the Boonsboro turnpike on the Pry farm and Bishop Russell's place. Sykes' division of the Fifth Corps was at Porterstown, while the Ninth Corps was between Mt. Carmel Church and the Geeting farm or Bishop Russell's.

Soldier Stevens, a member of the Sixth Corps, describes the scenic beauty of the area.

> Among the delightful and fertile valleys which beautify the State of Maryland, none is more charming than the one through which the Antietam winds its tortuous course. Looking from some elevation down upon its green fields, where herds of sleek cattle graze, its yellow harvests glowing and ripening in the September sun; its undulating meadows and richly laden orchards; its comfortable farm houses, some standing out boldly upon eminences, which rise here and there, others half hidden by vines or fruit trees; the ranges of hills, rising on either side of the stream, diversified by charming vales or deep gullies; the turnpikes winding along the sides of the hills and through the valleys; the lovely stream itself, now flowing smoothly over its dark bed and anon tumbling noisily in rapids over a stony bottom, winding here far up to one range of hills and then turning back to kiss the base of the other; the whole scene is one of surpassing beauty, upon which the eye rests with untiring delight. Who would have selected this lovely valley as the scene of one of the most bloody struggles ever recorded? Who...would have dreamed that those stacks of grain, which dotted the fields here and there, would soon become the only protection from the heat of the sun and the storm of battle, to thousands of wounded bleeding men? or, that from those lovely groves of oak and maple, now reposing like spots of beauty upon the landscape, were to belch forth fire and smoke, carrying destruction to thousands? Yet, here on these smiling fields, and among these delightful groves, one of the grand battles which should decide the march of events in the history, not only of our own country but of the world, was to be fought. These green pastures were to be stained with blood, and these peaceful groves marred and torn by shot and shell.[48]

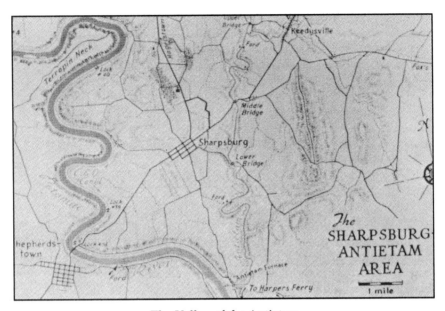

The Valley of the Antietam
Courtesy—The National Park Service

The Pry Farm
Courtesy—Fred Cross

CHAPTER VIII

TUESDAY, SEPTEMBER 16, 1862

—ARMY OF NORTHERN VIRGINIA—

This morning, a Mr. Grove in Sharpsburg invited Jackson, Longstreet, and Jeb Stuart to breakfast. The latter two accepted, but Jackson declined. Julia, Mr. Grove's daughter, thereby sent breakfast to Jackson's tent with one of Longstreet's aides. Jackson asked about the young lady who sent it.

Longstreet's aide did not know her name, but said, "It was a fair one."

Jackson wrote a thank you note saying:

Dear Miss Fairfield,

I have received the nice breakfast, for which I am indebted to your kindness. Please except my grateful appreciation....[1]

Confederate columns were moving up from Harpers Ferry to rejoin Lee at Sharpsburg on the banks of the Antietam.

August Dickert describes the march of this September Tuesday.

The sun poured down its blistering rays with intense fierceness upon the already fatigued and fagged soldiers, while the dust along the pikes, that wound over and around the numerous hills, was almost stiffling. We bivouaced for the night on the roadside, ten miles from Antietam Creek.[2]

E. P. Alexander arrived in Shepherdstown about noon today, along with the ordnance train. He was ordered to report to Lee at Sharpsburg. After crossing the Potomac, he came back and headed for Harpers Ferry with his empty wagons to collect all the ammunition that could be used and bring it to Sharpsburg. The unusable he was to take to Winchester. The Army of Northern Virginia was grateful for the expected increase. South Mountain had used a lot of it, and the ordnance wagons captured and burned by the Union cavalry was a tragic loss.[3]

After spending Monday in Martinsburg getting some repair work done on the horse artillery, George Neese left camp three miles from town, and moved to within a quarter of a mile of Shepherdstown and made camp. George says, "We camped on the farm near the residence of A.R. Boteler, Morgan Spring, a large and beautiful spring, is near his house."[4]

Neese remained here until Wednesday afternoon when his guns arrived from the Martinsburg repair shops. The morning and early afternoon hours were very anxious for George. All he could do was wait and wonder what was happening. "At times the artillery fire was so fierce and heavy that it sounded like one continual roar of thunder tumbling and rolling across the sky. The musketry fire was equally severe....The air between the lines must have been thick with flying lead." George did not see how the troops could survive such fire.

Then at 3:00 p.m. he started to the front. Progress was slow. The Potomac ford was rough and narrow, and the river was full of wagons coming and going. He noted that "Shepherdstown seemed to be full of our wounded. The entire distance from the river to the battlefield was crowded with ordnance wagons and ambulances." What a day in the Valley of the Antietam.[5]

Today a few shots from the long range guns of the Yankees whistled over the Confederates and fell on Sharpsburg, setting some fires. Riding through the town, looking for General Longstreet, William Owen "saw General Lee on foot, leading his horse by the bridle....He seemed perfectly unconscious of the danger. He directed us to keep the artillery ammunition for the enemy's infantry only." The Washington Artillery then made their headquarters in the Dutch Reformed Church. A lot of Confederate doctors were there. After supper, the men smoked their pipes, and slept soundly within the chancel area.[6]

An officer in the Eighth Virginia talked to Randolph Shotwell, saying that because of his wounded foot, he was excused to go into Sharpsburg in an effort to scrounge up some food for the men in the regiment.

The town looked deserted. All the businesses were closed. No children were to be seen, in fact, it looked as though the populace was in hiding. Then there was a noise that sounded like thunder. It was the Union artillery on the east bank of the Antietam. Soon several homes and a stable were in flames. Confederate couriers galloped through the streets of town.

Randolph shrank from entering houses. But after a time, hunger, and the thought of what the Yankees had done in Virginia, Shotwell went into two places and found nary a crumb. At the third place he fared a little better, finding some sugar cured hams in the attic, some jellies, and a huge ball of breaded dough. Entering the parlor, Randolph found another tall, skinny, barefoot Rebel with several hams and some other goodies. The North Carolina preacher's son sat down in one of the nice chairs and thought of the days that had been, of the war, of hunger, and the difficulty brought to the home in Sharpsburg.[7]

The shells from Union guns near the Middle Bridge were still falling on Sharpsburg. Shotwell thought that Pleasonton must not know there were only friendly women and children and the aged in town.

As he was going up Main Street, several big missiles tore through the tree tops making a terrible noise. One large "shell burst in the middle of the street near a hotel, killing...three Confederate soldiers, and wounding several others, including a (local) free negro." The wounded were removed to a porch, while the shells created a panic among the teamsters lounging in the area.

Then it was on to the Dunker Church and Pickett's command about one mile away. En route, Shotwell saw the ruins of a burned house that was still smoldering. About 9:00 p.m., he fixed a ham and dough ball for supper.

"Along the rolling ridges for miles, lay the two armies, one a mighty host, well armed, well fed," and well equipped. The other a "handful, weary, footsore, hungry, and in tatters, but resolute and vigilant."[8]

In the hollow of the valley was Sharpsburg, looking like "A Deserted Village." Not a light or lamp shone from the windows. Here and there sparks smoldered and flickered when fanned by the wind, aiding the reduction of the places hit by the shells in the afternoon.

At many places were the campfires with small groups of hungry, barefoot men roasting green ears of corn.

During the night the horses of the Jeff Davis Legion stampeded causing alarm and confusion. Fortunately for the Rebels, the animals ran to the rear, instead of toward the Yankees.

As the sun went down, cows roamed the fields, their progress made easier by the fences already torn down by men of war. Some of the fences had been destroyed in an effort to expedite the passage of troops. In other instances, the fence rails were being used for campfires. The smell of burning wood, the brewing of coffee, and preparation of pork drifted over the area. Many men prepared their last earthly meal.

—*ARMY OF THE POTOMAC*—

The day broke quiet and peaceful. The heavy mist covered the valley, and for a time hid the large masses of blue and gray troops from view. At first McClellan thought Lee had withdrawn. He sent a premature telegram to his wife saying he felt he had already delivered Pennsylvania and Maryland from the hands of the enemy. To General Halleck he sent the information that he could not see in the fog. He would do more as situation developed.[9]

It was to be a busy day. General Longstreet says:

> September 16, 1862, was a day of intense anxiety and unrest in the Valley of the Antietam. The people who lived in the farmhouses that dotted the golden autumn landscape in this hitherto quiet community had now abandoned their homes and given place to the armed forces. It was a day of marshalling and maneuvering of the gathering thousands....[10]

Some of the residents of Sharpsburg packed blankets, food, and precious belongings and headed elsewhere. Some went to Killingsburg Cave, north of town, along the Potomac. Others went to relatives, while some prepared shelters in their basements.

North of Sharpsburg is St. James Episcopal School. On the retreat from Gettysburg, it was to be right in the heart of the action, and in July of 1864 when Jubal Early marched to the gates of Washington, the school was again occupied by the men from the South.

But in September of 1862, Dr. John B. Kerfoot, president of St. James, and his staff acted as Good Samaritans. Kerfoot, along with Dr. Falk, and Rev. Henry Edwards, Rector of St. John's Episcopal Parish in Hagerstown, rode to Boonsboro and South Mountain with bandages, spirits, biscuits, and tobacco. In Boonsboro, they found four large hospitals caring for those who had fallen at Turner's Gap and in the Boonsboro skirmish. Then they rode to the top of South Mountain and found many Confederates remaining to be buried. They also discovered many seriously wounded Confederates at a nearby cabin.

Robert Westbrook and his mates in the 49th Pennsylvania found the day to be warm until noon, then cool and cloudy. They stayed in camp at the base of Crampton's Gap, and heard there was fighting going on near the Potomac.

While McClellan and Lee were making final preparations near Sharpsburg, Charles Wainwright of upstate New York was nearing

Frederick. Monday, while staying at the Willard Hotel, he received an order directing him to report to General Hooker to assume command of the artillery of the First Corps.

It was late Monday afternoon before Charles could get his wagon and staff started. When they arrived in Frederick they found great excitement that Tuesday afternoon in September. Everybody was talking about the great victory at South Mountain. Telegrams from McClellan at the front were posted in the hotel lobby. Citizens were praising Hooker for his gallantry at Turner's Gap, and lamenting the loss of Jesse Lee Reno.

Wainwright was tired and sought a hotel room. But they were all full. Finally, he found a very nice room in a private home.[11]

Just about every church and large building in Frederick was in use as a hospital, treating the soldiers wounded at South Mountain. Union troops captured and paroled at Harpers Ferry were also arriving in Frederick. A soldier told Jacob Engelbrecht that the bridge at Harpers Ferry was destroyed by blasting.

As Engelbrecht thought back over recent days, he came to the conclusion that "Our good city of Frederick, have seen as many Soldiers pass through their town, as perhaps any other town in the world in the Same Space of time....I do think if they were all strung out, Wagons, Cannons & all it would make one Continued String of at least fifty miles, if not more." Monday evening six more regiments passed through town on the way to join the main army and more were said to be on the way.[12]

Late that day General McClellan passed the campsite of the Ninth New York. He was on a brown horse and in the process of placing artillery batteries. "He was surrounded by several officers." Charles Johnson says, "This was the first time I have seen this great man."[13]

But great battles and the important things of life are affected by little things. It takes a tiny hinge to swing a big door, and at Antietam a small event occurred which affected the morale of the Second Corps. Oliver O. Howard, John Sedgwick, and General McClellan were standing together examining the Confederate position with the use of field glasses.

> when an officer in charge of McClellans headquarters' baggage train led his column of wagons to a pleasant spot on the slope, just behind us, in full view of our whole division. The enemy sent a few bursting shells into his neighborhood. This officer, much disturbed, quickly countermarched his train and hurried it off far out of range to the rear. It was done amid the

jokes and laughter of our men. Sedgwick, seeing the move, shook his head and said solemnly: "I am sorry to see that!"

McClellan himself did not go back that night; but the men thought that he did. Some of his staff never could understand how easily in times of danger the morale of an army may be injured."[14]

Marsena Patrick got up at 4:00 a.m., and routed his troops from their rest. However, two hours passed before the column moved. The road was pretty clear. Soon after reaching the fields of Antietam, Hooker ordered all troops under arms. At 5:00 p.m. Patrick's men crossed a very bad ford. Their destination was unclear. Confederate pickets hiding in corn fields popped away. It was 10:00 p.m. before Patrick's men were able to fall out. A light rain was falling, and most of the men tried to sleep with no food in their stomachs. A great battle was expected in the morning, and there was too much excitement to sleep.[15]

At 3:30, the 13th Massachusetts crossed the Upper or Hitt Bridge on the road to Bakersville, and turned to the left to advance on the Confederate positions. They came under heavy artillery fire, and then made camp on the Poffenberger Ridge, waiting for the dawn of the next day and a terrible battle.[16]

Rufus Dawes also took the opportunity to get a look at the Confederate position with Joe Hooker. The general estimated 40,000 Rebels on the banks of the Antietam.

The men from Wisconsin filled their haversacks with apples, and dropped in fields to sleep in a drizzle.[17]

Daniel MacNamara of the Ninth Massachusetts says that Lee's defeat on South Mountain brought great rejoicing to the folks in Washington County. Many thought he would cross the Potomac and not stay in Maryland.

MacNamara was delighted with the beauty of Pleasant Valley "arrayed as it was in all the gorgeous splendor of a plentiful harvest." It looked like a garden spot. Marching through Boonsboro and Keedysville, "we were met with welcome by the inhabitants."

The First Division of the Fifth Corps to which MacNamara belonged went into camp at Porterstown near the Middle Bridge, and soon had campfires going, preparing for supper. All around were the tents and campfires of the Army of the Potomac. The army was "in excellent spirits and confident of success."[18]

Later in the evening, after the pickets were posted, a medley of drums, bugles, and fifes rang out across the night air of autumn.

Men of the Fifth New Hampshire were detailed to destroy a dam at the Newcomer Mill near the Pry farm. The reasoning may have been to lower the level of the Antietam at the Pry Ford several hundred yards upstream.

Near sunset the men of the Fifth New Hampshire were marched to bivouac near the Pry house and McClellan's headquarters. This upset some of the men because they thought they would miss the battle, but the guard duty was just for the night. The men from New Hampshire had a morning engagement at the Sunken Road.[19]

Chaplain Quint and Colonel Dwight had ridden together on the way from South Mountain to the fields of Antietam. Monday night they slept together, and as Tuesday morning broke they were ready to catch up on paper work, when orders came to move. The distance was short, less than two miles, but the troops were drawn up in battle, and were not able to rest until 10:00 p.m. Colonels Andrews, Dwight, and Chaplain Quint used wheat stacks for their beds, and slept until wakened by cannon fire Wednesday morning.[20]

Morell's Division of the Fifth Corps moved up to a point near Porterstown that day. Later in the day the Ninth Corps advanced from the Old Sharpsburg Road and the Geeting farm to Jacob Miller's and Henry Rohrback's, ready to hit the southern end of Lee's line in the morning. The poor farmers wondered what was going to happen to their crops and animals. It was almost like a bad dream. Seven days ago it was quiet and peaceful. Now there were soldiers, guns, and the dread of battle.

Dr. James Oliver reached the Locust Spring farm today. Little did he realize that he would spend the next six weeks of his life in the area taking care of wounded men. Later in the day he went to Henry Rohrback's, feeling that this farm would be closer to the line of combat.

The 35th Massachusetts found this to be a lovely day. The area reminded some of the fellows of the Berkshires. It would have been a great day to rest. But every now and then the Confederates lobbed some shells into their midst, disturbing their sleep and peace. At sundown the men moved over a ridge and made a fine camp using straw from a large stack.[21]

Monday the 118th Pennsylvania left the banks of the Monocacy and marched through the streets of Frederick. They were very much impressed with the old city, the clean roads, the well paved streets, and the substantial stores and houses. It looked like a fertile and prosperous place.

The sun was hot and the dust was thick. The road was in rough shape, ground down by the men and wagons of those who had marched that way earlier. The ground on both sides of the road was bare due to the marching of the infantry. Troops always had to give way to vehicles. It was 6:00 p.m. when the 118th stopped marching close to the eastern base of the Catoctins.[22]

By 6:00 a.m. the men of the 118th Pennsylvania were on the road again. The men were impressed with the beauty of South Mountain. As they came down Braddock Mountain, beneath them for miles "lay the beautiful valley, dotted with barns and houses. Its stacks of grain, its tall, waving corn, and bright green pastures, told of the plenty of a toiling, prosperous community....The scene...was a rare landscape of mountain, and valley, hill and dale, stream and village."

The Pennsylvanians became agitated in Middletown. The handles had been removed from all the pumps. Troops had been marching through the village for a week and helping themselves to the water. The residents were fearful that the thousands using their wells would cause them to go dry, so they removed the handles. Some of the Pennsylvanians threw dirt and rocks into the wells until they were told the reason for the removal of the pump handles.[23]

Newton Curtis of the 16th New York took a break from his hospital work to go to the Confederate hospital in Burkittsville, looking for Mississippians who might have known his brother Andrew Jackson Curtis, a former resident of Vicksburg.

Andrew had died in 1858 but had loved Vicksburg and had many friends. As a result, quite a few corresponded regularly with Newton and the family in the North.

At the hospital, Curtis learned that there were no troops from Mississippi at Crampton's Gap. A North Carolinian was very hostile to Newton, telling him that he lamented the loss of his right arm, "Now I cannot fight the Yanks as well as I did with two arms." Newton spoke regrets. But the man from the Tarheel State shouted that he hated the Yankees, and followed Curtis with streams of profanity.

Newton found another fellow, a man with grey hair, too old really for combat service. The man was sad and beaten. He had lost his wallet and would be unable to buy a few things in the military prison. Curtis gave him a greenback.

Elsewhere in the hospital was a sixteen- or seventeen-year-old boy. His wound was not serious. But he was homesick and filled with anxiety about his mother and younger brothers and sisters. His dad had been killed in an earlier battle, and apparently it was his duty to care for the family.

Curtis suggested that he accept a parole and promise not to take up arms against the North again. He replied that he could not make such a promise, "if he did his mother would disown him; nor would he willingly leave the colors. He wished to fight until victory for the South was won, and if he could not do that, to die on the field as his father had. He was to do neither. Two weeks later he died of disease. Such was the tragedy of the war, the feeling in the hearts of the participants, and the disruption of home and family life.[24]

Before bedding down, many of them wrote a final message home in the event they were numbered with the slain. There were no "dog tags" then, so the notes were pinned to their shirts, or placed in Testaments in the shirt pocket. Some were given to comrades who might be expected to survive. The sounds of sad, plaintive songs could be heard.

Just before the battle, Mother,
I am thinking most of you,
While upon the fields we're watching.
With the enemy in view.

Comrades brave round me lying,
Filled with tho'ts of home and God;
For well they know
That on the morrow
Some will sleep beneath the sod.

Farewell Mother, you may never
Press me to your heart again;
But oh, you'll not forget me, Mother,
If I'm numbered with the slain.

As the shades of darkness fell, Captain George W. Bachelder of Company C, 19th Massachusetts Infantry and 2nd Lt. Edgar M. Newcomb shared the same tent somewhere on the Pry farm. Captain Bachelder filled the young lieutenant in on all the details of company matters and procedure, saying he did not expect to survive the battle. His premonition was correct. Bachelder fell in the West Woods, and Newcomb survived, only to be numbered with the slain at Fredericksburg.[25]

Joseph Mansfield, the new commander, and the oldest Union officer on the field, ate supper at the home of Jacob Cost. Then he went over reports and made plans about the morning. Soon orders came telling him to cross the Antietam, move closer to Hooker, and be prepared to move to his support early in the morning. Miles Huyette describes the move.

We formed and...crossed the stream on a stone bridge...The only sound was of scattered picket firing at the front and the mingled noise of men and artillery being rushed into position. After midnight we arrived at the George Line farm....We were massed "in column by company," in a cornfield; the night was close, air heavy...some rainfall. The air was perfumed with a mixture of crushed green cornstalks, ragweed, and clover. We made our beds between rows of corn and did not remove our accouterments.[26]

CHAPTER IX

SEPTEMBER 17, 1862, AND AFTER

With the misty dawn of Wednesday morning came the greatest struggle ever to occur in a single day on the Continent of North America. At daybreak the troops of Joseph Hooker moved out from the fields of Joseph Poffenberger to assault the positions held by the men of Thomas Jonathan "Stonewall" Jackson.

The objective of the attack was the high ground around the little Dunkard Church and the West Woods. The right flank of Hooker's attack was on the Hagerstown Road, and the left along the Smoketown Road.

Cannon on Poffenberger Ridge supported the advance of the men in blue. The 4th U.S. Artillery took a position near the haystacks on the D.R. Miller farm and opened additional fire.

General Hooker spotted the rays of the morning sun gleaming on the bayonets of Confederate troops in Miller's cornfield. Orders were given to rake the field with artillery fire. Hooker says, "Every stalk of corn in the northern and greater part of the field was cut as closely as could have been done with a knife, and the slain lay in rows precisely as they had stood in their ranks a few moments before. It was never my fortune to witness a more bloody, dismal battlefield.

The fighting raged back and forth from dawn to about 7:20 a.m. The First Corps suffered heavy losses, and the Twelfth Corps under J.K.F. Mansfield came down the Smoketown Road from the Line farm to support their comrades. Lee threw in Hood and his Texans. Bloody hand to hand combat followed, and General Mansfield fell mortally wounded.

Smoke covered the field, some of it from the Mumma barn. Standing between the two armies, the barn was fired to keep it from becoming a stronghold for the Yankees. By 9:00 a.m. the fighting died down. Both sides had suffered great losses.

But the lull was just for a moment. Fresh new troops were arriving. As things quieted down around the Dunkard Church, Edwin Sumner and the Second Corps were crossing at the Pry Ford and heading for the scene of conflict. The Second Division under John Sedgwick was advancing unsupported and without scouts in front.

Straight ahead it came into the West Woods, arriving about the time fresh new Confederate troops under Lafayette McLaws and Walker got into position. Confronted on three sides, the Confederates poured a withering fire into the ranks of the men in blue. And in less than half an hour, Sedgwick's Division was almost wiped out. Two thousand, two hundred, fifty men were dead or wounded.

So the third phase of the battle was over. First there had been Hooker's attack, followed by Mansfield, then Sedgwick. Now two more Union divisions were coming through the Neikirk farm and heading for a strong Confederate defensive position in a sunken country road. On through the Roulette farm they came until they reached the hill overlooking the lane. A tremendous fire fight followed, with hundreds falling on both sides. For a while the center of the Confederate line was in danger of being broken, but it held, although the fighting produced what was to become known as "Bloody Lane."

Meanwhile the Union cavalry and elements of the Fifth Corps were in position on the Sharpsburg-Boonsboro Road, awaiting the command to split the middle of Lee's line. Now was the time. But the order did not come, and a golden opportunity was gone forever.

Still another battle, one more separate phase of Antietam, was unfolding. South of the town near the Rohrback ridge, Georgia troops were holding at bay the Union Ninth Corps. They had the advantage of a steep slope and natural rifle pits.

At 1:00 P.M. Rodman's Division forded the Antietam and struck the Confederates in the flank, while other Union forces stormed across the bridge. The Confederates fell back. It was a dark moment. Lee was in great danger. A few more yards and the Harpers Ferry Road and perhaps his line of retreat would be gone.

But it was not to be. In one of the most dramatic events of the war, A.P. Hill, leaving Harpers Ferry early in the morning, came up the Virginia (West Virginia) side of the river, forded the Potomac, and came to the field of action via the Miller's Saw Mill Road.

In the Union advance, a gap occurred in the line, and into this gap, Hill, picturesque in his red battle shirt, threw his infantry and artillery, pushing the men in blue before him. Hill's forced march and counter attack saved the day.

The battle was over, but the plight of the suffering was not. Twenty-three thousand, four hundred men from the North and the

South had fallen in the woods, in the fields and along the Antietam, making it "America's Bloodiest Day."

McClellan had been so close. It seemed as though the Army of Northern Virginia could have been wiped out. Five separate attacks, instead of one coordinated assault had been made by the Army of the Potomac. All had been partially successful with the exception of Sedgwick's move. But a little bit more with his superior numbers, and an attack all along the line would have made it impossible for Lee to hold on. Victory was within McClellan's grasp. However, the story was "almost, but not quite."

In the midst of all the action, the Sixth Corps came up from Pleasant Valley. Robert Westbrook says the column marched through Rohrersville and turned to the left and marched to the top of a hill overlooking Keedysville. For a while they were able to watch the drama of battle unfolding below them. General Hancock said, "Boys, do as you have done before: be brave and true, and I think this will be your last battle." It might have been had Hancock been in command.

James Longstreet says:

> For fourteen long hours more than one hundred thousand men, with five hundred pieces of artillery, had engaged in titantic combat. As the pall of battle smoke rose and cleared away, the scene presented was one to make the stoutest heart shudder. There lay upon the ground, scattered for three miles over the valleys and the hills or in improvised hospitals, more than twenty thousand men. Horace Greeley was probably right in pronouncing this the bloodiest day in American History.[1]

Colonel Palfrey, an officer from Massachusetts, echoes the thoughts and feelings of many.

> The blessed night came...but the murmur of the night wind, breathing over the fields of wheat and clover was mingled with the groans of the countless sufferers of both armies.[2]

Throughout the night men in hospitals, and those still in the West Woods and on the hills near Burnside Bridge called out for water and attention. All through the night the lanterns of the ambulance crews looked for the living among the dead and sought to relieve human suffering and misery. By "dim and flaring lamps the work went on during America's 'longest night'."

Colonel Cross of the 5th New Hampshire says, "Gladly did we see the sun go down on the field of battle, and the dull clouds of war roll away to the west. Firing ceased. In place of the din of arms, we now heard a perfect chorus of groans and cries of pain and distress from the thousands of wounded that covered the ground."[3]

Among the fallen was Lieutenant Colonel Wilder Dwight of the Second Massachusetts Infantry. Just before the battle, between 6:00 and 7:00 a.m. he jotted a note to his mother,

> Dear Mother,—It is a misty, moisty, morning; we are engaging the enemy, and are drawn up in support of Hooker, who is now banging away most briskly. I write in the saddle, to send you my love, and to say that I am well so far.

Then the Second went into action, and the young Colonel galloped up and down the lines waving a captured Rebel battle flag to inspire his men. While telling his men to be careful and to protect themselves, he was shot in the left hip.

While the battle continued to rage, and in the midst of great pain, Wilder started to write again—to his mother:

> I am wounded so as to be helpless. Good by, if so it must be. I think I die in victory. God defend our country. I trust in God, and love all to the last. Dearest love to father and all my dear brothers....

> Mother, yours,

> Wilder

The note speaks for itself, and was to be repeated many times during the rest of the day and in the weeks to come as many succumbed to their wounds. The letter was stained by Dwight's blood, and he added a final thought, "All is well with those that have faith."[4]

Dwight was removed from the field and taken to the Jacob Thomas farm about three miles from the West Woods. There at dark he received word of the Union success, and about midnight on Friday he expired in Mr. Thomas's bedroom. The body was brought to Frederick and then shipped home to Boston.

The tragedy of the day is seen in the notes of Colonel Cross and Surgeon Child. They, like all the men at Antietam lost loved ones. One of their close friends who fell was Lieutenant Gay, an officer for just four days. He was a young man of great talent, cheerful, and loved by all who knew him. He was struck in the top of the head by a shell. Although in a coma, he lived for several hours. Another Union soldier robbed him of his sword, watch, and other items before he was returned to an aid station. Surgeon Child stayed with him, and held his hand, lamenting the fact that he was helpless.

Lieutenant Gay was buried on the battlefield with military honors. The guns were still firing down at Burnside Bridge. With muffled drums, and uniforms smeared with powder, the men of the Fifth took him to his grave. There was sorrow on every face. The path was past wounded men with ashen faces waiting to be collected. Nearby the stretcher bearers and surgeons were hard at work.

Cross and Child were also saddened by the loss of General Richardson. He was a favorite with the men of the Fifth New Hampshire. "It was a sad day for the Army of the Potomac when a rebel shot struck him down. If officers and soldiers ever weep, they of the fifth did that day when Gay and Richardson were sacrificed on our country's altar."[5]

On a lighter, but a sad note, a large black dog was chasing the Confederate cannon balls falling in the Bloody Lane area. The dog had just reached one and was pressing it with his legs and nose, when it exploded. The dog and a cloud of dust flew into the air. The nose and lower jaw of the dog were blown away, but he survived.

Before the 155th Pennsylvania resumed the march this morning, the men made a last trip into the apple and peach orchard on the seminary grounds in Urbana and stuffed their haversacks and pockets.

When the troops reached the Monocacy River and a halt was called, the men availed themselves of a good bath in the river.[6]

For some reason they had left Washington with loaded weapons. Now although they were getting closer to the action, the officers told them to unload. Some did so by engaging in so-called target practice. The men from Pennsylvania did not do so well that September day. Many not only missed the target, but the big trees upon which the targets had been placed. In their defense though, it was the first time some had ever fired a gun.

Then General Humphreys made them "fall in." There were reports of a life and death struggle across the mountain. And the men saw scenes of conflict at Monocacy. They saw the timber, debris, and the wreckage of the railroad bridge blown up by the Confederates. They also noticed the corpse of a black man. Supposedly he had been used by the Confederates to apply the torch that caused the explosion, and did not get away in time.

Near Frederick General Humphreys received an order which made him angry. Because Halleck and McClellan still feared for the safety of Washington, he was to remain in Frederick and act as a deterrent should a Rebel force appear. Humphreys hit the ceiling, but he had to obey orders. So while the fighting was raging along the Antietam Creek, the 8,000 Pennsylvanians spent the day in and around Frederick. Late in the day the order was rescinded, and the troops started out again. The new order read:

> We are in the midst of the most important and extended battle of the war. The rebels are desperate. We have driven them

some distance, but it is of vital importance to get up all our troops. Come as soon as possible, and hurry up with all haste. Do not render the command unfit for service, but force your march.

Thus while the ambulance crews were working in the Miller Cornfield, in the West Woods, and on the hills near Burnside Bridge, the new troops from Pennsylvania were engaging in a forced march to Antietam. The need, and patriotism, inspired them to make a great effort. Few halts were made, and they kept on. Some fell by the ways due to extreme exhaustion.

During the last hour of the march, they had the pleasure of seeing approximately one thousand Confederate prisoners being taken to the rear. In Boonsboro they met the ambulances bringing the wounded from Antietam to the rear. They passed the ambulance bearing the body of General James K.F. Mansfield who had fallen in the attack of the Union Twelfth Corps. Passing by in another ambulance was the body of Colonel James H. Childs of the Fourth Pennsylvania Cavalry who had fallen in the morning of the previous day. He too was from Western Pennsylvania. The men mourned his death, and its shadow cast a pall over them.[7]

About 7:00 a.m. General Humphreys rode into the Pry farm and reported to General McClellan that his division was "present and accounted for." The men had done well. One thousand of the 8,000 had fallen along the route due to exhaustion and disease. But for men just two weeks in the service, they had done well. And believe it or not, McClellan ordered these new troops who had just completed an all night's march to replace elements of the Fifth Corps at the Middle Bridge as the reserve of the Army of the Potomac.

During the day of the eighteenth, Hunter McGuire and other Confederate doctors took the wounded to Shepherdstown. And under the cover of night, Lee's army retreated via the Miller's Saw Mill Road and a glen on the Grove farm and crossed to the south side of the Potomac. Some say that Major Harman, Jackson's Quartermaster "cussed it over," while others say that Lee prayed it over. Jed Hotchkiss was so tired he laid down in the street of Shepherdstown, near a fire made by some weary comrades in arms.

The nineteenth was bright and pleasant. Lee was across the river not far from Shepherdstown. The Fifth Corps moved forward and gave some pursuit. Ferry Hill, the lovely home of the Douglas family overlooking the Potomac, became a wasteland as wagons and guns of the Army of the Potomac rolled into position on the hills and little elevation of the farm.

David Strother rode into Sharpsburg with General McClellan. "Little Mac" was not feeling well. Perhaps Lee's escape upset him, thus he was riding in an ambulance, pulled by four gray horses.

The little farming village had been riddled with shot and shell. David notes that scarcely a building escaped. In a brick house on the square, there were six holes made by cannon balls. No doubt this was the Grove home. "Several horses are lying dead in the street and stables." Some homes were plundered, especially those where the residents went elsewhere during the action. All things considered, Officer Strother felt the town "escaped remarkably well."

For some reason, General McClellan stopped in Sharpsburg and went into a house for a while. Whether he rested or received reports, it's hard to tell. And one must conjecture which house he entered. Nothing has turned up in the memoirs of the folks of Sharpsburg to describe his brief stop.

On Thursday twenty-five ambulances arrived in Frederick with wounded from Antietam. The Lutheran Church, the Methodist Church, the old and new German Reformed Churches on West Church Street, the old and new Protestant Episcopal Churches, the Presbyterian Church, City Hotel, United States Hotel, Winchester Female Seminary, the Roman Catholic Novitiate, and Schools Number 70 and 72 were in use as hospitals. During the next weeks other buildings were added to the list, and sometimes as many as 100 ambulances a day arrived in Frederick from the fields of Antietam. If the men were badly wounded they could haul but two or four. However, if they could sit up, then six to eight were hauled. Engelbrecht says that there were millions of dollars worth of medical and military supplies in the city.[8]

While the battle was going on, Charles Wainwright was still in Frederick. Conversing with the local people, he was told that Lee's army had been exceptionally well behaved. The men from the South had bought a lot of shoes and leather with Confederate money. The lady of the house where Charles was staying sold the Rebels some honey. As Wainwright walked through the town, he saw a lot of gray-clad prisoners at the Frederick County Court House.

On Thursday, Charles Wainwright arrived at Antietam to assume command of the artillery of the First Corps. At Keedysville, he turned right and took the Hitt, or Upper, Bridge to Hooker's position on the Joseph Poffenberger Ridge. From the time he crossed South Mountain, he passed ambulances taking the wounded from Antietam to Frederick.

Wagon trains of supplies and wounded were still coming and going through Middletown. Two weeks earlier it had been tranquil, but now standing in the path of the Blue and the Gray, there was suffering and heartache. George C. Rhoderick reported in the September 19 issue of *The Valley Register*,

Our town is at present one vast hospital. About 1,200 wounded, including some of the Rebels, of Sunday's battle, have been brought here, and all the churches, lecture rooms, school rooms and many rooms of private homes are being used as hospitals. Our citizens, especially the ladies, are untiring in their attention to those unfortunate, whilst our resident physicians are rendering all the aid in their power to mitigate the sufferings of the wounded....About fifty deaths have already occurred in the hospitals here....[9]

Quite a number of volunteer surgeons arrived to help. And *The Register* states that "all public buildings and many private houses in Burkittsville...are also filled with wounded."

John H. Brinton was among the doctors ordered to the front to help the Army of the Potomac in the battle that was sure to come. In Frederick he met the Surgeon General of the U.S. and Sir William Muir, Deputy Inspector-General of the British Army. He was tanned, jovial, and "as round as a barrel."

Brinton did not stay long in Frederick. He was headed to the front. At Middletown he found a large number of wounded being cared for by Dr. William Thomson.

Several days after the battle, Deputy Muir arrived in Keedysville to see the American system of caring for the wounded. Dr. Muir stayed at a hotel in Keedysville. He was very much impressed with the wife of the innkeeper. Once when some reinforcements were marching past to join McClellan, Muir forgot himself and slipped his arm around the waist of his hostess.

During the days following the battle, the 14th Connecticut, along with many other regiments, was involved in the disagreeable task of burying the dead. The havoc of battle was everywhere. A pall of gloom hung over the lovely Valley of the Antietam, and the bivouac of the living and the dead.

On Saturday, the twentieth, most of the Second Corps underwent an inspection. On Sunday, the twenty-first, worship services were held in most of the regimental areas. Reverend Kerfoot from St. James School held services at Army Headquarters, and also at Mt. Airy where the Fifth Corps was encamped.

The men of the 14th Connecticut met in the lovely oak grove where they were camped, with "flag draped drums for a pulpit and the inspiring music of the band serving as church bell and orchestra....None will forget that impressive occasion. The horrible experiences of the week, the death of their comrades...of boyhood days, brothers and relatives were very vivid to them in these hours of quiet reflection."

After the battle many people traveled to Antietam. Many were relatives coming to look for wounded or dead husbands, sons, brothers, or sweethearts. In some cases, they proved a nuisance and hindered the work of the doctors. In other instances, they were most welcome. In the latter category was George Templeton Strong, a prominent New York lawyer, Episcopal layman, and Treasurer of the Sanitary Commission, an organization which was similar to the Red Cross of today.

Strong reached Hagerstown about 9:00 p.m. There was not room to be had in the local hotels. Officers and men from the army camped in the streets. Finally accommodations were found with a Dr. Dorsey. The physician and his wife were ardent Unionists, but they had a son in the Confederate army. The Dorseys related stories of the occupation of Hagerstown by Longstreet's men, and said how dirty the men were. However, the Rebel soldiers had been in excellent spirits and bragged that they were going to capture Philadelphia.

Monday morning, September 22, Mr. Strong took an ambulance and rode off for Sharpsburg. Several miles north of town they encountered the terrible stench from the dead horses and decaying bodies. "Long lines of trenches marked the burial places; scores of dead horses...lay all around." One little brick house in Sharpsburg had a dozen shot-holes in it. The Valley of the Antietam, despite the smell of battle, reminded Strong of Berkshire County, "only more luxuriant and exuberant."[10]

In Sharpsburg, George found the little church which was being used as a hospital for the 118th Pennsylvania, a unit which had suffered heavy losses at the Shepherdstown Ford. Approximately fifty men were lying on straw on the floor of the church.

Army wagons, ambulances, beef cattle, officers, and men thronged the streets of Sharpsburg. In the midst of all of this, who should appear but Mrs. Arabella Griffith Barlow, looking as though she were walking down Broadway. She was in the area to care for her wounded husband, Colonel Francis Barlow.

Strong went to McClellan's headquarters, and also to Mt. Airy to visit General Porter. At McClellan's headquarters, twenty Confederate regimental flags captured on the fields of Antietam were on display.

Mr. Strong went to Keedysville to visit the wounded from French's Division of the Second Corps. He found these men as well as those at Mt. Airy on straw, "in their bloody stiffened clothes...some in barns and cowhouses, some in the open air. It was fearful to see."

After these two visits lasting several hours, Strong and a friend walked over a portion of the battlefield. "We traced the position in which a rebel brigade had stood or bivouacked in line of battle for half a mile by the thickly strewn belt of green corn husks and also cobs, and also, 'sit venia loquendi,' a ribbon of dysenteric stools just behind."

It was getting dark now, and Strong could see signal lights from Harpers Ferry. After a quick supper of bologna sausage, he and his companion drove to Dr. Dorsey's in Hagerstown.[11]

Like Lincoln, some of the soldiers had a lot of doubts about McClellan. On the nineteenth, Charles Wainwright, the artillery officer from the Hudson Valley of New York, rode with General Meade to visit Sharpsburg and then to see General Hooker at the Pry house. The general was recovering from his wound in the foot. He was in good spirits, but expressed regret at McClellan not renewing the attack on Thursday.[12]

While at the Pry farm, Wainwright saw General Israel B. Richardson who had fallen at Bloody Lane. He had been shot through the bowels and was in a great amount of pain. His groans could be heard throughout the house. "Fighting Dick" died at the Pry farm on November 2. Some say that his ghost haunted the house for a while.

Things were not very pleasant for Charles. On Saturday afternoon, the twentieth, Charles rode to the Potomac to see where Porter's men had crossed. "The whole road from Sharpsburg to the river was lined with abandoned guns, caissons and wagons; while every house, barn and shed was filled with rebel wounded, many more lay under trees, or wretched apologies for tents....Sharpsburg...is a small place, with very comfortless looking houses, though most of them are stone or brick; a few have holes through them, made by stray cannon balls, and all are crowded with rebel wounded." Once again Wainwright stopped at McClellan's headquarters.

On the thirtieth, Wainwright reported John Reynolds in charge, and the headquarters tents were moved from near the battlefield to a high knoll where the West Virginia countryside could be seen, although not the Potomac itself. The tents were all in a row, facing west.

The 24th Michigan was one of the last units to arrive at Antietam. They had been hauled in cattle cars from Detroit and Wayne County to Washington. Then it was on to the Monocacy River south of Frederick. While camped in a field near the railroad, the train carrying Mr. Lincoln on his return from Antietam passed by. The President stood at the end of one of the cars and waved to the men from Michigan. They in turn gave him rousing cheers. Ironically, several years later, some of these same men would be on a train with Mr. Lincoln, serving as guards of honor on the funeral train. It was a Saturday the men from Michigan would never forget.

On Sunday, October 5, the lads from the midwest went into the old city of Frederick. They were very much impressed with the town. However, they found "just about every church or public place in the town was filled with the wounded from South Mountain and Antietam battles."

On Monday, October 6, the lads from Michigan left their camp-sites on the banks of the Monocacy and headed west. Orson Curtis says, "Passing through Frederick City, we had a right royal greeting from the people." Due to a late start, the trek was just over the Catoctin Mountains to Middletown, where camp was made in a pasture.[13]

Tuesday morning the march continued through the "rich and cultivated" Middletown Valley. "All about us were the evidences of the late battle (South Mountain) shells lying around, trees and fences cut down." They saw the area where Gibbon's brigade had been engaged for four hours, fighting even into the moonlight. Now they were on the way to become a part of that famed unit. After camp was made, the men walked over the battlefield.

The men from Michigan took the short walk to Fox's Gap and visited with Mr. John Wise. From him they got a first-hand account of the battle. "His log house was pitted with bullets like small pox scars." The men were saddened to hear about the 17th Michigan. Two weeks prior to South Mountain they were still back home in Michigan. But on Sunday, September 14, twenty-eight of its members had been killed at Fox's Gap. They saw the tree under which General Reno died. Military accouterments, especially canteens, were all over the place, and they saw a pile of knapsacks marked "1st S.C." Their owners were in a nearby garden under the earth. "These scenes were food for serious reflections. How long ere we, too, would be actors on the field of deadly combat and fill soldiers" graves?

On Wednesday, the eighth, the 24th Michigan passed through Sharpsburg and moved to a place they named Camp Harbaugh. This was near the river and "the spires of Shepherdstown peered out of the woods across the Potomac....Near us were the excavations through the canal banks by which Lee and his army escaped after the battle. Nearby was a large pile of unburied amputated limbs. Every barn and shed about us was filled with the wounded enemy...left by Lee after his retreat....Near our camp was a barn filled with them....They expressed an undying hatred for the Union and were willing to march and fight, though shoeless and half clad."[14]

Thursday brought the official entrance of the 24th Michigan into the Army of the Potomac. George McClellan had asked for more western troops to complement the men from Indiana and Wisconsin. John Gibbon inspected the regiment. The ranks were full, and with the heavy losses in the Iron Brigade, they seemed almost as many in number as the rest of the brigade. "Our suits were new; theirs were army worn. Our Colonel extolled our qualities, but the brigade was silent. Not a cheer. A pretty cool reception, we thought. We had come to reinforce them, and supposed they would be glad to see us. Neither was satisfied with the other."[15]

The men from Michigan were joining a top notch outfit. And the Iron Brigade "had a right to know before accepting our full fellowship if we, too, had the mettle to sustain the honor of the brigade."

In the following weeks drills, dress parades, and inspections were the order of the day. This was life on the banks of the Potomac after the men from Michigan had completed the march to Antietam.

Charles Johnson, a member of Hawkins' Zouaves, had fallen wounded near Burnside Bridge and was taken to the Jacob Miller farm for treatment. Many a day he had nothing to eat but coffee and crackers. Occasionally he was given a small piece of delicious pie. The report was that excellent care was being given the wounded in Frederick and Middletown. He and his comrades could not wait to go.

Finally on September 29, a train of ambulances came to the Jacob Miller farm and took 100 of the wounded. Charles was overjoyed to be one of the number. "We started about nine o'clock and took the same road the army used in their advance." Charles notes the grand view of the Middletown Valley. "But it cannot compare with the same view we had from nearly the same elevation and position on the Seventeenth [fourteenth], when this magnificent valley, then teeming with a mass of armed men, was covered with that glorious spread of mingling colors of crimson and gold, with the different hues of varying Nature in Autumn."

Charles goes on to say, "How different now is this peaceful valley grown in the short interval of time. And how sad. The thunderclap of war has now rolled...." Two weeks ago, "I was...then hastening over this same road with thousands and thousands of others. Artillery was shaking this mountain gorge...I was full of life and vigor....I placed my confidence in McClellan, and was eager to do my duty to the letter....Now the campaign is ended. I had fondly hoped (it might terminate the war). Maryland is free...and the Nation rejoices in a great victory, as it mourns over the countless dead. I am returning with many others, helpless, to the little city of Frederick, seeking tenderness and care. The same city we left...before daylight two weeks ago, with musket in hand, hastening to the scene of action."[16]

The road back was different. Great battles had been fought. Troops had marched on the "Roads to Antietam"; they had faced each other, and many had given their "last full of devotion." And still the war continued.

Two weeks after the battle, Abraham Lincoln came. John T. Trowbridge made the journey in 1865. He traveled by stage from Hagerstown to Boonsboro and then made the trip to South Mountain. John walked to the tree where Reno breathed his last. He gazed upon the Catoctin Valley, "like a poem in blue and gold, with its patches of hazy woods, sunlit misty fields, and the Catoctin Mountains rolling up behind." He noticed gravestones of the fallen being knocked over by cows grazing on the hillside.

Then it was on to Keedysville, "a cluster of brick and log houses which were turned into hospitals after the battle." He saw the German Reformed Church and the pit behind it, "five feet long, five feet deep, and two feet wide, just full of arms and legs."

Next stop was Sharpsburg and a tour of the battlefield. A light shower fell, and Trowbridge pondered his visit. He took shelter in a house on the road to Burnside Bridge. The lady told him she fled the day before the battle, but she wished she had stayed. When she returned, her home had been plundered and everything of value taken. She said that both the blue and gray took about all they could.

The final stop was the ground purchased for the National Cemetery. The war had been fought by brothers. And America was the chessboard upon which the conflict of liberty was played.[17]

On July 6, 1978, another distinguished American made a pilgrimage to Antietam. President Jimmy Carter, the first President from the South since the Civil War, came to see the Valley of the Antietam. At each stop he asked about the involvement of the Georgia troops, and at Burnside Bridge where the Georgians held the Yankees for so long, he surveyed the scene of battle, and quiet pastoral scene.

Fred Cross, the Massachusetts State Archivist made many trips to Antietam. He had a feel for history. Writing on the occasion of his first visit in the summer of 1903, he said:

> Sharpsburg. What myriad memories awaken at that word....A sleepy old town near the crest of a rolling plateau in Western Maryland. Verdant fields on every hand rich with all the fruit and grains nature so bountifully produced in that fruitful zone...[18]

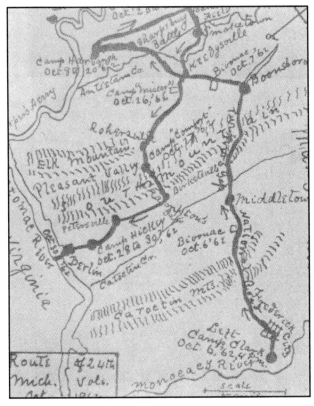

The Twenty-Fourth Michigan Marches to Antietam
Courtesy—Orson Curtis

While touring the battlefield, Cross stopped at Bloody Lane and wrote "an empty theatre—the lights extinguished, the music silent, and the actors gone. While I sat musing on the scene that once had been."[19]

The actors are gone, the scene is silent, but travel the **"ROADS TO ANTIETAM"** and discover a priceless part of our American heritage.

The Lutheran Church in Sharpsburg
Courtesy—The National Park Service

Back to Virginia

Courtesy—Garnet Jex

CHAPTER X

GLEANINGS

THE WEATHER

Monday, September 1	Rain, cool, damp.
Tuesday, September 2	Clear and cool.
Wednesday, September 3	"A fine day."
Thursday, September 4	"A fine day, cool at night."
Friday, September 5	"A very fine bright day, but quite warm."
Saturday, September 6	Warm and dusty.
Sunday, September 7	Fair and warm, Hotchkiss says very warm.
Monday, September 8	Fair and nice.
Tuesday, September 9	Warm, cloudy, hot and dusty.
Wednesday, September 10	Fair and warm.
Thursday, September 11	Cloudy, looked like rain, some rain in p.m.
Friday, September 12	Cloudy and warm.
Saturday, September 13	Fair, pleasant and nice.
Sunday, September 14	Pleasant but warm in the afternoon. Chilly, autumn fog at night.
Monday, September 15	Pleasant.
Tuesday, September 16	Cloudy, warm, somewhat humid. Drizzle in the evening.

From David Strother
    CCXIII, Feb., 1868, pp. 273–280, Owen, Hotchkiss Diary,
        and Cuffel, *Durell's Battery*.

ROUTES OF THE
ARMY OF THE POTOMAC

RIGHT WING
FIRST AND NINTH CORPS

FIRST CORPS
Joseph Hooker, Commanding

September 4	Upton's Hill
September 6	Leesborough
September 9	Brookville
September 12	Ridgeville, New Market, the Monocacy.
September 13	Frederick
September 14	South Mountain, north of Turner's Gap.
September 15	Keedysville area
September 16	Crossing the Antietam, Joseph Poffenberger's.

NINTH CORPS
Jesse Lee Reno, Commanding

September 4	Seventh Street Road
September 6	Leesborough
September 9	Brookville
September 10	Damascus
September 11	New Market
September 12	Frederick
September 13	Middletown
September 14	Fox's Gap, Old Sharpsburg Road
September 15	Along Dog Street and Geeting Road
September 16	Primarily on the Rohrback farm, near the Lower Bridge.

THE CENTER WING
SECOND AND TWELFTH CORPS

SECOND CORPS
Edwin V. Sumner, Commanding

September 4	Tennallytown
September 6	Rockville
September 9	Middlebrook
September 10–11	Clarksburg
September 12	Urbana

September 13   Frederick
September 14   Beyond Middletown
September 15–16 Fields on both sides of the Boonsboro-
                 Sharpsburg Road, on the Russell and Pry farms.

TWELFTH CORPS
J.K.F. Mansfield, Commanding

September 4   Tennallytown
September 6   Rockville
September 9   Middlebrook
September 10   Damascus
September 11   Damascus
September 12   Ijamsville Crossroads
September 13   Frederick
September 14   Middletown and the National Road
September 15   Boonsboro-Keedysville
September 16   The Cost and the Line farms.

FIFTH CORPS
Fitz John Porter, Commanding

George Sykes' division of regulars brought up the rear of the army, and followed the center column, as did the new units coming to join the army. Thus the route was via Rockville, Urbana, Frederick, and the National Road.

SIXTH CORPS
William B. Franklin, Commanding

September 2–6*   In the Alexandria area.
September 7   The Long Bridge to Georgetown to Rabbitt's farm
                 beyond Tennallytown.
September 8   Muddy Run
September 9   Seneca Run beyond Barnestown
September 10   Barnesville
September 12   The Monocacy and on to Buckeystown
September 13   Foot of the Catoctins near Jefferson.
September 14   Jefferson-Burkittsville, attack on Crampton's
                 Gap.
September 17   On to Sharpsburg. It is hard to follow the direct
                 route. Most likely it was to Rohrersville, Mt.
                 Briar and thence to Porterstown.
                 The Route of the Army is in *Official Records*,
                 XIX, Pt. 1, 40.

*Primarily from Slocum's report.

ROUTES OF THE
ARMY OF NORTHERN VIRGINIA

September 4–6	Crossing the Potomac River.
September 7–9	Camped around Fredericktown.
September 10	Army moved to carry out Order No. 191.
	McLaws to Burkittsville.
	Main Body of troops near Boonsboro.
September 11	Jackson to the Potomac and Williamsport.
	Longstreet toward Hagerstown.
	McLaws and Walker moving to fulfill their tasks.
September 12	Jackson completes work at Martinsburg.
	Walker and McLaws proceeding as ordered.
September 13	McLaws carried Maryland Heights.
	Jackson enveloping Harpers Ferry.
	Cavalry pushed back from Braddock Heights.
	Hill strengthens rear guard.
September 14	Investure of Harpers Ferry completed.
	Battle in all three passes of South Mountain.
	Longstreet hurried back from Hagerstown.
	Late at night, Lee orders retreat.
September 15	Longstreet's infantry crosses Antietam at dawn.
	Harpers Ferry falls.
	Jackson's men ordered to Sharpsburg.
	A.P. Hill takes care of surrender.
September 16	Lee strengthens his position on the banks of the Antietam.
	Some of Jackson's command arrives.
September 17	McLaws arrives from Maryland Heights and Harpers Ferry, while A.P. Hill arrives in the nick of time in the afternoon.

ROADS TO ANTIETAM

August 29–30

Confederates win Second Battle of Bull Run.

Monday, September 1

Fighting at Chantilly. These two battles clear the way for the Maryland Campaign.

September 1–6

Union forces fall back to Washington to regroup.

Tuesday, September 2

George B. McClellan placed in command of the Army of the Potomac.

Wednesday, September 3

Confederates march toward Leesburg.

September 4–6

Army of Northern Virginia crosses the Potomac. The invasion begins.

Saturday, September 6

Frederick occupied and Confederate generals in camp south of the city.

Sunday, September 7

The Confederate army encamps around Fredericktown. Jackson attends church. The Union army begins its northward movement from the Rockville area.

Monday, September 8

Lee issues his proclamation to the people of Maryland. General Pendleton enjoys a great day in Frederick among his former parishioners. Cavalry skirmishes occur. Jeb Stuart and his cavalry have a grand ball in a big hall in Urbana.

Tuesday, September 9

Lee issues Order No. 191, calling for a division of his army and the capture of Harpers Ferry. McClellan moves a few more miles to the north, advancing on three roads.

Wednesday, September 10

The Army of Northern Virginia tramps throughout the day through the street of Frederick, heading westward for Maryland Heights and Boonsboro. Frederick had never seen such a day. And supposedly Barbara Fritchie waved her flag.

Thursday, September 11

Lee makes his headquarters at the foot of South Mountain. Jackson heads for the Potomac. McClellan continues his slow advance. Hearing Union forces were heading south from Harrisburg, Lee has to make another division of his army to meet this supposed threat.

Friday, September 12

Cavalry skirmishes continue. Advanced elements of the Ninth Corps reach the Monocacy and charge into Frederick. Confederate forces proceed to envelop Harpers Ferry.

Saturday, September 13

A gala atmosphere prevails in Frederick as the Army of the Potomac enters with sighs of relief from the citizens and shouts of welcome. A copy of Lee's Order dividing his army is found, giving McClellan the chance of a lifetime. The Sixth Corps reaches Jefferson. The Ninth Corps crosses Braddock Mountain and makes camp in Middletown Valley. D.H. Hill watches in dismay and awe from his rearguard position on South Mountain.

Sunday, September 14

Union forces continue to march through the streets of Frederick as the church bells ring. The Ninth Corps attacks Fox's Gap, while the First and the Sixth assault Turner's and Crampton's. Lee hurries Longstreet back from Hagerstown. Jackson completes the encirclement of Harpers Ferry. But the day on the mountain goes against the Confederates, and Lee gives the order to withdraw.

Monday, September 15

Lee takes a position on the banks of the Antietam Creek. Harpers Ferry falls. In the afternoon, Union forces start to flow into the Antietam valley. McClellan makes his headquarters at the Pry farm. The area is filled with "a hundred circling camps."

Tuesday, September 16

A day of preparation for both armies as positions are consolidated and additional forces brought up. McClellan plans his attack.

NOTES FROM DR. STEINER

Dr. Steiner has Jackson's infantry of five thousand entering Frederick, and marching up Market Street, and encamping north of town. This would have been the units which occupied Worman's Mill, then at the junction of the Emmitsburg and Baltimore roads.

There was some music, but the band wasn't much. They played "Dixie" and, of course, "My Maryland." "Each regiment had a square red flag, with a cross, made of...blue stripes....On the blue stripes were placed thirteen white stars."

Like all the other eyewitness accounts, Steiner was not impressed with the appearance of Jackson's men. "A dirtier, filthier, more unsavory set of human beings never strolled through a town—marching it could not be called without doing violence to the word....All were...dirty and repulsive. Their arms were rusty....Faces looked like they had not been acquainted with water for weeks; hair, shaggy and unkempt, seemed entirely a stranger to the operations of brush or comb. A motlier group was never herded together. But these were the...deliverers of Maryland from Lincoln's oppressive yoke."

Although a provost marshal was appointed and guards assigned to the stores, the stores were soon packed, and in the crowds, many soldiers simply shoplifted. The men in dirty gray knocked on the doors of homes and begged for food. They ate it like they were famished.

Steiner says in his notes that the shoe stores were forced to stay open on Sunday. Forage was obtained for the Confederate mules and horses by simply asking the farmers and then paying for it with Confederate notes.

Being a physician, the plight of the Confederates really struck Steiner.

> Uncleanliness and vermin are universal. The odor of clothes worn for months, saturated with perspiration and dirt, is intense....They look stout and sturdy, able to endure fatigue, and anxious to fight in the cause they have espoused....They all believe in themselves as well as in their generals, and are terribly in earnest. They assert that they have never been whipped, but have drive the Yankees before them whenever they could find them....Their army is plainly intended for an advance into Pennsylvania, and they speak freely of their intention to treat Pennsylvania very differently from Maryland....

On Tuesday, the ninth, Dr. Steiner reports the Confederates were still trying to recruit soldiers. But they were having very little luck. One look at Jackson's ragged, dirty men would be enough to change your mind about the glory of serving in the Confederate army.

Again, the possibility of the Barbara Fritchie story arises. A minister told Steiner that an aged woman came out of her house as the Rebels were passing by and berated the Confederates for dragging an American flag in the dust. She shouted, "My curses be upon you and your officers for degrading your country's flag."

Some horses were being taken by the Confederates from the farms around Frederick.

At 4:00 a.m. on Wednesday, according to Steiner, Jackson's command started their westward movement from Frederick. The march continued all day, sixteen hours, until 8:00 p.m. Three thousand black troops were in the ranks.

Some Confederate regiments had as few as 150 men in the ranks. But the men were in good spirits. They felt their Confederate notes were as good as gold, and their cause was right and just. A few folks waved and cheered as they left, but mostly the men from the South received cold, sullen stares.

Prominent in the Confederate line of march were 150 cannon bearing the U.S. mark. However, many ambulances, caissons, and spring wagons bore the same mark. A few Confederates had blankets, and some had toothbrushes sticking from button holes. One citizen of Frederick urged the Rebels to make the North feel the wrath of war when they reached Philadelphia.

Thursday, the eleventh, D.H. Hill with 8,000 men, the rear guard of the army, marched through the streets of Frederick. These men made the most positive impression on the people. They were better dressed, marched better, and had good music. They moved rapidly. Steiner felt this was because they knew the Yankees were on their tails.

Three of the buildings on the hospital grounds were taken over by the Confederates. Steiner lamented the fact that the sick men threw themselves on the beds with boots and filthy clothing. In a few hours, the neatness and sanitary conditions of Union management were gone. Some ladies of Frederick who were Southern sympathizers came to nurse the men.

Rumors came that the Army of the Potomac was on the way. Men and women prayed and hoped that this was true. They longed for the return of the men in blue.

The passing of some of Stuart's cavalry on Friday indicated there might be truth to the rumors. The cavalrymen were neater and cleaner than the infantry. They rode good horses. The riders, like the foot soldiers boasted of their achievements. They said only one regiment, the First Michigan, had dared to cross swords with them. Stuart told Hospital Steward Fitzgerald to tell the Yankees that he would punish them if they were mean to Southern sympathizers in Frederick.

Late in the afternoon, when Union cavalrymen struck Stuart at the intersection of Market and Patrick Streets, many saddles were emptied. Residents of Frederick sought for a good vantage point.

Then, as described earlier, Union infantry entered Fredericktown, and there was great rejoicing. Soldiers from Ohio were almost mobbed. Burnside arrived and was cheered as a hero. The people of Frederick had been delivered from bondage. And a member of the Washington family is said to have unfurled the first Union flag to greet the Union troops.

No business was done on Saturday. Few days in the history of Frederick have been as big as this second Saturday in September. Everyone felt jubilant and congratulated himself and his neighbors that "the United States troops were once more in possession." Steiner also describes the great welcome received by McClellan, and the carnival-like atmosphere.

Bragging on his native Frederick, Steiner says,

> To Frederick belongs the high honor of having given the first decided, enthusiastic, whole-souled reception which the army had met since its officers and men had left their families and homes to fight the battles of their country....In Frederick it was received as a band of brothers, fighting for the welfare of the whole country and, whether successful or unsuccessful, entitled to the warmest demonstrations of good feeling possible.

The Army of the Potomac exhibited no vindictive feeling toward "the secession citizens of the town." No arrests were made of those expressing favorable Southern sentiments.

In the afternoon, Dr. Steiner found McClellan and a large part of the Union army encamped on the Steiner farm west of Frederick. The physician was able to note that it was just a temporary camp.

Steiner was very much impressed with the control the Confederate officers had over their men. He notes that Jackson's name was held in veneration. The dirty faces and ragged clothing of the Rebels also made a profound impression upon him. He contrasted this with the condition of the Union army. He was sorry that his colleagues in the Southern army had to rely largely upon captured medical supplies to alleviate human suffering.

On Sunday, Steiner was proud to watch General A.S. Williams and the Twelfth Corps march through the streets of Frederick. The men really looked like soldiers; they were eager to engage the enemy.

Dr. Andrew's report to Steiner is also included in the little booklet. Andrew speaks with profound admiration of the folks in Middletown, saying they furnished food, tore up sheets and table cloths for bandages. Andrew reached the stone church on Monday, and hired a horse from a farmer to take him to Keedysville. There he obtained a room in the home of Christian Keedy, and aided in the treatment of the wounded at Antietam, returning to Middletown for additional supplies.

LEE'S INJURY

In a letter written later, General Lee relates, "My hands are improving slowly, and with my left hand, I am able to dress and undress myself, which is a great comfort. My right is becoming of some assistance, too, though it is still swollen and painful. The bandages have been removed. I am now able to sign my name. It has been six weeks to day since I was injured, and I have at last discarded the sling."

So this was mid-October, and Lee suffered all the way through the Maryland Campaign with difficulty. This letter appears in the *Recollections of Robert E. Lee.*

NOTES

CHAPTER I
EARLY SEPTEMBER

1. Benjamin P. Poore, *The Life and Public Services of Ambrose E. Burnside* (Providence, 1882), p.157.
2. Charles Johnson, *The Long Roll* (East Aurora, N.Y., 1911), pp. 176–177.
3. Poore, p. 158.
4. William M. Owen, *In Camp and Battle With the Washington Artillery of New Orleans* (Boston, 1885), p. 157.
5. Susan Lee, *Memoirs of William Nelson Pendleton* (Philadelphia, 1885), p. 209.
6. Idem.
7. David S. Sparks, *Inside Mr. Lincoln's Army: The Diary of General Marsena Patrick* (New York, 1964), p. 138.
8. Oliver Otis Howard, *Autobiography* (New York, 1907), vol. 1, p. 271.
9. Josiah M. Favill, *The Diary of a Young Officer* (57th N.Y.), (Chicago, 1909), p. 181.
10. Matthew J. Graham, *The Ninth Regiment New York Volunteers* (New York, 1900), p. 255. Several accounts verify the statement that a boat was ready for the departure of the cabinet. But other sources deny it.
11. *Battles and Leaders of the Civil War*, vol. II (New York), p. 550.
12. Charles F. Walcott, *History of the Twenty-first Massachusetts Volunteers* (Boston, 1882) p. 175. Also see Augustus Woodberry, *Major General Ambrose E. Burnside and the Ninth Army Corps* (Providence, 1867), p. 175.
13. David Strother, *A Virginia Yankee in the Civil War* (Chapel Hill, 1961), p. 99. Much of the material appeared in magazines after the war.
14. Idem.
15. Rufus Dawes, *Service with the Sixth Wisconsin* (Marietta, 1890), p. 76.
16. Jubal Early and R.H. Early, *LT. General Jubal Anderson Early, C.S.A.* (Philadelphia, 1912), p. 134. See also Early's reports in the O.R.
17. Johnson, p. 178.
18. Ibid., p. 179.

CHAPTER II
CROSSING THE RIVER

1. John Pelham to his parents. Quoted in William W. Hassler's, *Colonel John Pelham: Lee's Boy Artillerist* (Richmond, 1960), p.77.
2. John Divine and Others, *Loudoun County and the Civil War* (Leesburg, 1961), p. 41.

3. J.G. Hamilton ed. *The Papers of Randolph Shotwell* (Raleigh, N.C.), vol. I, p. 309. Quoted hereafter as Shotwell.
4. Ibid., p. 310.
5. Heros Von Borcke, *Memoirs of the Confederate War for Independence* (New York, 1938), vol. I, p. 185.
6. Idem.
7. Jed Hotchkiss Papers, Library of Congress.
8. Henry Kyd Douglas, *I Rode with Stonewall* (Chapel Hill, N.C., 1940), p. 153.
9. Ibid., p. 154.
10. Early, O.R. pt. 1, p. 966.
11. Ibid., p. 35.
12. Shotwell, p. 310.
13. Jacob Engelbrecht Diary, Frederick, Maryland. This excellent description of life in Frederick has just recently been printed.
14. Ibid., p. 822.
15. Ibid., p. 952.
16. O.R. pt. II, p. 208.
17. Ibid., p. 185.
18. Ibid., p. 186.
19. Benjamin W. Crowinshield and D.H.L. Gleason, *History of the First Regiment Of Massachusetts Cavalry Volunteers* (Boston, 1891), p. 71.
20. Dawes, p. 45.
21. Ibid., p 46.
22. Franklin Sawyer, *A Military History of the Eighth Regiment Ohio Vol. Infantry* (Cleveland, 1881).
23. Engelbrecht Diary.
24. Lee to Davis, O.R. pt. 2, p. 590.
25. O.R. pt. 1, p. 1,011.
26. Ibid., p. 885.
27. Susan Lee, pp. 210–211.
28. William T. Poague, *Gunner with Stonewall* (Jackson, Tenn., 1957).
29. Engelbrecht Diary.
30. Shotwell, p. 313.
31. Ibid., p. 319.
32. Sparks, p. 140.
33. O.R. pt. II, p. 191.
34. Ibid., pp. 192–193.
35. Ibid., p. 198.

CHAPTER III

"THE CLUSTERED SPIRES OF FREDERICKTOWN"

1. Edward A. Moore, *The Story of a Cannoneer Under Stonewall Jackson* (Washington, 1907).
2. Owen, p. 131.
3. O.R. pt. 1, p. 1,011.
4. John Worsham, *One of Jackson's Foot Cavalry* (New York, 1912), p. 82.
5. George M. Neese, *Three Years in the Confederate Horse Artillery* (New York, 1911), p. 113. This is an excellent book on Chew's Battery.
6. Douglas, p. 148.
7. Ibid., p. 150.
8. Jackson to his wife. See Mary Anna Jackson, *Memoirs of Stonewall Jackson* (Louisville, 1895), p. 332.
9. Susan Lee, p. 211.

10. Strother, p. 102.
11. McClellan to his wife, and George B. McClellan, *McClellan's Own Story* (New York, 1887).
12. O.R. pt. II, p. 201.
13. Idem.
14. Ibid., p. 203.
15. The Papers of Dr. James Oliver, Chewsville, Maryland. Dr. Oliver was from Athol, Massachusetts, and had a distinguished career with the Ninth Corps.
16. *History of the Thirty-fifth Regiment Massachusetts Volunteers, 1861–1865* (Boston, 1884), p. 20.
17. Graham, pp. 255–257.
18. *35th Massachusetts*, p. 21.
19. Paul Jones, *The Irish Brigade* (New York, 1969), p. 136.
20. Favill, p. 182. See also Jacob Cole, *Under Five Commanders* (Patterson, N.J., 1905). Favill and Cole were members of the 57th New York. Their books, like others connected with the same regiment, are very much alike, in some cases almost word for word. Favill's was published in 1909 but is more polished.
21. H.R. Dunham Journal, found in the barn of the Hoffman Hospital barn after the battle. Dunham died at the Hoffman farm. The Journal is in the hands of a resident of Keedysville.
22. Wilder Dwight, *The Life and Letters of Wilder Dwight* (Boston, 1891), pp. 287–288.
23. Susan Lee, p. 211.
24. Augustus Dickert, *History of Kershaw's Brigade* (Newberry, S.C., 1899), p. 146.
25. *Rebellion Record*, Doc. 202. p. 607.
26. Von Borcke, p. 189.
27. *Southern Historical Society Papers*, X. p. 511
28. *Southern Historical Society Papers*, X. pp. 508–509.
29. Letter of James Gillette of the 71st New York.
30. Neese, p. 113.
31. Ibid., p. 115.
32. John Hampden Chamberlayne, *Ham Chamberlayne—Virginia Letters and Papers* (Richmond, 1932), p. 104.
33. Engelbrecht Diary.
34. O.R. pt. 1, pp. 815, 825.
35. W.W. Blackford, *War Years with Jeb Stuart* (New York, 1946), p. 140. The old academy is still standing near the Peter Pan Inn at Urbana, Maryland. Until recently, Urbana was much like it was in 1862.
36. John Dooley, *Confederate Soldier: His War Journal* (Washington, D.C., 1945), p. 25.
37. William Runge, ed., *Four Years in the Confederate Artillery: The Diary of Private Henry Robinson Berkeley* (Chapel Hill, 1961), p. 26.
38. O.R. pt. II, p. 208.
39. Johnson, p. 180.
40. O.R. pt. II, pp. 209–213.
41. Charles E. Davis, *The Story of the Thirteenth Massachusetts Volunteers* (Boston, 1894), p. 131.
42. Charles G. Page, *History of the Fourteenth Regiment Connecticut Volunteers* (Meriden, Conn., 1906), p. 26.
43. Charles Cuffel, *Durell's Battery in the Civil War* (Philadelphia, 1900), p. 78.
44. Edwin Marvin, *The Fifth Regiment Connecticut Volunteers* (Hartford, 1889), p. 237.
45. O.R. pt. II, p. 191.
46. O.R. pt. 1, p. 912.

47. Catherine S.T. Markell Diary for September 1862.
48. Ibid., p. 208.
49. The Dunham Journal.
50. Cuffel, p. 78.
51. Strother, p. 102.
52. Earnest L. Waitt, *History of the Nineteenth Regiment Massachusetts Volunteer Infantry* (Salem, Mass., 1906), p. 126.
53. O.R. pt. 1, p. 219.
54. Ibid., p. 224.
55. Ibid., p. 227.
56. Johnson, p. 176.
57. Dwight, p. 87.
58. George F. Noyes, *The Bivouac and the Battlefield* (New York, 1863), p. 156.

CHAPTER IV
ADVANCE AND MANEUVER

1. Douglas, p. 151.
2. Jacob Engelbrecht Diary.
3. Owen, p. 133.
4. John W. Schildt, *September Echoes* (Middletown, 1960).
5. Dooley, p. 27.
6. Ibid., p. 29.
7. Douglas, pp. 153–154.
8. O.R. pt. I, p. 852.
9. Ibid., p. 912.
10. O.R. pt. II, pp. 601–605.
11. Ibid., p. 245.
12. Edward P. Tobie. *History of the First Maine Cavalry* (Boston, 1887), p. 97.
13. Strother, p. 103.
14. Johnson, p. 103.
15. Sparks, p. 141.
16. Noyes, p. 158.
17. Noyes, p. 26.
18. Jones, p. 139.
19. Sawyer, p. 70.
20. O.R. pt. II, p. 209.
21. Ibid., p. 233.
22. Ibid., p. 239.
23. Dooley, p. 31.
24. O.R. pt. I, p. 953.
25. Ibid., p. 852.
26. Ibid., pp. 815–825.
27. Neese, p. 117.
28. Strother, p. 104.
29. Sparks, p. 142.
30. Noyes, p. 158.
31. Edward O. Lord, *History of the Ninth Regiment New Hampshire Volunteers* (Concord, 1895), p. 50.
32. *Thirty Fifth Massachusetts*, p. 23.
33. Neese, p. 118.
34. Papers in possession of Rev. Austin Cooper.
35. Strother, p. 105.
36. Waitt, p. 128.
37. Noyes, p. 109.

38. John Gibbon, *Personal Recollections of the War* (New York, 1928), p. 71.
39. Lord, p. 53.
40. Graham, p. 260.
41. Dawes, p. 78.
42. Lord, p. 55.
43. Johnson, p. 182.
44. O.R. pt. II, p. 416.
45. Graham, p. 260.
46. Engelbrecht Diary.
47. O.R. pt. I, p. 209.
48. Abner Hard, *History of the Eighth Cavalry Regiment Illinois Volunteers* (Aurora, Ill., 1888).
49. Buell and Johnson, *Battles and Leaders of the Civil War* (New York), vol. II, p. 584.
50. Graham, p. 261.
51. Johnson, p. 182.
52. Graham, p. 262.
53. Ezra D. Simons, *History of the One Hundred Twenty-fifth New York State Volunteers* (New York, 1888), p. 130.

CHAPTER V
SATURDAY, SEPTEMBER 13, 1862

1. Douglas S. Freeman, *Lee's Lieutenants* (New York, 1934), vol. II, p. 187.
2. O.R. pt. I. p. 863.
3. Idem.
4. Hotchkiss Diary.
5. Angela Davis Papers, Hagerstown, Md.
6. Dooley, p. 32.
7. O.R. pt. I, p. 416.
8. Ibid., p. 432.
9. Hard, p. 176.
10. Gleason, p. 74.
11. Strother, p. 105.
12. McClellan to his wife.
13. Strother, p. 106.
14. Oliver C. Bobyshell, *The Forty Eighth in the War....*(Philadelphia, 1895), p. 74.
15. Lord, p. 55.
16. Ibid., p. 58.
17. 35th Massachusetts, pp. 25–26.
18. Sawyer, p. 77.
19. Cole, p. 78.
20. Favill, p. 183.
21. The Dunham Journal.
22. Page, p. 27.
23. Gleason, p. 75.
24. Milo Quaife ed. *From the Cannon's Mouth: The Civil War Letters of General A. S. Williams* (Detroit, 1959), p. 121.
25. O.R. pt. I, p. 479.
26. Julian W. Hinkley. *A Narrative of Service with the Third Wisconsin Infantry* (Madison, 1912).
27. Dwight, p. 291.
28. Edmund R. Brown. *The Twenty-seventh Indiana Volunteer Infantry*, n.p. 1899. p. 228.
29. Hillman Hall. *History of the Sixth New York Cavalry* (Worcester, 1908), p. 59.

30. Simon, pp. 29–30.
31. George H. Washburn. *A Complete History and Record of the One Hundred and Eighth Regiment, New York Volunteers* (Rochester, 1894), p. 19.
32. Robert Westbrook, *History of the Forty-ninth Pennsylvania Volunteers* (Altoona, 1884), p. 124.

CHAPTER VI
SUNDAY, SEPTEMBER 14, 1862

1. *Battles and Leaders*, vol. II, p. 564.
2. Dooley, p. 35.
3. Owen, p. 136.
4. Dooley, p. 36.
5. Shotwell, p. 332.
6. Neese, p. 120.
7. Ibid., p. 121.
8. Letter found by Rev. Austin Cooper, noted Church of the Brethren historian in an old book in Burkittsville, 113 years after the skirmish.
9. O.R. pt. I, p. 140.
10. Ibid., p. 147.
11. O.R. pt. II, p. 608.
12. Ibid., p. 609.
13. Ibid., p. 604.
14. O.T. Reilly, battlefield guide who published a folder with pictures and commentary on Antietam.
15. Shotwell, p. 330.
16. Edwin P. Alexander, *Military Memoirs of a Confederate* (New York, 1907), p. 229.
17. O.R. pt. I, p. 210.
18. Ibid., p. 458.
19. Thomas T. Ellis. *Leaves From the Diary of an Army Surgeon* (New York, 1864), p. 13.
20. 35th Massachusetts. pp. 26–27.
21. Thompson in *Battles and Leaders*, vol. II, p. 558.
22. *The Valley Register*. Middletown, Md., September 19, 1862.
23. Todd, pp. 235–236.
24. Dawes, p. 79.
25. David Thompson in *Battles and Leaders*, vol. II, p. 557.
26. Lord, pp. 69–70.
27. Strother, p. 106.
28. Simon, p. 513.
29. Oliver Papers.
30. Davis, p. 133.
31. Livermore, p. 116.
32. Sawyer, p. 72.
33. Page, p. 27.
34. William Child, *A History of the Fifth Regiment New Hampshire Volunteers* (Bristol, 1893).
35. Dunham Journal.
36. Marvin, p. 273.
37. Jones, p. 138.
38. Alonzo Quint, *The Record of the Second Massachusetts Infantry* (Boston, 1867). p. 130.
39. Ibid., p. 131.

40. O.R. pt. I, p. 291.
41. Dawes, p. 80.
42. Gibbon, p. 76.
43. Dawes, p. 81.
44. William Pickerall, a member of the Third Indiana Cavalry in a letter to the *Valley Register*, Middletown, Md., September 1908.
45. Hard, p. 178.
46. Hall, p. 60.
47. Ellis, p. 251.
48. Curtis, p. 174.
49. Charles Coffin in a dispatch to the *Boston Journal*.
50. Henry Humphreys, *Andrew Atkinson Humphreys: A Biography* (Philadelphia, 1924). pp. 68–69.
51. *Antietam to Appomattox with the One Hundred and Eighteenth Pennsylvania Volunteers* (Philadelphia, 1892). p. 34.
52. Francis W. Dawson, *Reminiscences of Confederate Service*, 1861–1865 (Charleston, S.C., 1882). pp. 64–65.

CHAPTER VII

MONDAY, SEPTEMBER 15, 1862

1. Neese, p. 124.
2. Hotchkiss Diary.
3. Freeman, *Lee's Lieutenants*, vol. II, p. 204.
4. James Longstreet. *From Manassas to Appomattox* (Philadelphia, 1896). p. 216.
5. O.R. pt. I, p. 951.
6. Owen, p. 139.
7. Freeman, p. 379.
8. Shotwell, p. 395.
9. *Battles and Leaders*, vol. II, p. 667.
10. O.R. pt. I, p. 53.
11. Ibid., p. 200.
12. Hard, p. 182.
13. Livermore, p. 120.
14. Ibid., p. 122.
15. Ibid., p. 123.
16. Page, p. 34.
17. Child, pp. 117–119.
18. Favill, pp. 184–185.
19. Gibbon, p. 79.
20. Dawes, p. 78.
21. Dunham Journal.
22. Waitt, p. 135.
23. Stowe Journal.
24. Howard, pp. 276–277.
25. Gleason, p. 77.
26. Tobie, p. 98. According to Scharf's *History of Western Maryland*, Mount Pleasant was located at the foot of South Mountain, northeast of Boonsboro, now Route 66, and was a "small, but thriving village." P. 1267.
27. Sparks, p. 145.
28. Noyes, p. 183.
29. Ibid., p. 185. Strange's death is reported in O.R.
30. Ibid., p. 189.

31. Ibid., p. 191.
32. O.R. p. 417.
33. Todd and Husey, p. 236.
34. Strother, p. 108.
35. Lord, pp. 89–90.
36. Durell's Battery, p. 76.
37. O.R. p. 630.
38. Johnson, p. 188.
39. Lord, p. 93.
40. Graham, p. 296.
41. Strother, p. 108.
42. O.R. pt. I, p. 107.
43. Brown, p. 233.
44. Hard, p. 182. See footnote 26 and the reference to Mount Pleasant. There are several homes in the Valley of the Antietam by the name of Mount Pleasant, but Hard was referring to the little community near Boonsboro.
45. 155th Pennsylvania, p. 69.
46. Idem.
47. Oliver W. Norton, *Army Letters* 1861–1865 (88th Pa.) Chicago, 1903. p. 119.
48. George T. Stevens, *Three Years in the Sixth Corps* (Albany, 1866). pp. 142–143.

CHAPTER VIII
TUESDAY, SEPTEMBER 16, 1862

1. Douglas, p. 167.
2. Dickert, p. 150.
3. Alexander, p. 242.
4. Neese, p. 123.
5. Ibid. p. 124.
6. Owen, p. 141.
7. Shotwell, p. 350.
8. Idem.
9. O.R. p. 78.
10. Longstreet, p. 217.
11. Allan Nevins, ed. *The Personal Journals of Colonel Charles S. Wainwright*, 1861–1865 (New York, 1962), p. 98.
12. Engelbrecht Diary.
13. Lord, p. 188.
14. Howard, p. 291.
15. Sparks, p. 145.
16. Dawes, p. 135.
17. Dawes, p. 83.
18. Daniel G. McNamara, *The History of the Ninth Regiment Massachusetts...Infantry* (Boston, 1899). p. 209.
19. Child, p. 126.
20. Dwight, p. 289.
21. 35th Massachusetts, p. 36.
22. 118th Pennsylvania, p. 36.
23. Ibid., pp. 36–37.
24. Curtis, p. 177.
25. Waitt, p. 132.
26. Miles C. Huyette, *The Maryland Campaign and the Battle of Antietam* (Buffalo, 1915). pp. 27–28.

CHAPTER IX
SEPTEMBER 17, 1862, AND AFTER

1. Longstreet, p. 218.
2. Francis W. Palfrey, *The Antietam and Fredericksburg* (New York, 1882), p. 81.
3. Child, p. 124.
4. Dwight, p. 293.
5. Child, p. 125.
6. 155th Pennsylvania, p. 75.
7. Ibid., p.73.
8. Engelbrecht Diary.
9. Wainwright, p. 101.
10. Allan Nevins, ed. *Diary of the Civil War, 1860–1865. George T. Strong* (New York, 1962), p. 260.
11. Ibid., p. 261.
12. Wainwright, p. 103.
13. Curtis, p. 62.
14. Ibid., p. 64.
15. Ibid., p. 65.
16. Johnson, p. 200.
17. John T. Trowbridge, *The Desolate South*, 1865–1866 (Boston, 1956). p. 24.
18. The Papers of Fred Cross, State Archivist for Massachusetts in the early 1900's.
19. Idem.

BIBLIOGRAPHY

MAIN SOURCE

OFFICIAL RECORDS, WAR OF THE REBELLION. Washington, 1880–1891. Vol. 19, Parts I and II.

PRIMARY SOURCES

The Rev. Austin Cooper Papers, Burkittsville, Maryland.
The Fred Cross Papers, Boonsboro, Maryland.
The Angela Davis Papers, Hagerstown, Maryland.
The H.R. Dunham Journal, Keedysville, Maryland.
The Jacob Engelbrecht Diary, September 1862, Frederick, Maryland.
Catherine Susan Thomas Markell Diary.
The Dr. James Oliver Papers, Chewsville, Maryland.
The Dr. Lewis Steiner Papers, Baltimore, Maryland.
The Jonathan Stowe Journal.

NEWSPAPERS

The Baltimore Sun.
The Boston Journal.
The Middletown *Valley Register.*

BOOKS

Alexander, Edward Porter. *Military Memoirs of a Confederate*. New York, 1907.
Battles and Leaders of the Civil War, eds. Robert U. Johnson and Clarence C. Buell. Four Vols. Volume II used in the study of the Maryland Campaign. New York, 1884–1888.
Blackford, William W. *War Years with Jeb Stuart*. New York, 1946.
Bobyshell. *The Forty-eighth in the War*....Philadelphia, 1895.

Borcke, Heros Von. *Memoirs of the Confederate War for Independence*. New York, 1938, vol. I.

Brown, Edmund R. *The Twenty-seventh Indiana Volunteer Infantry in the War of the Rebellion*. n.p., 1899.

Bruce, George A. *The Twentieth Regiment of Massachusetts Volunteer Infantry*, 1861–1865. Boston, 1906.

Chamberlayne, C.G. *Ham Chamberlayne—Virginian, Letters and Papers of an Artillery Officer*. Richmond, 1932.

Child, William. *A History of the Fifth Regiment New Hampshire Volunteers*. Bristol, 1893.

Cook, Benjamin F. *History of the Twelfth Massachusetts Volunteers*. Boston, 1882.

Cuffel, Charles. *Durell's Battery in the Civil War*. Philadelphia, 1900.

Curtis, Orson B. *History of the Twenty-fourth Michigan*. Detroit, 1891.

Davis, Charles E. *The Story of the Thirteenth Massachusetts Volunteers*. Boston, 1894.

Dawes, Rufus. *Service With the Sixth Wisconsin Volunteers*. Marietta, 1890.

Dawson, Francis W. *Reminiscences of Confederate Service*. Charleston, 1882.

Dickert, Augustus. *A History of Kershaw's Brigade*. Newberry, S.C., 1899.

Divine, John. *Loudoun County and Civil War Collection*. Waterford, Va.

Dooley, John. *Confederate Soldier: His War Journal*. Washington, 1945.

Douglas, Henry Kyd. *I Rode With Stonewall*. Chapel Hill, N.C., 1940.

Dwight, Wilder. *The Life and Letters of Wilder Dwight*. Boston, 1891.

Ellis, Thomas. *Leaves From the Diary of an Army Surgeon*. New York, 1864.

Favill, Josiah. *The Diary of a Young Officer*. Chicago, 1909.

Freeman, Douglas S. *Lee's Lieutenants, A Study in Command*. 3 Vols. New York, 1943.

Freeman, Douglas S. *Robert E. Lee, A Biography*. 4 Vols. New York, 1935.

Gibbon, John. *Personal Recollection of the Civil War*. New York, 1928.

Gordon, John B. *Reminiscences of the Civil War*. New York, 1903.

Graham, Matthew J. *The Ninth Regiment New York Volunteers*. New York, 1905.

Hall, Hillman. *History of the Sixth New York Cavalry*. Worcester, 1908.

Hamilton, J.G. ed. *The Papers of Randolph Abbott Shotwell*. 3 Vols., Raleigh, N.C., 1929.

Hard, Abner. *History of the Eighth Cavalry Regiment Illinois Volunteers*. Aurora, Ill., 1888.

Hinkley, Julian. *A Narrative of Service With the Third Wisconsin Infantry.* Madison, 1912.

Owen, William. *In Camp and Battle With the Washington Artillery of New Orleans.* Boston, 1885.

Page, Charles G. *History of the Fourteenth Regiment Connecticut Volunteers.* Boston, 1894.

Palfrey, Francis W. *The Antietam and Fredericksburg.* New York, 1882.

Pickerall, William. Letter to the *Valley Register.*

Poague, William T. *Gunner With Stonewall.* Jackson, Tenn. 1957.

Poore, Benjamin P. *The Life and Public Services of Ambrose E. Burnside.* Providence, 1882.

Quaife, Milo M., ed. *From the Cannon's Mouth, The Civil War Letters of General Alpheus S. Williams.* Detroit, 1959.

Quint, Alonzo. *The Record of the Second Massachusetts Infantry.* Boston, 1867.

Reilly, O.T. *Antietam.* Hagerstown, 1906.

Runge, William H. ed. *Four Years in the Confederate Artillery: The Diary of Private Henry Robinson Berkeley.* Chapel Hill, 1961.

Sawyer, Franklin. *A Military History of the Eighth Regiment Ohio Volunteer InfantrY.* Cleveland, 1881.

Schildt, John W. *September Echoes.* Middletown, Md., 1960.

Simons, Ezra D. *History of the One Hundred Twenty-fifth New York State Volunteers.* New York, 1888.

Sparks, David, ed. *Inside Mr. Lincoln's Army: The Diary of General Marsena Patrick, Provost Marshal General, Army of the Potomac.* New York, 1964.

Stevens, George T. *Three Years in the Sixth Corps.* Albany, 1866.

Strother, David. *A Virginia Yankee in the Civil WaR.* Chapel Hill, 1961. This is sort of a compilation of Strother's many magazine articles after the war.

Thirty Fifth Massachusetts Volunteers. Boston, 1884.

Tobie, Edward P. *History of the First Maine Cavalry.* Boston, 1887.

Todd, William. *The Seventy-ninth Highlanders, New York Volunteers.* Albany, 1886.

Trowbridge, John T. *The Desolate South, 1865–1866.* Boston, 1956.

Waitt, Ernest L. *History of the Nineteenth Regiment Massachusetts Volunteer Infantry.* Salem, Mass., 1906.

Walcott, Charles F. *History of the Twenty-first Massachusetts Volunteers.* Boston, 1882.

Washburg, George H. *A Complete History...of the One Hundred and Eighth Regiment N.Y. Volunteers.* Rochester, 1894.

Westbrook, Robert. *History of the Forty-ninth Pennsylvania Volunteers.* Altoona, 1884.

Woodberry, Augustus. *Major General Ambrose E. Burnside and the Ninth Army Corps*. Providence, 1867.
Worsham, John. *One of Jackson's Foot Cavalry*. New York, 1912.

INDEX